JAVASCRIPT + CSS
+ DOM MAGIC

by Makiko Itoh

New Riders

201 West 103rd Street, Indianapolis, Indiana 46290
An Imprint of Pearson Education
Boston • Indianapolis • London • Munich • New York • San Francisco

JavaScript + CSS + DOM Magic

International Standard Book Number: 0-7357-1132-1

Library of Congress Catalog Card Number: 2001087311

Printed in the United States of America

First Printing: May 2002

06 05 04 03 02   7 6 5 4 3 2 1

Interpretation of the printing code: The rightmost double-digit number is the year of the book's printing; the rightmost single-digit number is the number of the book's printing. For example, the printing code 02-1 shows that the first printing of the book occurred in 2002.

Trademarks

Warning and Disclaimer

Publisher
David Dwyer

Associate Publisher
Stephanie Wall

Executive Editor
Steve Weiss

Production Manager
Gina Kanouse

Managing Editor
Sarah Kearns

Acquisitions Editor
Theresa Gheen

Development Editor
Ginny Bess Munroe

Project Editor
Jake McFarland

Technical Editors
Suzi Arnold
Cal Henderson

Copy Editor
Chrissy Andry

Indexer
Angie Bess

Product Marketing Manager
Kathy Malmloff

Publicity Manager
Susan Nixon

Manufacturing Coordinator
Jim Conway

Book Designer
Steve Gifford

Cover Designer
Aren Howell

Proofreader
Sarah Cisco

Compositor
Kim Scott

Media Developer
Jay Payne

About the Author

 **Makiko Itoh** is a principal of PRODOK Engineering (**www.prodok.com**), a development and consulting company based near Zürich, Switzerland, whose clients range from small companies to international corporations and government agencies in Germany, Switzerland, and the United States. Prior to making the switch to web development, Makiko was a print graphics designer for several years. She combines a knowledge of scripting and programming issues, which are needed for interactivity and dynamic presentation, with an innate understanding of what designers demand visually. Makiko contributes to several web publications and is the editor-in-chief of Wise-Women (**www.wise-women.org**), a site dedicated to encouraging women web developers and designers.

Originally from Japan, Makiko now divides her time between Switzerland and the United States, where she is a frequent speaker at various technical conferences such as Seybold Seminars and Web Design World. In her spare time, she likes to travel even more. You can follow her latest activities via her personal web site, **www.makikoitoh.com**.

About the Technical Reviewers

These reviewers contributed their considerable hands-on expertise to the entire development process for *JavaScript + CSS + DOM Magic*. As the book was being written, these dedicated professionals reviewed all the material for technical content, organization, and flow. Their feedback was critical to ensuring that *JavaScript + CSS + DOM Magic* fits our readers' need for the highest-quality technical information.

Suzi Arnold is the founder of think inkless (**www.thinkinkless.com**), a web development and digital design studio established in 2000. She has been developing web sites since 1996. Hired as the first employee for a major job board, Suzi spent the ensuing years training and managing its production team. She finished her "corporate" life as Web Producer for the interactive division of an international advertising agency.

Cal Henderson is a web applications developer from London. By day, he is the technical director of new projects at emap (**www.emap.com**). By night, he works for a whole host of web sites and communities, including the Javascript and DHTML playground, pixelflo (**www.pixelflo.com**), and his personal site, i:am:cal (**www.iamcal.com**). In his spare time, Cal writes Windows software (**www.iamcal.com/software**), and he develops web publishing tools.

*Special thanks to **Chris Falvey (www.mediabasement.com)** for lending his advice, late hours, technical sweat, and absoulte faith in New Riders and this project.*

—New Riders

DEDICATION

For my role model, my mother Michiko Ebina—the bravest woman I know.

ACKNOWLEDGMENTS

As a first-time author, I would like to first and foremost thank my acquisitions editor, Theresa Gheen, and my development editor, Ginny Bess Munroe, and everyone at New Riders Publishing for their almost infinite patience and guidance.

My deepest gratitude goes to my technical editors, Suzi Arnold and Cal Henderson, for their sharp eyes and comments that made this book so much better, as well as to Chis Falvey, Peter-Paul Koch, and Doc Ozone for their earlier involvement; and to my dear friends, Shirley Kaiser and Carole Guevin, for their wonderful designs. You all rock!

Special thanks to Molly Holzschlag, who pointed me to this project in the first place; David Fugate, my agent at Waterside Productions for his patience and advice; to Nick Finck for getting me started with this writing;

and to list mom Dori Smith and the wonderful members of the Wise-Women mailing list. And to all my friends and family who encouraged and pushed me along as I struggled with the mighty task of completing this book… It couldn't have been done without you: Wanda Cummings, my sisters Mayumi and Megumi, my mother and father, Michael Manson, and Sarah, who is now in heaven.

To the people responsible for the background entertainment that kept me more or less sane as I worked on this book: Panic Software for Audion, Apple for making the iPod, Pizzicato Five, Fantastic Plastic Machine, Ella Fitzgerald, Smoke City, Yumi Matsutoya, Billy Joel, Kiroro, aiko, Pink, Sugar Soul, Iron Chef, Radio FG, the BBC, and the whole Star Trek franchise. Arigato!

Last and not least, to my partner in crime, Max Wyss: There aren't words adequate enough to express how I feel about all the things you do for me.

TELL US WHAT YOU THINK

As the reader of this book, you are the most important critic and commentator. We value your opinion and want to know what we're doing right, what we could do better, what areas you'd like to see us publish in, and any other words of wisdom you're willing to pass our way.

As an Executive Editor for the Creative Media team at New Riders Publishing, I welcome your comments. You can fax, email, or write me directly to let me know what you did or didn't like about this book—as well as what we can do to make our books stronger.

Please note that I cannot help you with technical problems related to the topic of this book, and that due to the high volume of mail I receive, I might not be able to reply to every message.

When you write, please be sure to include this book's title and author as well as your name and phone or fax number. I will carefully review your comments and share them with the author and editors who worked on the book.

Fax: 317-581-4663

Email: **steve.weiss@newriders.com**

Mail: Steve Weiss
          Executive Editor
          New Riders Publishing
          201 West 103rd Street
          Indianapolis, IN 46290 USA

Visit Our Web Site: www.newriders.com

On our web site, you'll find information about our other books, the authors we partner with, book updates and file downloads, promotions, discussion boards for online interaction with other users and with technology experts, and a calendar of trade shows and other professional events with which we'll be involved. We hope to see you around.

Email Us from Our Web Site

Go to **www.newriders.com** and click on the Contact Us link if you…

- Have comments or questions about this book.
- Want to report errors that you have found in this book.
- Have a book proposal or are interested in writing for New Riders.
- Would like us to send you one of our author kits.
- Are an expert in a computer topic or technology and are interested in being a reviewer or technical editor.
- Want to find a distributor for our titles in your area.
- Are an educator/instructor who wants to preview New Riders books for classroom use. In the body/comments area, include your name, school, department, address, phone number, office days/hours, text currently in use, and enrollment in your department, along with your request for either desk/examination copies or additional information.

INTRODUCTION

Ever since graphical web browsers were unleashed, the World Wide Web has evolved in leaps and bounds. But arguably, the last two to three years have been the most exciting, and yet frustrating, period of time to be a web designer.

Since the introduction of graphical web browsers, designers could stick to programming in plain old HTML and tweaking their GIFs and JPEGs. Now, however, even pure designers must deal with a lot more. They are now presented with a bewildering array of possibilities and technologies. Recent advances in browser technology and increasing demands from web users and developers have made many "tried and true" authoring methods, if not obsolete, then on their way to becoming so. Indeed, it's a challenging time for web designers and developers alike.

The foundation of any good web page is well-formed HTML or XHTML markup. Making web pages come to life is the task of Cascading Style Sheets (CSS) for visual presentation and JavaScript for dynamism. And the glue that ties everything together is the Document Object Model (DOM). These are the core client-side technologies (the things that work in the browser rather than on the server) of the World Wide Web.

This book is filled with practical examples of ways to use these technologies on real web sites. I've placed a great emphasis on showing you exactly how CSS, the DOM, and JavaScript are used together. If you've been confused and even intimidated by all of these technologies, this book will help clear up some of that confusion and give you the confidence to enhance your web sites and your skills. My goal is to get you to regard CSS, JavaScript, and the DOM as tools that enhance your creativity and expand your range as a web designer.

Why Do It Yourself?

With the availability of visual editors, such as Macromedia Dreamweaver and Adobe GoLive, for creating web sites, you might be wondering why you should bother to create your own scripts, not to mention your own HTML or XHTML markup. Visual editors are wonderful tools that can greatly speed up your creation process. However, relying solely on cut-and-paste scripts and the like puts a creative barrier between you and your creation. When you must rely on a ready-made script to accomplish something, you are forced to use the method chosen by the author of the script. When you know how to create or at least modify a script on your own, you can adapt and change things to suit your needs.

When it comes to CSS, you must create a unique stylesheet for your particular site or page. You can't simply copy someone else's stylesheet without knowing the rules. A solid knowledge of the rules and syntax of both CSS and JavaScript, and most importantly of the way they work together, is essential to fully master the art of web page creation. It will also help you to use visual editors more effectively.

WHO I AM

I'm not a professional, full-time writer. I design and build web sites for a living, and I'm also hired by other companies to help them implement these web technologies on web sites or in web-based applications in a practical, workable way. My background is in print design, so I'm very aware of the need for visual feedback and control that is a characteristic of many designers. While I always keep an eye on emerging technologies, I'm also always aware of the pressures of deadlines and the demands of clients. I hope that my experiences and battle scars will help you in your every day efforts to turn out web sites that are visually pleasing and functional.

WHO YOU ARE

This book is written for the web designer and creative professional with a fairly good knowledge of HTML, design principles, and basic web site construction. Chances are you have already started looking into using CSS on your sites, and you might have hacked a few scripts that you've picked up here and there. This is not a book for total beginners, but it doesn't assume that you're a programming whiz either.

In keeping with the aim of the Magic series, this book takes a very visual and "hands-on" approach. If you've been daunted by the more detailed, yet non-visual approach of most books about CSS, JavaScript, and the DOM, or if you have been confused about how they actually work together on "real" web pages, this book is for you.

In addition, since this book is intended for visual designers and creative people, I've concentrated primarily on the visual effects you can create with JavaScript, CSS, and the DOM. For example, JavaScript is a powerful scripting language that can be used for a variety of purposes, but for this book I've kept the focus on the parts of web page construction that are most likely to fall under the responsibility of the designer, such as navigation interfaces.

HOW TO USE THIS BOOK

This book is divided into four parts. The projects in each part can stand on their own, but they are also presented in a way so that the principles and methods introduced in one are built on in subsequent projects. If you are unsure about any of the subjects covered, you'll get the most out of the book by making your way systematically through the projects. Take your time working on the projects and play around with them until you understand what's going on.

If you are more experienced, you can skip around in the book. For example, if you already know how to control text appearance with CSS, you could skip Project 1 of Part 1, "Real-Life CSS"; if you can do basic JavaScript rollovers and can control framesets and windows in your sleep, skip Part 2, "JavaScript Level 1: Basic JavaScript." You can also use this book like a cookbook to pick up quick solutions to urgent problems.

WHAT'S IN THIS BOOK

This book is broken down into the following parts:

- **Part I, "Real-Life CSS."** This section starts with the foundation: valid, well-formed HTML/XHTML markup. Then, you'll learn how to use CSS on several levels, from basic text appearance control to CSS-P (using CSS for positioning and layout).

- **Part II, "JavaScript Level 1: Basic JavaScript."** This section covers the page-enhancing JavaScript that works in all JavaScript-capable browsers. Here you will find scripts for image swapping (rollovers), dealing with frames, and controlling browser windows.

- **Part III, "JavaScript Level 2: Dynamic HTML."** These scripts work in 4.x and later versions of Microsoft Internet Explorer and Netscape Navigator/Communicator. It's the kind of JavaScript that is often called DHTML. This section tackles the different DOMs for the various browsers, browser sniffing, and script branching methods, and discusses some "best practices" for implementing many popular dynamic methods such as scrolling "windows," popup text, dropdown menus, and more.

- **Part IV, "JavaScript Level 3: The Latest DOM Methods."** This section covers just a few of the exciting scripting possibilities of the newest browsers that support the DOM recommended by the World Wide Web Consortium (**www.w3.org**), also known as the *W3C DOM*. These scripts work in version 5 and later versions of Microsoft Internet Explorer, Netscape 6.x, and Mozilla. You'll also learn some transitional strategies to employ as you update your site construction methods to take advantage of the most current browsers, while accommodating older browsers.

- **The CD.** The companion CD for this book contains a wealth of extra materials, including all of the files used for the projects and more. Please consult the "What's on the CD-ROM" appendix at the end of the book for more details.

THE COMPANION WEB SITES

This book is accompanied by two companion web sites. You'll find bonus content, including sample chapters and additional projects (including the code) at **www.newriders.com**. New Riders also provides the errata, links, updates, resources, and a lot more. In addition, there is an author-maintained companion web site for this book, which is located at **www.createwebmagic.com**.

ASSUMPTIONS AS I WROTE THIS BOOK

I wrote this book with the following underlying assumptions in mind:

- **You already have a good working knowledge of HTML.** You should have at least built a few web pages before you try to tackle this book.

- **You're not necessarily a programmer by trade.** I don't assume that you've had a lot of programming experience. It's a big plus if you have done some programming, however, especially for the object-oriented projects in this book.

- **You know what good design principles are.** This book can make you a better designer by increasing your understanding of the tools you use, but it won't prevent you from making awful-looking pages. Ultimately, to make good web pages you have to have a good sense of what visual design is.

- **You want real projects for real web sites.** Most of the projects in this book have a practical application, and they can be adapted for use right away on real web pages.

- **You're interested in creating cross-browser, multi-platform web sites—within reason.** If you've created even just one web site, you know that one of the big headaches of web design is dealing with cross-browser incompatibilities. Throughout the book, you'll see alerts for particular problems, especially those associated with version 4 browsers. In addition, the focus of this book is on methods that work on at least all the latest versions of the browsers from Netscape and Microsoft, and that work on Windows, Mac, and Unix/Linux platforms. Therefore, there isn't much discussion of methods that work in only one browser or on one particular platform.

- **You're interested in learning about and coding for the browsers that support web standards.** No book about web site creation can avoid the subject of web standards. This point warrants further explanation, which you'll find in the following section.

WEB STANDARDS

There are two organizations that create standardized, open specifications for various web-related technologies. The main organization is the World Wide Web Consortium, or W3C. The W3C has created the specifications for markup (HTML/XHTML/XML), CSS, and the DOM, among other things. The other organization of note is the ECMA, which has specified a standardized version of JavaScript/JScript called ECMAScript.

Up until fairly recently, however, browser makers have simply incorporated their own versions of CSS, JavaScript (or JScript, in Microsoft-terms), and proprietary DOMs. Even proprietary HTML markup has been introduced. Nothing is as frustrating as when the page you painstakingly created to work just so in one browser fails completely when viewed in another. Recently, browser manufacturers have finally started to listen to the demands of people who create web sites to support a common set of specifications, or standards. The latest versions of Microsoft Internet Explorer for Windows and the Mac, as well as the latest incarnations of the Netscape browser, support the standard specifications created by the W3C for CSS Level 1 (and partial support for CSS Level 2), HTML 4.01/XHTML 1.0 markup (the currently recommended markup language is XHTML 1.0 Transitional), and DOM Level 1 (and partial support for DOM Level 2). These browsers also support a flavor of the latest version of ECMAScript-262.

One of the most important aims of this book is to actually show you what standards-compliant markup and CSS look like and to demonstrate how a standardized DOM simplifies scripting tasks. Browser support for standards is getting much better, but it's still not 100%—as you will see from the many browser-specific workarounds in this book. Another aim of this book is to eliminate as many cross-browser incompatibility headaches as possible.

To read the standards documents themselves, visit the W3C web site at **www.w3c.org**. The ECMA site is located at **www.ecma.ch**. You might also be interested in the activities of the Web Standards Organization (**www.webstandards.org**), a group interested in getting the browser manufacturers to support standards.

THE TOOLS YOU'LL NEED FOR THIS BOOK

The following list briefly covers what you'll need to work through the projects in this book:

- **A good text editor.** It's possible to write scripts and stylesheets with NotePad or SimpleText… but why torture yourself? Good programmer's text editors are inexpensive and will save you countless hours of extra work and headaches. The CD includes demo or Lite versions of several of the most popular text editors available for Windows and Mac. For this book, BBEdit on the Mac and Notepad Pro on Windows were used.

- **A graphics program.** I used Adobe Photoshop with Image Ready or Macromedia Fireworks to create the graphics in this book, but you can use other programs. Several hints about how to use these programs to your best advantage when creating dynamic web pages have been included, too.

■ **At least two of the latest versions of the most popular browsers.** For the purposes of following the lessons and projects in this book, it's highly recommended that you work with the most current version of either Microsoft Internet Explorer (version 6 or later) or Netscape (version 6 or later). The most recent versions of both browsers are included on the CD. In addition, it's highly recommended that you download the latest stable version of Mozilla from **www.mozilla.org**. Netscape 6 is based on Mozilla, as are some other lesser known browsers.

The latest browsers adhere more strictly to W3C recommended standards than older browsers do. I consider it best to become familiar with the way things should work and then worry about dealing with the bugs and workarounds necessary for older browsers. All the projects in this book were tested on Internet Explorer 5.0 and up on Windows and Mac, and on Netscape 6 and Mozilla.

Fans of alternative browsers such as Opera and iCab may wonder why these browsers aren't included in the list of testing browsers. There are a couple of reasons for this: first, the number of people who use these alternate browsers is very small. Second, while both browsers offer a lot of promise, their support for all the W3C standards is not quite up to par—at least as of this writing. Opera, for example, offers excellent support for CSS, but not for the W3C DOM—which makes scripting for this browser rather difficult. The browser landscape is constantly changing, however, so things may have already changed by the time you read this book. Always test your pages in as many browsers as you can, concentrating on the browsers that most of your site visitors use.

■ **Your imagination.** Programming can be as creative as visual design, though you'll have to use some other parts of your brain. Hopefully, you can take the concepts explained here and come up with your own creations.

CONVENTIONS USED IN THIS BOOK

Every computer book has its own style of presenting information. As you flip through the book, you'll notice that there's an interesting layout going on here. Because most of you are really into graphics, the project openers contain some cool eye candy. The real meat of the projects starts on the next page. Take a look.

In the left column, you'll find step-by-step instructions for completing the project, as well as succinct but valuable explanations. The text next to the number contains the action you must perform. In many cases, the action text is followed by a paragraph that contains contextual information. Note that if you want to perform the steps quickly and without any background info, you only need to read the text next to the step numbers.

In the corresponding columns to the right, you'll find code and/or screen captions, illustrating the steps. You'll also find Notes and Tips, which will provide you with additional contextual information or customization techniques. Expanded notes about important subjects are contained in Sidebars.

At the end of many of the projects, you'll find unique customization information. Each *Magic* project is designed to be highly customizable and practical; therefore, I provide many tips and examples of what you can do with the techniques you've learned so that you can apply them to your own work quickly and easily.

Finally, the code printed in the book uses a code continuation (or carriage return) character (➡) to indicate when a line of code must break on the printed page, but should not break in your text editor. Keep in mind that code only really comes to life when it's actually used. I recommend that you load up the example code from the CD into a text editor and browser, and try it out for yourself as you go through each project.

DESIGNING A PAGE
WITH CSS

"To stay sharp we must find new

grindstones to whet and sharpen our

potential and keep us at our brightest,

most penetrating best."

—ROBERT KALL

APPLYING CSS STYLES TO A BASIC HTML PAGE

Use CSS style rules to transform the appear-

ance of a basic HTML page. This project

shows you how to create an About Us page

for a fictional jazz and swing band. If you have

never tried to use CSS on your pages before,

this is the ideal project to start you on

your way.

Designing a Page with CSS

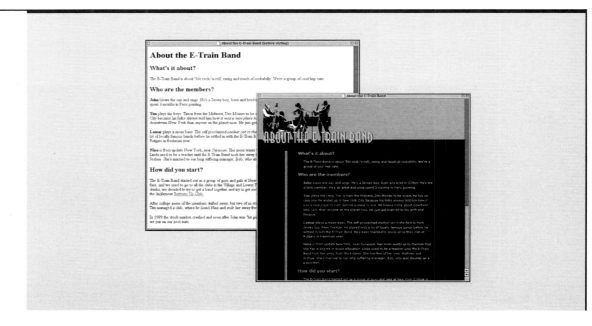

GETTING STARTED

In this project, you will create a well-formed HTML page using tags that should be familiar to you. Then you'll apply Cascading Style Sheet (CSS) style rules to transform the text appearance, change colors and background, and adjust margins. Finally, you'll be given the opportunity to add some extra touches to enhance the page. Note that the book uses only one background graphic for the page—all other appearance changes are accomplished with CSS.

CREATING A WELL-FORMED HTML PAGE

Your first task is to turn a basic text document into well-formed HTML—the base to which CSS style rules are applied. The following steps will guide you through this process.

1 Create the copy for the web page or examine the copy that you have been given. If necessary, mark it up so that you know which lines are headers, which sections will be paragraphs, and so on.

CREATING WELL-FORMED CSS THAT IS READY FOR HTML MARKUP

Before you apply CSS style rules or create JavaScript for your pages, it's critical to lay a good foundation. In web terms, this means creating well-formed markup with HTML or XHTML and understanding the Document Object Model (DOM). Think of the markup as the framework of your page and the DOM as the wiring and plumbing. CSS makes the page look good, and JavaScript adds life to it. All of these parts work together to create a well-designed, dynamic web page.

The keys to creating CSS-ready, well-formed HTML markup are as follows:

1. Close opened HTML tags.

   With the exception of a few tags, most HTML tags should be closed. This means that if you open a paragraph with a **<p>**, you must close it with a **</p>**. When applying CSS style rules to HTML elements, open tags might cause styles to be displayed incorrectly.

HTML tags should be thought of not just as tools for layout, but as wrappers around content or as "containers." HTML tags are used to identify parts of the web page as scriptable and styleable objects.

2. Take care not to overlap tagged elements.

   For example, this is incorrect:

   <p>text**<b>**more text**</p></b>**

   This is correct:

   <p>text**<b>**more text**</b></p>**

3. Eliminate most presentation tags from your markup.

   This chiefly means avoiding the use of the **<font>**...**</font>** tag for indicating how the text looks, but it also can mean not using style attributes in a tag, such as **bgcolor**, **margin** values, and **border** values. For this project, we've avoided all such attributes in the HTML tags.

2 Convert the text document into a well-formed HTML document. Use familiar HTML tags such as **<h1>**, **<h2>**, and **<p>** to indicate headers and paragraphs.

On this page, the **<h1>** tag has been used for the top-level headers, and **<h2>** has been used for all subsequent headers. Use inline elements such as **<b>** and **<em>** to indicate inline text that should stand out. Make sure that all the tags are closed properly to prevent CSS problems.

```
<!DOCTYPE HTML PUBLIC "-//W3C//DTD HTML 4.01//EN"
   "http://www.w3.org/TR/REC-html40/strict.dtd">
<html>
<head>
   <meta http-equiv="content-type" content="text/html;charset=ISO-8859-1">
   <title>About the E-Train</title>
</head>

<body>
<h1>About the E-Train Band</h1>

<h2>What's it about?</h2>

<p>The E-Train Band is about '50s rock-'n-roll, swing and touch of rockabilly.
We're a group of cool hep cats.</p>

<h2>Who are the members?</h2>

<p><b>John</b> blows the sax and sings. He's a Jersey boy, born and bred in Clifton. He's
the oldest member. He's an artist and once spent 3
months in Paris painting.</p>
```

continues

Using HTML Tidy: A good way to check your pages to see if they are well formed is to run them through an *HTML/XHTML lint program*. HTML/XHTML lint programs parse a document, checking to see if there are any unclosed tags.

The most popular lint program is HTML Tidy by Dave Raggett. It is available for just about every computer platform in existence and is tremendously useful—and it's free. See **http://www.w3.org/People/Raggett/ tidy/** for the version most suited for your needs.

You also might want to validate your document using an HTML validation program. See the "About DOC-TYPE" section later on in this project for more about how validation works.

After you have checked for well-formed HTML, the page is ready to style with CSS.

Note: At this stage, you should not be concerned about the design of the page because this will be applied later with CSS styles. This might take some getting used to, but it also teaches you to think of the page contents and structure as being separate from the visual design of the page. Ensuring that the page is readable without any CSS means that the page contents are readable with non-CSS browsers, such as text browsers.

continued

```html
<p><b>Tim</b> plays the keys. Tim is from the Midwest, Des Moines to be exact. He has no
idea how he ended up in New York City because his folks always told him how   <em>it was a
nice place to visit, but not a place to live </em>. He knows more about downtown New York
than anyone on the planet now. He just got married to his girlfriend Melanie.</p>

<p><b>Lamar</b> plays a mean bass. The self proclaimed <em>coolest cat in the East</em> is
from Jersey too, from Trenton. He played with a lot of locally famous bands before he
settled in with the E-Train Band. He's been married to Joyce since they met at Rutgers in
freshman year.</p>

<p><b>Nina</b> is from upstate New York, near Syracuse. Her mom wants us to mention that she
has a degree in music education. Nina used to be a teacher until the E-Train Band took her
away from the kiddies. She has two of her own, Matthew and Joshua. She's married to our long
suffering manager, Bob, who also doubles as a babysitter.</p>

<h2>How did you start?</h2>

<p>The E-Train Band started out as a group of guys and gals at New York College in the mid-
80s. We were all blues and jazz fans, and we used to go to all the clubs in the Village and
Lower East Side together. Since we couldn't afford to pay for our drinks, we decided to try
to get a band together and try to get some gigs. After a few months, we did. Our first gig
was at the (in)famous <a href="http://www.example.com">Bottoms Up Club.</a></p>

<p>After college some of the members drifted away, but two of us stayed in the Village. John
got a job as a stockbroker, and Tim managed a club, where he found Nina and stole her away
from the band she was in. Lamar joined a year later.</p>

<p>In 1989 the stock market crashed and soon after John was "let go" from his Wall Street
job. As he traded in his blue suits, we put on our zoot suits.</p>


<h2>Do you have a new CD?</h2>
<p>Yep. It's our 10<sup>th</sup> CD and it's
called <b>Swing Low</b>, available from <a href="http://www.example.com">Artista Records.
</a></p>


<h2>When's your next gig?</h2>

<p>Check out our <a href="http://www.example.com">World Tour Schedule.</a></p>
</body>
</html>
```

CREATING THE LAYOUT

After the basic page structure is established, it's time to design the layout of the page. This page requires a simple design with a restrained color palette that is reminiscent of the Jazz Age. A one-column layout is used to present the text contents to keep the design streamlined.

1 Using your favorite graphics programs, make a layout mockup of your page.

In this case, a combination of Adobe Illustrator and Photoshop has been used to create the layout.

2 Based on the mockup, create a color palette and note the RGB color values for each color.

This page uses black for the base color, a very pale gray (RGB #eeeeee) for the foreground, golden yellow (#ffcc00) for the headers and the accent text, and an orange (#ff9900) for the second accent color. The color combination is intended to invoke a sophisticated mood reminiscent of the 1930s.

Create a mockup in Photoshop. Use a one-column layout for the text. Note the RGB values of the colors that you'll use in the CSS stylesheet later.

Note: Setting up your color palette with the corresponding RGB hex codes at this stage makes it much easier to create a uniform look. It's useful to note the color values now given that you will be using them in your CSS stylesheet.

3 Create a page banner graphic that will be used as the background image for the page. Make it 1200 pixels wide. Use line art as the basis of the logo element, staying within the color palette for the page. Save the graphic as a GIF.

By setting the width of the graphic to 1200 pixels, you ensure it's wide enough to stretch across the top of the browser window on most monitor displays. By keeping the color palette constrained and by using line art, you'll be able to keep the file size small—a mere 9k.

Create a "banner" graphic that is wide enough to stretch across the top of the browser window.

Note: The bottom of the banner graphic is black, the same color as the intended background color of the final page. The graphic will blend in with the background seamlessly.

APPLYING CSS FONT STYLES

The capability to quickly specify and change the font styles for a whole page is one of the main advantages of using CSS. You'll never go back to the **<font>** tag again.

1 Set up the **<style></style>** tags in the head section of the page.

The comment **<!-- -->** tags hide the contents from older browsers. The CSS style rules will be written within these tags.

```
<head>
        ....other head tags....
        <style type="text/css" media="Screen">
        <!--
                ...style rules go here....
        -->
        </style>
</head>
```

2 Set the font face for the whole page by specifying the same font face values for the **font-family** property for the **<body>**, **<h2>**, **<p>**, and **<div>** elements.

Several fonts are listed in order of preference. Gill Sans is the first choice—if the user has this font installed, the page will be displayed in this font. However, given that Gill Sans is not a commonly installed font, the second choice is Verdana. The final font specified is the default sans-serif. Users who do not have either Gill Sans or Verdana installed will see the browser default sans-serif font.

```
body, h2, p, div {
        font-family: 'Gill Sans', verdana, helvetica, sans-serif;
        }
```

The shorthand method of specifying a single style rule for multiple elements or selectors. Separate the font names with commas and put quotation marks around font names with spaces.

It's also possible to specify the style rule for each element (selector).

```
body {
        font-family: 'Gill Sans', verdana, helvetica, sans-serif;
        }
h2 {
        font-family: 'Gill Sans', verdana, helvetica, sans-serif;
        }
p {
        font-family: 'Gill Sans', verdana, helvetica, sans-serif;
        }
div {
        font-family: 'Gill Sans', verdana, helvetica, sans-serif;
        }
```

Note: When you want to specify the same font for the entire page, it's enough to simply specify it for the body element because all current browsers support CSS inheritance (where style rules applied to a parent element get passed down to a child or are nested elements within the parent element). Netscape 4.x, however, does not support inheritance rules very well. Therefore it's safer to specify any applicable style rules for all the major elements/selectors on the page, as we have done here.

Use this shorthand method when specifying the same style rules for multiple elements/selectors all at once. If you prefer, you can specify the font-family value separately for each element/selector instead of using this shorthand method. The code shows both methods.

3 Specify the **font-size** and **line-height** rules for individual selectors. Apply these styles to each element selector.

On this page, the **h2** elements have a **font-size** value of 15 pixels, and the **p** elements have a **font-size** value of 11 pixels with a leading (**line-height**) value of 18 pixels.

Note: Tag selectors and font-family names are case-insensitive.

When specifying a specific font name with spaces in it (such as Gill Sans), surround the whole name with quote marks. If specifying a one-word font face name (such as Helvetica), the quote marks are not needed.

4 Check the page in your main testing browsers and fine tune the **font-size** and **line-height** values if necessary.

Note that no style rules have been applied to the **h1** element. We will apply a special rule to this element later.

```
p {
    font-size: 11px;
    line-height: 18px;
}
h2 {
    font-size: 15px;
}
```

Specify the **font-size** and the **line-height** properties in pixels. In this case, the **font-size** for the p (paragraph) element/selector is 11px, and the **line-height** (the spacing from baseline to baseline of each line of text) is specified at 18px. The **h2** element/selector size is 15px.

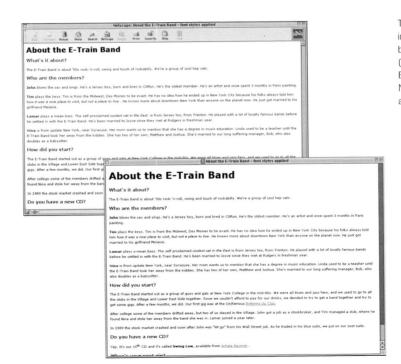

The font face, size, and leading (**line-height**) appear to be the same in Netscape 4.75 (on the left) and Internet Explorer 5.0 (on the right). No style rules have been applied yet to the **h1** element.

SPECIFYING FONT AND LINE HEIGHT SIZES

On this page, **font-size** and **line-height** values are specified in pixel units. Specifying these values in pixels is the safest choice when your goal is to make the page look the same, as much as is possible, in all CSS-aware browsers.

Odd pixel values for **font-size** can cause problems in Netscape 4.x on Windows, which usually makes them one pixel smaller. Check your page in Netscape 4.x, and if the font size seems too small, size it up to 12px or more.

Never specify **line-height** in anything other than pixels to avoid running into more Netscape 4.x problems. Specifying **line-height** in **em**, for example, can cause the lines to overlap each other in certain situations.

APPLYING COLOR STYLES AND BACKGROUND IMAGES

Your page starts to take shape as you apply color values and add a background banner graphic—by applying **background** and **color** style rules.

1 Working from the basic color palette, specify a black background (RGB value **#000000**) for the page. Make the main **p** (paragraph) text light gray (RGB value **#eeeeee**).

Note that you are adding **background-color** and **color** styles to both the **body** and **p** tag selectors.

> **Note:** Specify the **background-color** and **color** rules for both the **body** and **p** elements/selectors. While this is not necessary for current browsers that support CSS inheritance properly, it's necessary for Netscape 4.x, which does not.

```
background-color: #000000;
color: #eeeeee;
```

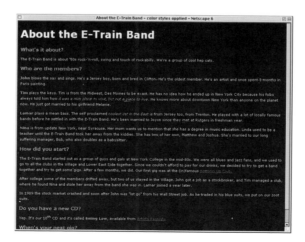

The page with color styles applied to the header, bolded and emphasized text.

2 Specify the first accent color value (golden yellow, RGB value **#ffcc00**) for the **h2**, **b**, and **em** elements.

```
color: #ffcc00;
```

The CSS style rules up to this point with the color style rules.

SPECIFYING COLOR VALUES

Color values are case-insensitive. You can specify the color value in the following ways:

- In hex code in the format **#rrggbb** (where **rr** is the 2-character code for the red value, **gg** is the green value, and **bb** is the blue value) or **#rgb** (the first character of the red, green, and blue hex code values).

- In the format **rgb** (**red,blue,green**). Use the normal integer values for **red**, **blue**, and **green** within the parentheses, not the hex values.

- Some colors can be specified by name. (I never found this to be too practical except for colors such as black and white because I can never remember which colors are which names. Specifying colors by RGB value is also more precise, considering that you can say exactly which "red" you mean to use—the pink-red or the brown-red!)

For example, the golden yellow used here can be specified either as **#ffcc00**, **#fc0**, or **rgb** (**255,204,0**).

Don't use quotation marks around the color hex values. (Some HTML-friendly text editors have a feature that makes it possible to drag a color from a palette to the document to auto-insert a color value but may insert quotation marks too. Remember to delete these when using the color values in CSS.)

```
p {
    font-size: 11px;
    line-height: 18px;
    color: #eeeeee;
}
h2 {
    font-size: 15px;
    color: #fc0;
}

b,em {
    color: #ffcc00;
}

body,p,
h2 {
    font-family: 'gill sans',verdana,helvetica,arial,sans-serif;
}

body {
    background-color: #000000;
    color: #eeeeee;
}
```

3 Add colors to the **a** element. In the default (unclicked) state, make the **a:link** pseudo-elements the alternate accent orange color (**#ff9900**).

4 Specify the appearance of two other **a** element pseudo-classes, **:visited** and **:hover**. Place the **:visited** rules above the **:link** rules. For the **:hover** pseudo-element, use a pale yellow (**#ffff99**) **background-color**.

A **background-color** value is specified for the **:hover** state to provide immediate visual feedback to the user when she moves the mouse over it.

5 Specify that link text should be underlined by applying the **text-decoration: underline** rule to the **:link** pseudo-element. Specify that visited links should not be underlined by applying the **text-decoration: none** rule to the **:visited** pseudo-element.

Note: Put pseudo-element style rules in this order: **:visited**, **:link**, then **:hover**. This is necessary because of cascade order rules in CSS.

```
a:visited {
     text-decoration: none;
     color: #ffff99;
     background-color: black;
     }
a:link {
     text-decoration: underline;
     color: #ff9900;
     background-color: black;
     }
a:hover {
     color: black;
     background-color: #ffff99;
     }
```

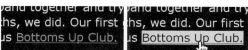

Set different style rules for **a:link** (left, the default view of hyperlink text), **a:hover** (center) and **a:visited** (right). The visited link has no underline (**text-decoration: none**) and is a pale yellow color, making it recede visually.

6 Add the background image to the **body** tag selector and set the **background-repeat** value to **no-repeat**.

```
body {
     background-image: url(etrainlogo.gif);
     background-repeat: no-repeat;
     }
```

TRANSFORMING HYPERLINK TEXT WITH TEXT-DECORATION AND TEXT-TRANSFORM

Hyperlink text is underlined by default. Many designers prefer to remove the underline. To do this, specify **text-decoration: none**. However, keep in mind that Netscape Navigator 4.x does not recognize the **:hover** pseudo-element. Therefore, if you do get rid of the underline, make sure that hyperlinks are clearly marked in some other way.

Another **text-decoration** value that's available in current browsers is **overline**. This places a line above the text. On its own it looks rather silly, but you can combine it with underline to create a line above and below a piece of text.

Text-transform is another property that can be used to make text, such as hyperlink text, stand out. The possible values for this property are **lowercase** (turns all characters to lower case),

uppercase (turns all characters to upper case), and **capitalize** (turns just the first character of each word to upper case).

The following style rules are displayed:

```
a:link {
        text-decoration: overline underline;
        }

a:hover {
        text-transform: uppercase;
        }
```

An **a** element (hyperlink text) with **text-decoration** set to **overline underline** stands out on the page (left). The hover state (right) changes the text to upper case with **text-transform: uppercase**.

The **background-repeat** rule specifies whether the background image should be repeated (stepped) over the page and in which direction. In this case, the background image is not repeated, so the **background-repeat** value is set to **no-repeat**.

> **Note:** Note that **background-attachment** is not recognized in version 4 browsers; however, this should not overly influence the page design.

> **Note:** Background style rules may be specified one-by-one, as is done here, or in "shorthand" format all at once. The order is as follows:

```
selector {
        background: background-color url(path/to/
        background/image) background-repeat background-attachment
        background-position;
        }
```

Not all properties need to be specified. (We'll cover **background-attachment** later on in this project and **background-position** in Project 2, "Incorporating CSS in a Table-Based Layout.") For this page, we can specify the background styles as follows:

```
body {
        background: black url(etrainlogo.gif) no-repeat;
        }
```

7 Check the results in a browser. The text is overlapping the background image, which is not desirable. This will be remedied in the next step.

The text contents overlap the background image at this point.

ADJUSTING THE MARGINS AND PADDING TO REFINE THE LAYOUT

By adding **margin**, **padding**, and **border** property styles, you can fine tune the layout of your page without resorting to tables.

1 Place the entire text contents (everything that is contained within the **<body>**...**</body>** tags) in a **div** element with the **id main.**

This puts the contents of the page into one big block. CSS style rules that specify the margins, border, and padding are applied to this block.

2 Specify **margin-top**, **margin-left**, and **margin-right** property values for the **#main** selector.

3 Add a strong **border** to the left side of the text block. Specify the width, style, and color of the left border with the **border-left-width**, **border-left-style**, and **border-color** properties.

Note: The **border-left-color** property would be the logical one to use here, but unfortunately it's not recognized by Netscape 4.x. Use **border-color** instead if you want a border to appear in Netscape 4.x. The **border-style** (**border-left-style**, **border-right-style**, and so on) properties are also ignored by Netscape 4.x, which only displays solid single-line borders.

Note: id selectors are case-sensitive. Remember to put a hash **#** mark in front of the **id** selector name but not in front of the **id** attribute in the HTML tag. The HTML tag for the **div** looks like this:

<div id="main">...</div>

Note: The **margin** properties are used to specify how far the block of text should be from the top, left, right, and bottom sides of the browser window. The **margin-top** value should be slightly larger than the height of the banner graphic.

Keep in mind that this will restrict the margin widths but not the actual width of the text block. For example, if the browser window is 800 pixels wide, the text block will be 550 pixels wide; if the window is 1100 pixels wide, the text block will be 850 pixels wide. If you want to restrict the actual width of the text block itself, set the width property value like so: **width:** 500px.

The **margin-bottom** property is also available. However, Netscape 4.x might incorrectly add the **margin-bottom** value to the top of the element, which will make the top margin too much. Therefore, it's not used on this page.

4 Specify a **padding-left** value to put some white space between the edge of the text and the border.

```
#main {
        margin-top: 200px;
        margin-left: 100px;
        margin-right: 150px;
        margin-bottom: 50px; /* only recognized by a few browsers */
        width: 500px;

        border-left-width: 10px;
        border-left-style: double;
        border-color: #ffcc00;
        padding-left: 30px;
```

5 Indent the **p** elements by specifying a **text-indent** property value.

Indenting the **p** elements emphasizes the headings.

```
/* Indent all paragraphs. */
p {
        margin-left: 20px;
        }
```

Note: To indent (shift to right) a whole block of text, use the **margin-left** property as we've done here. To indent only the first line of a block of text, use the **text-indent** property.

The text contents are now placed appropriately in relation to the graphic, and a double border has been applied to the left side, emphasizing the Art Deco feel.

PROVIDING FOR TEXT READERS AND CLEANING UP THE STYLESHEET

Having both the main header text, "About the E-Train Band," and the text in the image is redundant for viewers using graphical browsers (the majority of site visitors). The easy solution for this is to simply eliminate the header text. However, the drawback is that text-only browsers or screen readers have nothing to read because we can't provide **alt** text for the background image. We will use the **display** CSS property instead.

1 Hide the **h1** element by specifying **display: none**.

The **display** property can be used to completely hide any element by setting the value to **none**. This is a great way to hide redundant text in CSS-capable browsers while still providing alternate text for non-CSS browsers such as text browsers.

2 Clean up and edit the final stylesheet if necessary. Check the results in a browser and correct any errors.

STYLESHEET TROUBLESHOOTING TIPS

Ensure you have answered these questions with the appropriate solutions and watch out for these common stylesheet errors:

- Are all the brackets closed properly?

- Are all colons and semicolons correct? Remember that a colon terminates the property name, and a semicolon terminates each style rule (for example, **property:** value**;**).

- Most CSS properties and selectors are case-insensitive, but ID selectors are case-sensitive. Therefore, if you have an HTML element with the **id myElement**, the corresponding selector in the stylesheet must be **#myElement**—not **#myelement** or **#MyElement**!

- Don't put quotation marks around color hex values.

If you have corrected all of these things and everything displays fine in all browsers except Netscape 4.x, refer to the Netscape 4 troubleshooting tips in Project 5, "JavaScript Rollovers."

```css
/* This will hide the h1 element when the page is viewed in
CSS-capable graphical browsers. */
h1 {
    display: none;
    }
```

The final stylesheet.

```html
<style media="screen" type="text/css">
<!--
p  {
    font-size: 11px;
    line-height: 18px;
    color: #eeeeee;
    margin-left: 20px;
    }
h2 {
    font-size: 15px;
    color: #fc0;
    }

h1    {
    display: none;
    }

b,em {
    color: #ffcc00;
    }

body,p,h2 {
    font-family: 'gill sans',verdana,helvetica,arial,sans-serif;
    }

body {
    background-color: #000000;
    color: #eeeeee;
    background-image: url(etrainlogo.gif);
    background-repeat: no-repeat;
    }

a:visited {
    text-decoration: none;
    color: #ffff99;
    background-color: black;
    }
```

continues

About the E-Train Band

What's it about?

The E-Train Band is about '50s rock-'n-roll, swing and touch of rockabilly. We're a group of cool hep cats.

Who are the members?

John blows the sax and sings. He's a Jersey boy, born and bred in Clifton. He's the oldest member. He's an artist and once spent 3 months in Paris painting.

Tim plays the keys. Tim is from the Midwest, Des Moines to be exact. He has no idea how he ended up in New York City because his folks always told him how *it was a nice place to visit, but not a place to live.* He knows more about downtown New York than anyone on the planet now. He just got married to his girlfriend Melanie.

Lamar plays a mean bass. The self-proclaimed *coolest cat in the East* is from Jersey too, from Trenton. He played with a lot of locally famous bands before he settled in with the E-Train Band. He's been married to Joyce since they met at Rutgers in freshman year.

Nina is from update New York, near Syracuse. Her mom wants us to mention that she has a degree in music education. Linda used to be a teacher until the E-Train Band took her away from the kiddies. She has two of her own, Matthew and Joshua. She's married to our long suffering manager, Bob, who also doubles as a babysitter.

How did you start?

The E-Train Band started out as a group of guys and gals at New York College in the mid-80s. We were all blues and jazz fans, and we used to go to all the clubs in the Village and Lower East Side together. Since we couldn't afford to pay for our drinks, we decided to try to get a band together and try to get some gigs. After a few months, we did. Our first gig was at the (in)famous Bottoms Up Club.

After college some of the members drifted away, but two of us stayed in the Village. John got a job as a stockbroker, and Tim managed a club, where he found Nina and stole her away from the band she was in. Lamar joined a year later.

In 1989 the stock market crashed and soon after John was "let go" from his Wall Street job. As he traded in his blue suits, we put on our zoot suits.

Do you have a new CD?

Yep. It's our 10th CD and it's called **Swing Low**, available from Artista Records.

When's your next gig?

Check out our World Tour Schedule.

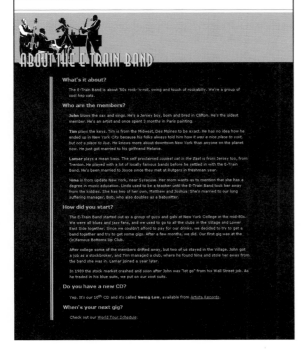

continued

```
a:link {
    text-decoration: underline;
    color: #ff9900;
    background-color: black;
    }
a:hover {
    color: black;
    background-color: #ffff99;
    }


#main {
    margin-top: 200px;
    margin-left: 100px;
    margin-bottom: 50px;
    margin-right: 150px;
    border-left-width: 8px;
    border-left-style: double;
    border-color: #ffcc00;
    padding-left: 30px;
    }
-->
</style>
```

The final page with the "About the E-Train Band" text hidden. It looks quite different from the original text version, yet the structure is exactly the same. The only additions have been the stylesheet and the background image. (The entire page weighs in at under 12K, with the single graphic being 9K in size and the HTML + CSS itself only 3.8K.)

About DOCTYPE

What is the **DOCTYPE** declaration, and how does it work? Up until recently this has been a fairly meaningless question as far as web designers were concerned because browsers ignored the **DOCTYPE** declaration. However, this has changed in the last couple of years. Now's the time to figure out how the **DOCTYPE** works.

The **DOCTYPE** element on an HTML page is used to declare what language a document uses, as well as the level of that language, and what type of Document Type Definition (DTD) that page is using.

There are two types of DTDs: *loose* or *transitional* and *strict*. A strict DTD follows set standards closely and does not allow for any errors, while a loose DTD allows for more leeway and interoperability. However, in practice this works in the following manner:

Note: The first major browser to recognize the **DOCTYPE** declaration as it was intended to be used was Microsoft Internet Explorer 5.0 for Macintosh. Currently Netscape 6 and other Mozilla-based browsers also recognize **DOCTYPE**, as does Microsoft Internet Explorer 6.0 for Windows.

1 Strict HTML or XHTML **DOCTYPE** declaration:

This causes the document to be rendered in Strict mode, adhering to the DTD.

```
<!DOCTYPE HTML PUBLIC "-//W3C//DTD HTML 4.01//EN"
"http://www.w3.org/TR/html4/strict.dtd">


<!DOCTYPE html PUBLIC "-//W3C//DTD XHTML 1.0 Strict//EN"
"http://www.w3.org/TR/xhtml1/DTD/xhtml1-strict.dtd">
```

2 Transitional or loose HTML **DOCTYPE** declaration with a URL:

This causes the document to be rendered in Strict mode, adhering to the DTD—because it points to the URL.

```
<!DOCTYPE HTML PUBLIC "-//W3C//DTD HTML 4.01 Transitional//EN"
"http://www.w3.org/TR/html4/loose.dtd">
```

3 Transitional or loose HTML **DOCTYPE** declaration without a URL:

This causes the document to be rendered in *Quirk* mode—meaning that the browser will render the page as best as it can.

```
<!DOCTYPE HTML PUBLIC "-//W3C//DTD HTML 4.01 Transitional//EN">
```

4 With no **DOCTYPE** declaration at all, the document is rendered in Quirk mode.

5 Transitional XHTML **DOCTYPE** declaration:

This causes the document to be rendered in Transitional XHTML mode.

```
<!DOCTYPE html PUBLIC "-//W3C//DTD XHTML 1.0 Transitional//EN"
"http://www.w3.org/TR/2000/REC-xhtml1-20000126/DTD/
xhtml1-transitional.dtd">
```

If you aim toward creating pages that follow World Wide Web Consortium standards, try to make pages that are as clean and well-formed as possible, specify a strict DTD, validate the page, and then view the page in a standards-compliant browser. (Currently, either Netscape 6.x/Mozilla or Microsoft Internet Explorer 5.0/Mac seem to be the most standards-compliant browsers available.) This will help you to educate yourself on what valid, standard code looks like.

> **Note:** If you are using HTML, use the HTML 4.01 **DOCTYPE**, not the older (4.0 and 3.2) **DOCTYPE**s. HTML 4.01 is the final version of the HTML specifications and includes all the DTDs of the prior versions.

However, for everyday production situations, using the Quirk mode option might still be your best bet—especially if you rely heavily on table-based layouts. Because web pages must work and display as intended in a wide variety of browsers, including those that render markup in quirky ways, it is almost impossible to use a strict DTD for all but experimental web sites.

For example, on a page that utilizes a table-based layout, common practices such as using single-pixel GIFs as "spacers" or including **width**, **height**, **bgcolor**, **colspan**, and **rowspan** attributes in the tags will prompt many complaints from the validator when the page is checked with a strict DTD specified. Displaying such a page in a W3C standards-compliant browser such as Netscape 6.x could be problematic.

> **Note:** Well-formed markup (as opposed to "valid" markup) is the most important aspect of creating a sound foundation for your web pages.

SIZING UNIT ISSUES

For this project, we've stuck to absolute pixel sizes for all size values. Pixel sizes are the most reliable for controlling appearance, especially in version 4 browsers. The disadvantage of using pixels is that the text cannot be resized in most browsers by the user (with the exception of Internet Explorer 5.0 + on the Mac, iCab 2.51 and later, Opera, and Netscape 6/Mozilla.) An alternative is to use relative sizes, such as **em**. This is less reliable but does allow the text to be resized by the user. Be careful with this and test your pages on a variety of platforms and browsers to make sure you're not getting unacceptable results.

Avoid using points (**pt**) when specifying font sizes. In version 4 browsers and older on the Mac, the display resolution is 72dpi (dots per inch), while in all Windows browsers and version 5 and later browsers on the Mac, it's 96dpi. This means a 12-point font is displayed at a much smaller size in older Mac browsers. At small point sizes, the text becomes unreadable. For on-screen representation it's best to stick to pixels. (In case you were wondering, points are also absolute units.)

48pt Times New Roman - Netscape 4

48px Times New Roman - Netscape 4

48pt Times New Roman - MSIE

48px Times New Roman - MSIE

48-point text in Netscape 4.7 (top) is smaller than 48-point text in Internet Explorer 5.0 (third line), but 48 pixel text is the same in both browsers.

INCORPORATING CSS IN A TABLE-BASED LAYOUT

"Simply pushing harder within

the old boundaries will not do."

—KARL WEICK

STYLING A TABLE-BASED LAYOUT WITH CSS

Like it or not, not all computer users upgrade

their browsers to new versions immediately. To

accommodate people who are still using version

4 browsers, it's still safer to use tables for lay-

ing out pages. Additionally, web designers are

far more familiar with using tables for page

creation. This project shows you how to incor-

porate CSS into a typical table-based layout

using the best features of each method.

Project 2

Incorporating CSS in a Table-Based Layout

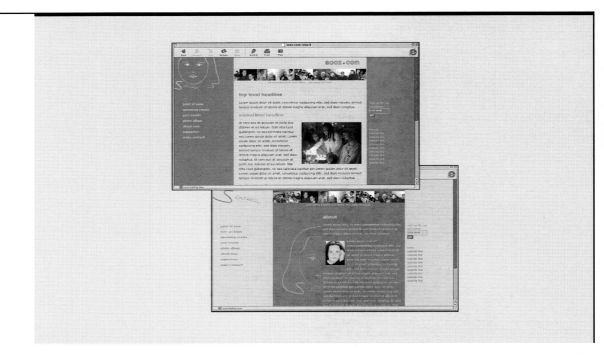

GETTING STARTED

Due to the need to create pages that display the same way in version 4 browsers as well as current version 5 and later browsers, in real-life situations designers are forced to use table-based layouts. However, that doesn't mean that designers can't put CSS to good use.

The example in this project uses a typical 3-column layout. It has a static "banner" element on top, content in the middle, and navigation and link elements in the two outside columns. It uses a combination of a table layout with "safe" CSS properties and values. There are two distinct areas of color in this design, so the **class** and **id** selectors are used for CSS style attributes.

Using CSS makes it much easier to change and update the look of the page, while using tables for the "bones" means the layout will not break up in browsers with partial support for CSS standards. Consider this approach if your client demands

that their site look good in Netscape Navigator 4.08 through the latest browsers. If you are leery of using CSS at all, this project will help you to ease into it without abandoning table-based layouts.

In this project, you'll learn how to

- Build a simplified table layout that uses **div** elements inside the table cells rather than nested tables

- Use **class** selectors to define separate styles for different groups of the same HTML elements

- Use **id** selectors to define styles for unique elements

- Refine and enhance the look of the page with CSS

- Create a page that still looks good in version 4 browsers and is enhanced in the latest browsers

PLANNING THE BASIC LAYOUT

When planning a table-based layout that uses CSS, it's important to figure out the logistics at the design mockup stage, even before you start to create the markup. Try to keep the number of nested **table** elements to a minimum. Where you might have used nested tables before, use **div** or **span** elements.

1 Based on the list of requirements given to you by your client, create a mockup of the layout of your page in your favorite image editor. Use the rulers and the layout grid if needed. Make notes where necessary.

Here, the required sizes for the base graphics, and where to use **rowspan** in the table layout are noted.

This page layout uses one simple **table** with **div** element blocks nested within table cells. The **div** blocks are indicated by black borders in the figure. The **div** blocks are used where previously designers might have used nested tables for blocks of content.

Note: When you are planning to use CSS in a table-based layout that must display properly in older browsers, it's safest to plan for positionable block-level elements, such as **div** blocks, to be placed inside table cells. **div** blocks are more flexible than nested tables because it's possible to specify **margin** or **padding** style rules for them, as you'll see later in this project.

2 Based on the page mockup, create the base graphics.

On this page there are six base graphics: the illustration logo, the site logo, the photo strip, the "connecting people" text beneath it, and the background "watermark" image behind the main content area. A single-pixel transparent "spacer" GIF is also used for certain table cells.

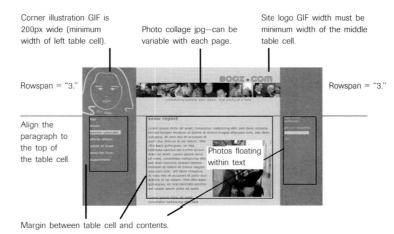

Corner illustration GIF is 200px wide (minimum width of left table cell).

Photo collage jpg—can be variable with each page.

Site logo GIF width must be minimum width of the middle table cell.

Rowspan = "3."

Rowspan = "3."

Align the paragraph to the top of the table cell.

Photos floating within text

Margin between table cell and contents.

Have a clear picture of your layout. Note the size of the base graphics, as they will work within the HTML markup. Except for the static content on the top of the page, the changeable content in the left, center, and right table cells are contained within **div** blocks, instead of using nested tables.

The base building block graphics, showing transparency where appropriate.

The corner illustration is made to the exact size of the minimum size of the table cell that will hold it. The site text logo and the "connecting people" text graphic are as wide as the minimum width of the inner table row (400 pixels) and as high as the table cells that will hold the graphics. The single-pixel transparent GIF is used to "hold open" any table cells that are visually empty.

Note: When creating a transparent GIF, choose a matte color for the graphic that matches the background color that the graphic will be placed onto. For the face illustration graphic in this project, the matte color is set to a medium gray, which matches the intended background color.

CREATING THE HTML TABLE LAYOUT AND EXTERNAL STYLESHEET

Once the layout design is nailed down and the base graphics are created, convert it to an HTML table-based layout. At the same time, set up an external stylesheet that will be linked to the HTML page.

1 Create the "bones" of the page using **table** elements and **div**s. Place the images and placeholder text where appropriate. Specify **border="1"** for the **table** tag so that you can see the outlines of the **table** elements. (This border is just temporary so that we can see exactly how the tables look. It will be eliminated later.)

Avoid using any **bgcolor** attributes in the table cell (**<td>**) elements.

Enclose the left, center, and right content elements in **div**s with unique **id**s: **left**, **main**, and **right**.

To make the position of the **div**s clearer, specify a temporary **div {border: 1px solid black}** style for them. This also will be eliminated later.

The text within the **#main div** should be contained within the appropriate headline (**<h1>**...**</h1>**, etc.) or paragraph (**<p>**...**</p>**) tags.

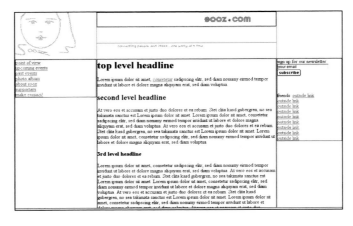

Create the "bones" of the page with a table. The table elements and **div** elements have temporary, visible borders so that we can clearly see the structure.

```
<!DOCTYPE HTML PUBLIC "-//W3C//DTD HTML 4.01//EN"
        "http://www.w3.org/TR/1999/REC-html401-19991224/strict.dtd">
<html>
<head>
        <meta http-equiv="content-type" content="text/html; charset=iso-8859-1">
        <title>Project 2 example: step 1, without the stylesheet</title>

        <style type="text/css" media="Screen">
```

continues

```
<!--
div {border: 1px solid black;}
-->
</style>
</head>
<body>
<table width="100%" border="1" cellspacing="0" cellpadding="0">
<tr>
<td class="seccolor" rowspan="3" width="25%"><img
src="images/corner.gif" alt="" width="200" height="150"
border="0"></td>

<td class="maincolor" width="55%" align="center"><div id="banner">
<img src="images/soozcom.gif" alt="" width="400" height="45"
border="0"></div></td>
<td class="seccolor" rowspan="3"  width="20%" "height="50"><img
src="images/clear.gif">
</td>
</tr>
<tr><td class="maincolor" id="photos" width="55%"><img
src="images/clear.gif" height="50" width="1"></td></tr>
<tr><td class="maincolor" width="55%"><img src="images/connecting.gif"
height="50" width="400"></td></tr>
<tr>
<td class="seccolor" valign="top">

<!-- left side navigation -->
<div id="left">
<a href="#">point of view</a><br>
<a href="#">upcoming events</a><br>
<a href="#">past events</a><br>
<a href="#">photo album</a><br>
<a href="#">about sooz</a><br>
<a href="#">supporters</a><br>
<a href="#">make contact!</a>
</div>
<!-- end left side navigation -->

</td>
<td class="maincolor">
<!-- start main content -->
<div id="main">

<h1>top level headline</h1>
```

```
<p>
Lorem ipsum dolor sit amet, <a href="#">consetetur</a> sadipscing
elitr, sed diam nonumy eirmod tempor invidunt ut labore et dolore
magna aliquyam erat, sed diam voluptua.</p>
<h2>second level headline</h2>
<p>
At vero eos et accusam et justo duo dolores et ea rebum. Stet clita
kasd gubergren, no sea takimata sanctus est Lorem ipsum dolor sit
amet. Lorem ipsum dolor sit amet, consetetur sadipscing elitr, sed
diam nonumy eirmod tempor invidunt ut labore et dolore magna aliquyam
erat, sed diam voluptua. At vero eos et accusam et justo duo dolores
et ea rebum. Stet clita kasd gubergren, no sea takimata sanctus est
Lorem ipsum dolor sit amet. Lorem ipsum dolor sit amet, consetetur
sadipscing elitr, sed diam nonumy eirmod tempor invidunt ut labore et
dolore magna aliquyam erat, sed diam voluptua.
</p>

<h3>3rd level headline</h3>


<p>
Lorem ipsum dolor sit amet, consetetur sadipscing elitr, sed diam
nonumy eirmod tempor invidunt ut labore et dolore magna aliquyam erat,
sed diam voluptua. At vero eos et accusam et justo duo dolores et ea
rebum. Stet clita kasd gubergren, no sea takimata sanctus est Lorem
ipsum dolor sit amet. Lorem ipsum dolor sit amet, consetetur
sadipscing elitr, sed diam nonumy eirmod tempor invidunt ut labore et
dolore magna aliquyam erat, sed diam voluptua. At vero eos et accusam
et justo duo dolores et ea rebum. Stet clita kasd gubergren, no sea
takimata sanctus est Lorem ipsum dolor sit amet. Lorem ipsum dolor sit
amet, consetetur sadipscing elitr, sed diam nonumy eirmod tempor
invidunt ut labore et dolore magna aliquyam erat, sed diam voluptua.
At vero eos et accusam et justo duo dolores et ea rebum. Stet clita
kasd gubergren, no sea takimata sanctus est Lorem ipsum dolor sit
amet.
</p>
<h4>4th level headline</h4>
<p>
At vero eos et accusam et justo duo dolores et ea rebum. Stet clita
kasd gubergren, no sea takimata sanctus est Lorem ipsum dolor sit
amet.
</p>
<!--end main content -->

</div>
```

continues

continued

```
</td>                                                    <a href="#">outside link </a><br>
<td class="seccolor" valign="top">                       <a href="#">outside link </a><br>
                                                         <a href="#">outside link </a><br>
<!-- right side bar -->                                  <a href="#">outside link </a><br>
<div id="right">                                          </div>
<form method="post">                                      <!-- end right side bar -->
sign up for our newsletter
<input type="text" name="email" value="your email"><br>  </td>
<input type="submit" name="submit" value="subscribe" src="images/go.gif"  </tr>
border="0">                                               <tr>
</form>                                                   <td class="seccolor" colspan="3" height="30">
<br><br>                                                  <p>&copy;2000-2001 Susan Kaup, www.sooz.com. Used with permission.</p>
friends:                                                  </td></tr>
<a href="#">outside link </a><br>                        </table>
<a href="#">outside link </a><br>
<a href="#">outside link </a><br>                        </body>
<a href="#">outside link </a><br>                        </html>
```

Note: To specify the temporary border style for the **div** elements, we've used the shorthand form of specifying border styles, that is, **border: 1px solid black**. The syntax is the width of the border, the style of the border, and the color of the border.

2 Establish two classes: **maincolor** and **seccolor**. In your HTML markup, apply the appropriate class attribute to each of the **<td>**s (table cells). The side column and bottom **<td>**s will have the class **seccolor**, and the middle column **<td>** will have the class **maincolor**.

3 Establish four **id** selectors: **photos**, **left**, **main** and **right**. The **id photos** selector is used for the **<td>** that will contain the photo strip graphic; **left** is used for the **<div>** that contains the left side navigation; **main** is used for the **<div>** that contains the main content; and **right** is used for the **<div>** that contains the right side navigation.

Note: For backward compatibility, use the **align=**, **valign=**, **height=**, and **width=** attributes in the **td** cells instead of using the **text-align**, **vertical-align**, **height** and **width** CSS attributes. For more details, see the "How It Works" section later in this project.

```
<td class="maincolor".....> or <td class="seccolor".....>
```

Note: Be sure to apply the **class** attribute to the **<td>** elements rather than the **<tr>** or **<table>** elements to avoid problems in version 4 browsers.

```
<td id="photos"> or <div id="left">  <div id="main"> <div id="right">
```

Note: Use a **class** selector when you want to apply a common set of style rules to multiple elements, and use an **id** selector when you want to apply a set of style rules to a single element on the page. **id**s are also used to identify single elements on a page in JavaScript, as you'll see later on in this book.

4 Create an external stylesheet. Open a new blank text document with no HTML tags. Save this with the filename **main.css**. Link to this stylesheet in your HTML page with the **<link>** tag in the **<head>** section.

```
<link rel="Stylesheet" href="main.css" type="text/css"
media="Screen">
```

USING EXTERNAL STYLESHEETS

By using an external stylesheet rather than putting the CSS style rules within the HTML page, it's possible to define the styles for an entire web site at once.

The external stylesheet file can be named anything you like—it does not have to have the **.css** suffix, although on some servers the **.css** suffix identifies it as a document of type **text/css**. However, it must be a plain ASCII (text) file and cannot contain any HTML tags. Don't use any **<style>** tags or HTML comment tags (**<!-- -->**) within an external stylesheet.

It's a good idea to annotate your stylesheets by inserting comments. To insert comments into a stylesheet (whether the stylesheet is external or included on the HTML page), enclose them in **/* */** tags.

It's common to save external stylesheets in a separate directory or folder. If you save your external stylesheet document to another folder on your site, be sure to specify the correct directory path in the **href=** attribute of the **<link>** tag of the HTML document. In addition, be careful if you are pointing to any image files in your external stylesheet. To avoid problems, it's safest to use absolute links or full server paths when pointing to images or pages within an external stylesheet.

Take this example of the directory structure of a typical web site. The external stylesheet file, styles.css, is in the directory includes. An image used as a background, pattern.gif, is in the directory images. The HTML file named index.html that uses the stylesheet is in the directory content.

If we use relative paths, the **<link>** tag in index.html and the relevant CSS style rule in styles.css look like this:

```
<link rel="Stylesheet" href="../includes/styles.css">
body {
        background-image: url(../images/pattern.gif);
        }
```

Using absolute paths, the **<link>** tag in index.html and the relevant CSS style rule in styles.css look like this:

```
<link rel="Stylesheet" href="/includes/styles.css">
body {
        background-image: url(/images/pattern.gif);
        }
```

CREATING STYLE RULES FOR THE CLASS SELECTORS

This page has two distinctive backgrounds: the main color, which is yellow, and the secondary color, which is gray. You will create style rules and use class selectors to apply these style rules to multiple elements on the page.

1 Define the background color and color attribute styles for the class selectors, **.maincolor** and **.seccolor**.

> **Note:** Class selectors are preceded by a "." (period) in CSS—that is, **.maincolor**.

```
.maincolor {
        background-color: #ffcc66;
        color: #33333;
        }

.seccolor {
        background-color: #666666;
        color: #ffcc66;
        }
```

2 Save these styles and preview your HTML page in a browser.

The backgrounds of the two side columns are now gray, and the middle column is yellow.

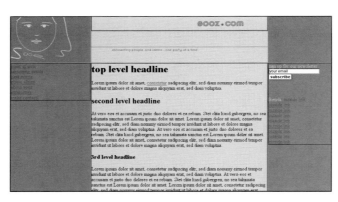

Use a class selector to apply the same style rules to multiple elements on the page. On this page the **<td>** elements that make up the sidebars have a class attribute of **.seccolor**, and the **<td>** elements that make up the middle column have a class attribute of **.maincolor**.

APPLYING FONT STYLES

Next, you will apply font styles to the text elements on the page.

1 Specify one **font-family** style for the entire page by applying the same rule for all the elements on the page. Be sure to include all of the HTML elements on the page that could include any text.

This method tends to be the safest to use when you must support version 4 browsers.

```
p,h1,h2,h3,h4,ul,ol,li,div,blockquote,body,table,td {
        font-family: verdana, arial, helvetica, sans-serif;
        }
```

2 Specify the same color style for all of the header elements (**<h1>**, **<h2>**, **<h3>**, and **<h4>**). Specify different **font-size** styles for each header element and **font-size**, **line-height**, and **color** styles to the **<p>** element.

> **Note:** Use absolute pixel sizes to specify the **font-size** and **line-height** attribute values—to avoid any problems in Netscape 4.x.

```
p,h1,h2,h3,h4,ul,ol,li,div,blockquote,body,table,td {
        font-family: verdana, arial, helvetica, sans-serif;
        }
h1, h2, h3, h4 {
        color: #336699;
        }
h1 {
        font-size: 18px;
        }
h2 {
        font-size: 16px;
        }
h3 {
        font-size: 14px;
        }
h4 {
        font-size: 12px;
        }
p {
        color: #000000;
        font-size: 12px;
        line-height: 20px;
        }
```

3 View the HTML page at this point.

The text in the main section looks the way we intend it to. The text in the side sections is displayed with the **font-family** we have specified, but the font size has not been specified yet.

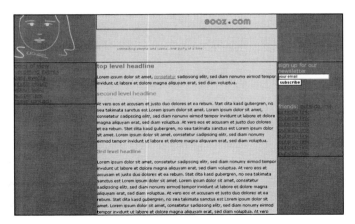

Font styles are applied to the page.

USING CLASS SELECTORS FOR DIFFERENT LINK TEXT

This design uses text navigation rather than graphical buttons for navigation. But that doesn't mean we don't want the navigation to look visually distinctive. To make the **<a>** elements (the link text) in the side sections look different from the **<a>** elements in the main content, we will use **class** selectors.

1 Create two **class** selectors: **nav** for the **<a>** elements in the left column and **outside** for the **<a>** elements in the right column, which are links mainly to outside sites (and of less importance than the main navigation links). Insert the appropriate **class** attributes into each **<a>** tag in the left and right columns. The default **a** element style will be used for links within the main body text.

> **Note:** For practical purposes, it's not necessary to specify a **background-color** style for all the elements. However, the W3C CSS Validator will complain if you do not specify a **background-color**. For elements that do not have a background color, specifying a transparent color value will suffice. Do not use the inherit color value—this will show up as an interesting lime green in Netscape 4.x.

```
<!-- left side navigation, showing class attributes inserted into tags. -->
<div id="left">
<a class="nav" href="#">point of view</a><br>
<a class="nav" href="#">upcoming events</a><br>
<a class="nav" href="#">past events</a><br>
<a class="nav" href="#">photo album</a><br>
<a class="nav" href="#">about sooz</a><br>
<a class="nav" href="#">supporters</a><br>
<a class="nav" href="#">make contact!</a>
</div>
<!-- end left side navigation -->
```

KEEP THE HTML IN THE EDITABLE AREA SIMPLE

Why not create a class for the **<a>** elements in the middle section also? For one thing, it's not necessary given that we can define style rules for the default **<a>** element. Another reason for not creating classes for HTML elements within the main content is that this is typically the part of a page that will be updated frequently by the client, long after the designer has completed the site. The client might know a little HTML—or you may be able to give him instructions about how to update the content—but it's quite likely that he will forget about adding any extra attributes to the tags. Even if you are editing the pages yourself, you could forget which classes to use where.

Therefore, it's usually a good idea to keep the markup tags for the main content section of a web page as basic as possible, without any associated **class** attributes. In addition, when building your page, make it very clear which area is editable and which area should not be touched by your client or anyone else. (Using comment tags is a good way of making clear what fits where.)

2 Create the style rules for the three different `<a>` element styles.

```css
a:link {
    color: #993333;
    background-color: transparent;
    font-weight: bold;
    text-decoration: none;
    }
a:visited {
    background-color: transparent;
    color: #666666;
    text-decoration: none;
    }
a:hover {
    background-color: transparent;
    color: #ffff99;
    background-color: #993333;
    }
a.nav:link, a.nav:visited {
    color: #ffcc66;
    background-color: #666666;
    font-weight: bold;
    text-decoration: none;
    }
a.nav:hover {
    color: #cccccc;
    background-color: #993333;
    }
a.outside:link, a.outside:visited {
    color: #ffcc66;
    background-color: #666666;
    text-decoration: none;
    font-weight: normal;
    }
a.outside:hover {
    text-decoration: underline;
    color: #ffcc66;
    background-color: transparent;
    }
```

3 Check the page in a browser again. To see the "hover" behavior, check the page in a version 5 or higher browser or in Microsoft Internet Explorer 4.x.

> **Note: hover** is not supported by Netscape 4.x. The page should still be navigable without the **hover** style.

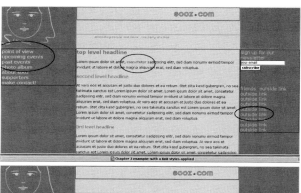

The link text is circled. The top screenshot shows default link styles, and the bottom screenshot shows the **hover** style.

APPLYING MARGIN AND PADDING STYLES TO THE divs AND THE BODY

Instead of using nested tables, the page uses **divs** to contain the text elements. The advantage of using **div** blocks rather than nested tables is that it's possible to apply **margin**, **padding**, and other style rules to the element.

1 Create style rules for the **id** selectors, **#left** and **#right**. Specify the same **margin-top** value and the appropriate **margin-left** and **margin-right** attribute values. Specify the **font-size** and **line-height** attribute values also.

```
#left {
    margin-top: 40px;
    margin-left: 20px;
    font-size: 12px;
    line-height: 24px;
}

#right {
    margin-top: 40px;
    margin-left: 10px;
    margin-right: 20px;
    font-size: 11px;
    line-height: 16px;
}
```

2 Create style rules for the **id** selector, **#main**. Specify a "white space" around the contents of the **div** by using the **padding** attribute. These style rules are applied to the **<div>** element with the **ID** main.

```
#main {
        padding: 0px 10px 10px 20px;
}
```

Note: When specifying different **padding** or **margin** values for the four sides of the elements on one line like this (as opposed to specifying each side separately—that is, **margin-top**, **margin-left**, and so on, as we did for the **#left** and **#right** selectors), start at the top side and work your way around clockwise. (Think of a clock that starts at 12 and stops at 3, 6, and 9.)

3 Create a **margin** attribute style rule for the **body** element. To get rid of the default browser margin, set the **margin** value to **0**. When all the **margin** values are the same, as in this case, you can specify one single number.

```
body   {
        margin: 0;
}
```

Bug Alert

Why use the **padding** attribute for the main **div** element here? Technically, using the **margin** attribute makes more sense because we want to specify a margin between the edge of the **<div>** block and the edge of the **<td>** that contains it. However, there is a bug in Netscape 4.x that will cause the width of a **<div>** element that contains long unbroken lines of text to stretch very wide when you specify margin values for it. Therefore, we're using the **padding** attribute here. Visually, the results are the same. For version 5 and later browsers, using the **margin** attribute works fine.

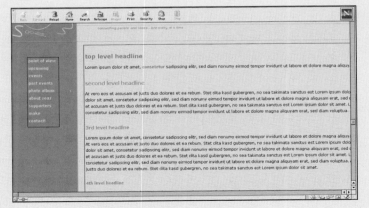

If you specify margin values for the main **div**, in Netscape 4 the **div** stretches way out horizontally.

Note: When all four sides of an element have the same **padding** or **margin** value, you can just specify one value as I did here.

Zero is the only number for which you do not have to specify a unit of measure such as **px** or **pt**.

Note: Specifying a **margin** value of **0** for the **body** element is the simple CSS way of getting rid of the default browser offset. However, this does not work in Netscape 4.x. If you want to get rid of that default browser offset in Netscape 4.x, the most straightforward way is to use the **marginwidth="0"** **marginheight="0"** attributes in the **<body>** tag. This is not valid HTML 4.01 markup, however.

4   View the HTML in a browser.

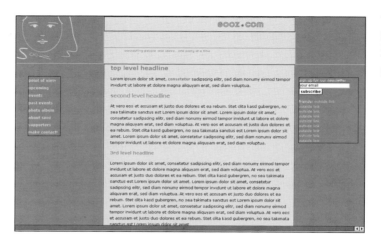

The page with **margin** and **padding** values set for the left, main, and right **<div>** elements. The browser default margin also has been eliminated.

APPLYING STYLES TO FORM ELEMENTS

Form elements are often overlooked in the overall page design because most designers find them boring. However, with CSS it's possible to improve the appearance of form elements.

Note: Netscape 4.x does not recognize CSS styles for form elements.

1   Create a class **textbox** for the **input** field and **submitbutton** for the **submit** button. Insert the **class** attributes for each in the HTML markup.

There are two **form** elements on this page: the text input field and the submit input button. Because both are **input** elements in HTML terms, it's necessary to set up separate classes for each to specify CSS styles for them.

```
<input class="textbox" type="text" name="email" size="30" value="your email">
<input class="submitbutton" type="submit" name="submit"
value="subscribe" border="0">
```

Note: class selectors are used for the **form** elements instead of **id** selectors, even though there's only one submit button and one text input box on this page. This allows you to use this external stylesheet throughout the site. If there is a form on another page with multiple buttons and text boxes, you specify the appropriate **class** attribute to multiple elements.

2 Specify the CSS style rules for the **submitbutton** and **textbox** input **class** selectors.

For the **submitbutton**, specify the text color (**color**), the background color (**background-color**), the border styles for each side of the element (**border-top**, **border-bottom**, **border-left**, and **border-right**); the style of the text (**font-family**, **font-weight**, and **font-size**); the **height** and **width**; and a **vertical-align** value to center the text vertically in the button box. Note that we have specified a solid border that's the same color as the background color of the submit button—that's to make the button seem a little bit bigger.

For the **textbox**, specify the text color (**color**), the background color (**background-color**), the border styles for each side of the element (**border-top**, **border-bottom**, **border-left**, and **border-right**); the style of the text (**font-family** and **font-size**); the **height** and **width**; a **vertical-align** value to center the text vertically in the text box; and **padding** to put a little space between the text and the edge of the text box on top and bottom. Note that we have given the text box a dashed border and the same background color as the area of the page where it will be located.

```
input.submitbutton {
        color: #ffffff;
        background-color: #993333;
        border-top: 2px solid #993333;
        border-right: 2px solid #993333;
        border-bottom: 2px solid #993333;
        border-left: 2px solid #993333;
        font-family: arial, sans-serif;
        margin-top: 2px;
        font-size: 11px;
        font-weight: bold;
        height: 20px;
        width: 60px;
        vertical-align: middle;
}

input.textbox {
        color: #ffffff;
        background-color: #666666;
        font-family: arial,sans-serif;
        font-size: 11px;
        border-top: 1px dashed #ffffff;
        border-right: 1px dashed #ffffff;
        border-bottom: 1px dashed #ffffff;
        border-left: 1px dashed #ffffff;
        height: 18px;
        width: 80px;
        vertical-align: middle;
        padding: 2px 0px 0px 2px;
}
```

Note: The border styles have been specified for each side. This is because if you specify a style for all borders at once, that is **border: 1px dashed #ffffff;** in Netscape Navigator 4.x, you will see a small, detached box floating near the input element to which you have applied the **border** style. Because Netscape Navigator 4.x does not recognize border styles for form elements when they are specified for each side of an element, it will ignore the style values.

Note: Although we've specified a **height** and **width** style for each **form** element in the stylesheet, it's still necessary to include a **size** attribute value in the **<input>** tag for the text box. This is to avoid a very wide text box from showing in Netscape 4.x, which doesn't recognize CSS styles applied to **form** elements. The **width** value specified in the CSS will override the size value in the browsers that do recognize CSS styles applied to form elements.

3 Check the results in a browser.

In Internet Explorer 5.x and up and in Netscape 6, the **form** elements are styled. In Netscape 4.7, they're not—but the Netscape 4.x site visitor would probably be unaware that anything was missing.

The **form** elements displayed in Internet Explorer 5.0 (left), Netscape 6.2 (center) and Netscape 4.75 (right).

Note: If you want to have a colorful **submit** button that displays in Netscape 4.x, you can use an **input** element of the type image, for example,

```
<input type="image" src="somegraphic.gif">
```

The disadvantage of using an image input button is that it only can have a submit action. You can't use an image for a reset button, for example.

CREATING DIFFERENT LOOKS FOR MULTIPLE PAGES USING ONE GRAPHIC

Details count in any design, and with some CSS style rules you can make a design come to life. For example, you can use a single graphic as a background image for a table cell for every page but vary the **background-position** to give a different view. Because the graphic is loaded the first time the visitor accesses a page, on subsequent pages the graphic displays in a snap. Creating fewer graphics also means less work for the designer.

1 Delete the temporary border style rule for the **div** elements by deleting the whole **<style></style>** section in the **<head>** section of the HTML page. Eliminate the table border by changing the **border** attribute value to **0** in the **<table>** tag.

```
<table width="100%" border="0" cellspacing="0" cellpadding="0">
```

2 Create an **id** selector called **photo**. Apply that **id** attribute to the empty table cell at the top of the page.

```
<td class="photo".....>
```

3 Specify **background** attribute styles for the **photo** selector. Use the photo strip graphic (stripcolor.jpg) for the **background-image**. Specify that the image should repeat horizontally only by giving the **background-repeat** attribute a value of **repeat-x**. Specify a **background-position** value of **0% 0%**.

```
#photo {
        background-image: url(images/stripcolor.jpg);
        background-repeat: repeat-x;
        background-position: 0% 0%;
        }
```

Note: The **background-position** can be specified with **x** and **y** coordinates as shown here or with values such as **top**, **center**, **bottom**, **left**, **center**, or **right**. Specifying, the **x** and **y** coordinates gives more flexibility.

4 Change the **x** coordinate of the **background-position** property value for each page to show a different part of the graphic. To make the **background-position** override the "default" **background-position**, place the style rule inline within the **<td>** element with the ID photo.

```
<td class="maincolor" id="photo" width="55%"
style="background-position: 30% 0%"><img
src="images/clear.gif" height="50" width="1"></td>
```

This allows for varying the design without having to load a separate graphic every time. Note that **background-position** is not recognized in version 4 browsers, but Netscape 4.x users will see the background graphic in its default position—so nothing will seem to be missing.

Place a single-pixel clear GIF with **height="50"**, the height of the background graphic in the **table** cell to keep it open. The background graphic will show through the clear GIF.

Here is the revised code for the photo strip **table** cell.

Note: Any style rules specified inline (as a **style** attribute within the HTML tag) will override the **style** rules specified elsewhere, such as in an external stylesheet or in the **<head></head>** section of the page.

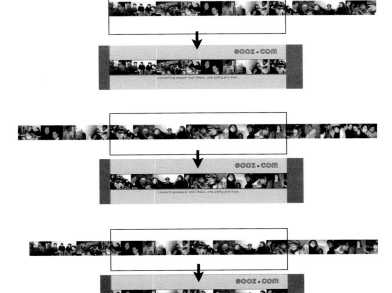

One long (1500-pixel wide) graphic is used as a background-image for the table cell, with the **background-position** set to different values for different pages on the site. From top to bottom: **background-position: 0% 0%; background-position: 30% 0%; and background-position: 60% 0%.**

ADDING BORDERS TO PAGE COLUMNS WITH CSS

Used with restraint, borders can add to the look of a page design. Previously, it was only possible to add the look of borders with complicated nested tabled and single-pixel GIFs used as "shims." With CSS, you can add or subtract borders easily.

1 Create two new class selectors for the side panels named **seccolorleft** and **seccolorright**. To give these two classes the same **color** property values as **seccolor**, group them together in the style rules. Specify only the **border** styles for the individual classes.

2 Change the class attributes in the HTML markup for the table cells where you want the appropriate border to appear, from **seccolor** to **seccolorleft** or **seccolorright**.

```
.seccolor, .seccolorleft, .seccolorright {
    background-color: #666666;
    color: #ffcc66;
}
.seccolorleft {
    border-right: 2px solid #cccccc;
}
.seccolorright {
    border-left: 2px solid #cccccc;
}
```

3 Review your page in a browser.

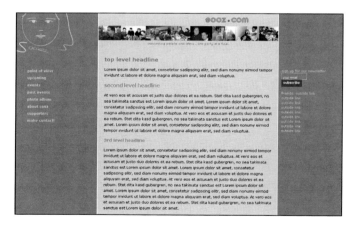

A subtle, light gray border has been added to the left and right side columns of the page.

CREATING STYLES FOR FLOATING PICTURE ELEMENTS

Many of the pages on this site will have photos interspersed with the text. Handling the positioning of graphics is much easier with CSS than with complicated table layouts.

1 Create two classes for graphics that will go to the left of the text and graphics that will go to the right. Name these **picleft** and **picright**.

2 Use the **float** property to define styles for these two **class** selectors. Add some padding so that there is sufficient "white space" around the graphic.

```
.picright {
    float: right;
    padding: 10px;
    }
.picleft {
    float: left;
    padding: 10px;
    }
```

3 Specify a **clear** attribute value of **both** to the header elements. This is necessary to prevent the header text from wrapping around a placed graphic.

```
h1, h2, h3, h4 {
    clear: both;
    }
```

Note: The style rule **clear: both** means that the element content will not wrap around graphics placed on either side. You also may use **clear: left** and **clear: right** if you want to specify that the text should not wrap around when a graphic is only on the left or right side.

4 Place some graphics in the text in **div** elements with the **class** attribute **picleft** or **picright**.

Take care that the floating **div**s are not nested within the paragraphs or headlines but placed in between the tags—to avoid problems in version 4 browsers.

Before (top) and after (bottom) creating float style rules for the **div** elements that contain the images. With float, the text flows around the graphic.

39

HOW IT WORKS: DEALING WITH VERSION 4 BROWSERS

This project shows a fairly conservative use of CSS that is mostly version 4 browser-safe. The keys here are to use a simple table layout to define the large sections of the page, but to use CSS box-level elements (using **div**) to define the inner areas. As long as the **div**s are contained within table cells, they will usually behave properly in legacy browsers.

Instead of struggling with the lack of CSS support in version 4 browsers, learn to live with them. As the screenshots here show, the pages do not look absolutely identical in Netscape Navigator 4.x and in version 5 and 6 browsers, yet the page is still acceptable, and nothing is obviously breaking up. The only things lacking are small cosmetic items such as the borders and the colored form elements.

Creating a similar page relying on older methods (such as using small table cells and nested tables for creating "borders") is a tremendous amount of work and also adds to the weight and complexity of the page.

The page viewed in different browsers—from top: Netscape 4.75; Internet Explorer 5.0/Windows, Netscape 6.2, and Internet Explorer 5.0/Mac. There are small differences in each browser, but the page still looks fine.

MODIFICATIONS: CREATING AN ALTERNATE LOOK

By changing the stylesheet, it's possible to quickly create a whole new look for the page. In this example, we created an alternate layout for the site's "about" page, where the colors are reversed. The complete stylesheet for this page as well as the original page are on the companion CD as well as on the companion website at http://www.createwebmagic.com.

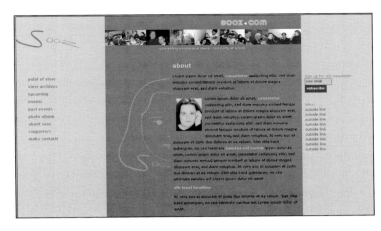

Modify the look of a page quickly by changing the stylesheet.

"Fall seven times, stand up eight."

—JAPANESE PROVERB

CREATING A SIMPLE LAYOUT WITH CSS-P

BOOKS.PRODOK.NET OPENING PAGE

The great promise of CSS is the ability to position elements around the screen using style rules (CSS-P). Since the introduction of version 5 and later browsers, it has finally become possible to use more CSS-P for laying out a web page. This project shows the possibilities of using CSS-P for page layouts right now, as well as some of the drawbacks.

Project 3

Creating a Simple Layout with CSS-P

GETTING STARTED

For this project, I have designed a page with a simple 2-column layout. The layout is created with CSS instead of relying on tables. By following along, you will see the various problems that you can be faced with when attempting to use CSS positioning properties for layout in currently available browsers. You also will learn some more style rules to apply to text elements.

In this project, you will learn about

- XHTML markup
- The position property values and how they are interpreted in browsers
- More ways to style text with CSS

In this project, you'll learn how to create a simple 2-column layout using CSS-P. The main requirement for this page is that it should be liquid and scaleable—it should resize and reposition itself when the browser window is altered.

44

CREATING THE XHTML BASE

For this project, we will use XHTML markup instead of HTML markup. XHTML is very similar to HTML markup, with just a few differences.

The disconcerting aspect of using CSS for many web designers who are used to creating layouts with tables and **<font>** tags is that there is no immediate visual feedback of the layout until the CSS is applied. Nevertheless, it's important to learn this way of assembling a web page to take full advantage of CSS. Create and tag the page content first and leave the visual layout for later.

1 Open a new XHTML page using the XHTML 1.0 Transitional **DOCTYPE**.

Put the header text content within **<h1>** tags and other text within **<p>** tags. Close all open tags: **
** should be **
, and **<img> tags should be closed with an **/>**.

Note: To ensure that the page will be readable in older, non-CSS-enabled browsers, it is always a good idea to use regular header (**<h1>**, **<h2>**, and so on), paragraph (**<p>**), and other recognized HTML tags to indicate the relevant portions of your text content.

Tip: On this page, we've specified several colors with CSS that are not one of the 216 web-safe colors. You can obtain the hex codes for these colors with the Eyedropper tool in many graphics programs such as Fireworks and Photoshop.

Colors outside of the 216 web-safe color palette won't be displayed properly on lower color depth monitors that can only display up to 256 colors. The number of such monitors in use is dwindling, but to be on the safe side, test your designs at many different color settings.

```
<!DOCTYPE html PUBLIC "-//W3C//DTD XHTML 1.0 Transitional//EN"
    "http://www.w3.org/TR/xhtml1/DTD/xhtml1-transitional.dtd">
<html xmlns="http://www.w3.org/1999/xhtml">
<head>
<meta http-equiv="content-type" content="text/html; charset=iso-8859-1">
<title>books.prodok.net</title>
<style type="text/css" media="Screen">
<!--
the CSS will go here.
-->
</style>
</head>
<body>

<div id="leftbox">
<p>
There is no such thing as
a moral book or an immoral book.
    Books are well written or
    badly written. That is all.
</p>

<p>--Oscar Wilde</p>

</div>

<div id="rightbox">
<img src="images/booksbig2.gif" alt="books.prodok.net" width="300"
height="45" border="0" />

<br />
```

continues

The Key Differences Between HTML and XHTML

Following is a list of differences between HTML and XHTML:

- The **DOCTYPE** declaration is required for XHTML. For most pages, use the XHTML Transitional DTD shown here, which is more flexible and tolerant of markup and does not strictly meet the stringent requirements of the XHTML Strict DTD.

- The **<html>** tag has an **xmlns** attribute pointing to a document on the W3C site.

- HTML is not case-sensitive, but XHTML is (because it's a subset of the case-sensitive XML markup language). All tags must be in lowercase.

- All XHTML tags must be closed. This includes replaced tags, such as **<meta>**, **
, and **<img>, which are not "closed" in HTML. In XHTML, these tags now look like this: **<meta.../>**, **
, and **<img.../>. (Always have a space between the last attribute within the tag and the ending tag.)

All XHTML files should be saved with the **.htm** or **.html** suffix, not **.xhtml**.

continued

```
<h1>Books we're writing</h1>

<p>Welcome to the prodok.net books portal. Here you will find links to the books we're
writing, as well as to the ones we use, read and recommend.
</p>

<p><a href="#">Check out what's new.</a></p>

<h1>books we're writing</h1>

<p>JavaScript + CSS + DOM Magic<br />
to be published by New Riders Publishing,<br />
spring 2002.</p>

<h1>books under development</h1>
<p>PDF Handbook for Designers</p>

<h1>books we use</h1>
<p><a href="#">newest review</a><br>
<a href="#">review index</a></p>

</div>

</body>
</html>
```

2 Create a **div** element with the **id leftbox**. Enclose the **<p>** element that contains the quotation in this **div** element.

This will be the positionable left-side block.

Tip: An easy way to convert an existing HTML markup to XHTML is to parse it with HTML Tidy, using the Convert HTML to XML option.

3 Create a **div** element with the **id rightbox**. Put the opening **<div>** tag at the top of the remaining content and put a closing **</div>** tag at the end. This will be the positionable right-side content block.

> **Note:** The **div** element is a generic, block-level element with no predefined style rules associated with it. Therefore, it's a good idea to use **div** to create blocks of positionable content.

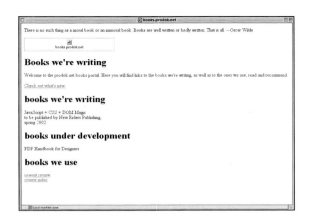

Check the page in a browser at this stage to ensure that the contents are readable without any styles applied. Here the image also is turned off to check the alt text in the **img** element.

CREATING THE STYLE RULES FOR THE BODY AND TEXT ELEMENTS

Before positioning the elements on the page, let's create the style rules for the **p**, **h1**, and **body** selectors.

1 Create font styles for the **p** and **h1** elements, as well as the **a** (link) pseudo-elements.

> **Note:** Instead of specifying each type of font style property separately, it's possible to use a type of CSS shorthand to specify all styles at once. The syntax is as follows:
>
> **font: font-weight font-size line-height font-style font-family;**
>
> It's not necessary to specify all the property values, but they must be listed in the correct order.
>
> When specifying a selection of **font-family** font faces in order, it's not always necessary to stick with the default font style type of your first typeface choice. Here for example, the first choice for the **p** element is Georgia, a serif font. But you'd rather see Verdana or another sans-serif font such as Helvetica or Arial displayed if Georgia is not available on the user's machine.

```
p {
        font: normal .9em/1.3em georgia, verdana, arial, sans-serif;
        color: #333333;
        }
h1 {
        font-family: georgia,verdana, sans-serif;
        font-size: 1.5em;
        color: #333333;
        }
h2 {
        font-family: georgia,verdana, sans-serif;
        font-size: 1.2em;
        color: #333333;
        }
a:visited {
        color: #333333;
        text-decoration: none;
        }
a:link {
        color: #333333;
        text-decoration: none;
        }
a:hover {
        text-decoration: underline;
        }
```

47

2 Use the `:first-letter` pseudo-element to change the **color** of the first letter in the **<h1>** elements.

> **Note:** Psuedo-elements let you set the style of a sub-section of an element without using a **<span>** tag. The `:first-letter` pseudo-elements refer to the first character of the text contents of any given element. Here, it's used to change the color of the first character of the **h1** header text—to add a little pizzazz.

```
h1:first-letter {
    color: #993333;
    }
```

3 Give the first **<p>** element in the markup a class attribute of **quote**. Apply the **font-style: italic** rule to the **p.quote** class selector to italicize the text. In addition, apply the **white-space: pre** style to make the text display exactly as it's typed. Finally, apply a unique **line-height** style and **color** style.

```
<p class="quote">
There is no such thing as
a moral book or an immoral book.
    Books are well written or badly written.
    That is all.</p>
<p class="author">--Oscar Wilde</p>
```

```
p.quote {
        font-style: italic;
        line-height: 18px;
        white-space: pre;
        color: #7b686a;
        }
p.author {
        font-style: italic;
        line-height: 18px;
        text-align: right;
        color: #7b686a;
        }
```

4 Give the second **<p>** element on the page a class attribute of **author**. Apply the same **font-style**, **line-height**, and **color** rules to the **p.author** class selector as the ones used for the **p.quote** class selector. In addition, give the element a **text-align: right** style.

> **Note:** The **white-space: pre** rule is the CSS replacement for the **<pre>** tag. Elements with this style are displayed exactly as they are typed. The one drawback to using the **white-space: pre** rule is that it's not supported properly by Internet Explorer 5.5/Windows and earlier, but this has been fixed in Internet Explorer 6.0.
>
> The **text-align** property aligns the contents of a given element to the left, center, or right of the element. In this case, the text contents of the element are aligned to the right.

5 Check the page in your target browsers. Adjust the font sizes in the CSS styles if needed.

The page with styles applied to the text elements. Note that the quotation text appears exactly as it's typed and that the author name is aligned to the right.

6 Specify the style rules for the **body** element. Add the **margin: 0px** style rule to get rid of the default browser window offset.

Because the background image should only repeat along the **y** axis (up–down), it's necessary to specify the style rules.

```
body {
      background-color: #eeeeee;
      background-image: url(images/bookscollage.jpg);
      background-repeat: repeat-y;
      margin: 0px;
      }
```

Note: Instead of specifying each type of background style property separately, it's possible to use a type of CSS shorthand to specify all styles at once. The syntax is as follows:

background: background-color background-image background-repeat background-attachment background-position;

For this page, the background property style is this:

background: #eeeeee
url(images/bookscollage.jpg) repeat-y;

Note that it's not necessary to specify all property values, but the values must be specified in the correct order.

POSITIONING THE ELEMENTS

A combination of CSS positioning rules is used to achieve the required layout.

1 Apply a temporary border to all **div** elements on the page by using a **border** style rule.

The temporary border lets us see the boundaries of the elements we're trying to position during the design process. It will be removed once we're happy with the results.

```
/* temporary black border on all div elements.
This will be removed later. */
div {
        border: 1px solid black;
        }
```

2 Apply an absolute position value style rule (**position: absolute**) for the **#leftbox** selector. Give **#leftbox top** and **left** values of **80px** to position the element 80 pixels down and 80 pixels across from the top left corner of the browser window. Apply a width value of **25%** so that it takes up 25% of the **width** of the parent element (the **body**).

```
#leftbox {
        position: absolute;
        top: 80px;
        left: 80px;
        width: 25%;
        background-color: transparent;
        }
```

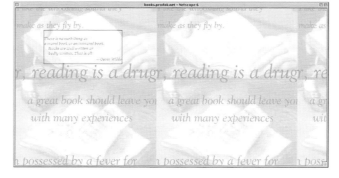

The absolutely positioned **div** element sits in the white area of the book in the background image. Even when the page is resized, it stays in the same position. Only the width changes, but because the quotation text has a **white-space: pre** style, it doesn't move.

USING THE position AND float PROPERTIES TO PLACE ELEMENTS

All elements on a page have a default **position** value of **static**. That simply means that an element appears exactly where it's typed on the page. When you want to shift elements around on the page with CSS, you will use other **position** values. The **position: absolute** and **position: relative** values are the ones you will use most frequently in CSS-P.

A **position: absolute** element stays "put" on the page, at the left/top and in some cases right/bottom coordinates you specify for it. An absolutely positioned element is positioned absolutely within the containing parent element: that is, if it's contained within a block **div** element and you specify a **top** position value of **100px**, then it will be positioned 100 pixels from the top of the parent. On this page, the containing parent element for the **#leftbox div** is the body, so it's positioned 80 pixels from the top and 100 pixels from the left of the browser window.

Absolutely positioned boxes are taken out of the normal "flow." This means they have no impact on the layout of other elements on the page except for any elements that are nested within that element. On this page you can see that the **leftbox div** stays in place even if you resize the page.

A **position: relative** element, on the other hand, is positioned according to the flow of the document. If the "normal" position of an element is at point x, and you specify a **left** position of **300px**, then the top left corner of the element is offset by 300 pixels.

The **float** property, which was introduced in Project 2, "Incorporating CSS in a Table-Based Layout," is used to specify whether a relatively positioned element should be positioned, or "floated," to the left or right of the parent. (The default value for **float** is **none**.) On this page, we've applied a **float: right** value to the relatively positioned **rightbox div** to position it to the right of the body.

---

3 Apply a relative position value style rule (**position: relative**) to the **#rightbox** selector. Specify **float: right** so that the element will float to the right side of the parent element (the **body**). Specify **0px** as the value for the **margin-top**, **margin-right**, and **margin-bottom** properties so that the element will be flush with the top, right, and bottom sides of the browser window.

Specify a **padding-top** value of **150px** and a **padding-left** value of **60px** so that the contents of the right-box element will be positioned 150 pixels from the top edge and **60px** from the left side of rightbox.

```
#rightbox {
        position: relative;
        float: right;
        margin-top: 0px;
        margin-right: 0px;
        margin-bottom: 0px;
        padding-top: 150px;
        padding-left: 60px;
        width: 45%;
        height: 1200px;
        z-index: 10;
        background-color: #f7f7f7;
        border-left: 5px double #7b686a;
        }
```

Specify a **width** value of **45%** so that the rightbox element's width will be 45% of the width of its parent element (the **body**).

Specify a **z-index** value higher than **0** or **1**—here we've set it to **10**. The **z-index** property specifies the 3-dimensional stacking order of elements on the page. Set it to a high enough number so that the rightbox element does not get overlapped by any other element on the page.

Specify a height value of **1200px** to make sure that the element will "stretch" long enough vertically to fill the browser window.

Finally, apply the **background-color** and **border-left** styles. Here we've specified a very pale gray for the background and a purple picked up from the background image for the border color.

4 Check the page in a browser at different browser window widths.

Note: If no **z-index** value is specified, the leftbox element might overlap the rightbox element, which is not acceptable in this case.

The page layout displayed in a browser window. When the window is resized, the rightbox element resizes itself to 45% of the browser window width. The only disadvantage of this approach is that the rightbox overlaps the leftbox when the window is very narrow.

Note: An absolute pixel value of **1200px** is specified for the **height** property, instead of a relative value such as **100%**. This is because of the different ways that browsers handle the question, "100% of what?"

The W3C CSS-2 specifications merely state that when an element's height is specified as a percentage value, it should be a percentage of the containing block's overall height. We're used to assuming that when we specify a height of 100% for an element whose parent is the body, it should be 100% of the browser window height. This is the way it's interpreted in Internet Explorer 5.x on both Windows and Mac. However, Netscape 6.x interprets 100% to mean 100% of the body height. The body height "stretches" just enough vertically to accommodate the contents. On pages like this where there isn't much content, you'll see that the bottom of the rightbox **div** is cut off in Netscape 6.

If your page has enough content to "stretch" the height of the **body**, this is not an issue. Another rather ugly workaround is to insert a large number of line breaks coupled with invisible non-breaking line spaces (the ** ** HTML entity) at the bottom of the text content.

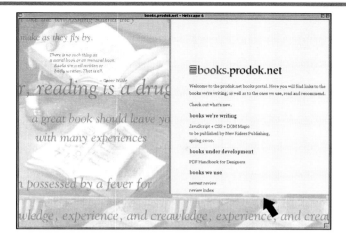

The rightbox **div** is cut short at the bottom in Netscape 6 when its height property is set to 100% specified.

REFINING THE LAYOUT

Now we'll add another refinement to the layout by adding a margin to the text block and changing the **line-height** value for one of the paragraphs.

1 In the XHTML markup, enclose the text contents in the rightbox **div** in another **div** with the **id** contents. Give a **class** attribute of **blurb** to the first **p** element.

```
<div id="contents">

<p class="blurb">Welcome to the prodok.net books portal.
Here you will find links to the books we're writing, as
well as to the ones we use, read and recommend.
</p>
<!-- the rest of the contents go here. Omitted here
for clarity. -->
</div>
```

2 This specifies CSS rules for the **#contents** selector that corresponds to the contents **div**. Specify a **margin-left** value of **25px** and a **margin-right** value of **70px**. This "indents" the whole contents **div** block by the specified **margin-left** value and also puts in adequate white space on the right side of the **div** block relative to the edge of the parent element (the **rightbox div**).

```
#contents {
    margin-left: 27px;
    margin-right: 70px;
}
```

3 Specify CSS rules for the **p.blurb** class selector. Specify a **line-height** value of **18px**. All **p** elements with the class blurb will inherit the style rules for the plain **p** element selector, but the **line-height** property value (set to **24px** originally) will be overridden by the new value.

```
p.blurb {
    line-height: 18px;
}
```

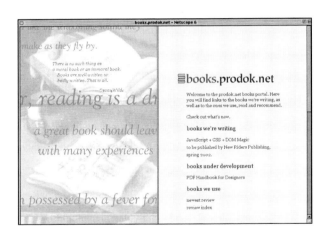

The text block now has wider left and right margins, and the blurb text line height is narrower.

MAKING ADJUSTMENTS FOR NETSCAPE 4.X

Using this method of laying out two columns works more or less in Netscape 4.x. However, a few additional adjustments are necessary.

1 Add the JavaScript **onresize** code to the **<body>** tag. This causes the page to reload itself if the browser window is resized. Without this, the page will totally collapse when the window is resized.

```
<body onresize="history.go(0)">
```

2 Delete the **background-color: transparent** style from the **#leftbox** selector. The **background-color: transparent** style is improperly displayed as black in Netscape 4.x.

Do not specify a **border** style together with a **background** style for any **div** element. When a **border** style is specified for **div** elements, Netscape 4.x will show a gap between the edge of the background color and the border. You can specify colors for either the border or the background, but not both.

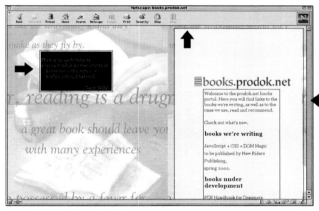

Netscape 4 CSS bugs: a transparent background is displayed as black, there is a gap between the edge of the background color and the border, and when the page is resized, the layout collapses totally. Additionally, the zero margin value for the body element is not recognized.

Note: In reality, it's not practical to rely on pure CSS-P when creating layouts for Netscape 4.x. In later projects, I'll show you different ways of coping with this problem using JavaScript and some CSS tricks.

CREATING ANOTHER TWO-COLUMN LAYOUT

The disadvantage of using the method described previously is that when the browser window is too narrow, the right column block overlaps the left column block. Creating a 2-column layout where both columns should be liquid, yet not overlap each other, is a little trickier.

For this example, more text has been added to the left column.

1 Delete the **white-space: pre** style rule from the **p.author** class element so that the text is displayed normally.

2 Change the style rules for the **#leftbox** selector. Specify a **position: relative** style, a **width** value of **45%**, and a **margin** value of **0** for a zero margin on all sides of the box. The **padding-top** value is set to **50px** so that the content starts 50 pixels from the top edge of the **div** block.

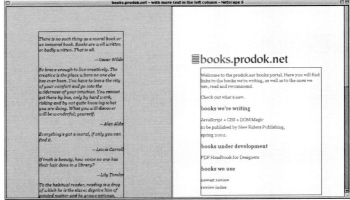

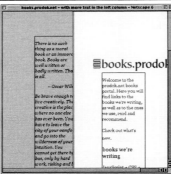

The same page with more text added to the **leftbox div**. Note that the right-box overlaps the leftbox when the browser window is narrow. (The background image has been omitted for clarity.)

3 Set the **padding-left** and **padding-right** values to **2%**. Specify a **float** value of **left**. Change the **background** property style rules to use the book collage graphic. (This is the same **background** style rule we used previously for the **body** element.)

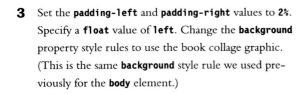

```
#leftbox {
        position: relative;
        width: 45%;
        margin: 0;
        padding-top: 50px;
        padding-left: 2%;
        padding-right: 2%;
        float: left;
        background: #eee url(images/bookscollage.jpg);
}
```

4 Change the **float** property value of the #rightbox selector from **right** to **left**. Change the **padding-left** and **padding-right** values to **2%** and **3%**, respectively.

```
#rightbox {
    position: relative;
    float: right;
    margin-top: 0px;
    margin-right: 0px;
    margin-bottom: 0px;
    padding-top: 2%;
    padding-left: 3%;
    width: 45%;
    height: 1200px;
    z-index: 10;
    background-color: #f7f7f7;
    border-left: 5px double #7b686a;
}
```

5 Change the **background** property value of the **body** to the same background color as the #rightbox selector.

```
body {
    background: #f7f7f7;
    margin: 0px 0px 0px 0px;
    padding: 0;
}
```

6 Check the results in a browser window.

> **Tip:** It's important to keep in mind that any border adds to the dimensions of the block if you use a temporary **div border** to mark the edges of **div** elements.

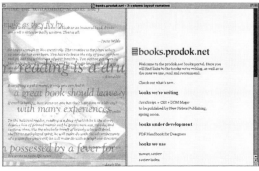

Two liquid columns that don't overlap each other when the browser window is resized.

How This Layout Works

The following list explains how this 2-column layout works:

- Both elements have the style **float: left**. Logically speaking, you might be inclined to use **float: left** for the **leftbox** element and **float: right** for the **rightbox** element. However this goes against the way the **float** property works according to CSS specifications. When **float: left** is set, it means that the element should be on the left of any following elements. Therefore, even though nothing follows the **rightbox div**, its **float** value should be set to **left** because it should stay on the left of anything that follows it.

- The two **width** values for the **leftbox** and **rightbox** plus the **padding-left** and **padding-right** values for each add up to **99%**, rather than **100%**. This is because of the **border** on the left side of the **rightbox** element. If the total of the widths, left and right margins, left and right padding values, and left and right border widths of the elements aligned next to each other exceed 100%, the blocks will collapse and just be displayed from top to bottom in the order they appear in the markup.

- The **background** image style is applied to the **leftbox** instead of keeping it with the **body** element. When block elements are aligned with this method horizontally, a tiny gap shows on the right side with the body background showing through. To avoid having this unsightly gap, set the **background** style rules for the **body** to the same values as the **rightbox** element.

Be warned, this layout will break if the browser window is resized to be too narrow.

If the background of the body differs from the right side block, the body background shows through on the right edge.

Modifications: A Single-Column, Centered Layout

I'll conclude this project by varying the **width**, **margin**, and **padding** property rules to create a simple, horizontally centered, single-column layout. There are several ways of accomplishing this seemingly simple task. Here are three possible methods.

Please note that none of these methods work in Netscape 4.x.

1 Delete the **rightbox div** and all its contents from the page. You should now have just the **leftbox div** block.

The goal: to create a liquid centered-column layout.

2 Re-apply the background image style to the **body** selector. Apply a solid background-color style to the **#leftbox** selector.

```
body {
        background: #eeeeee url(images/bookscollage.jpg) repeat-y;
        }
        #leftbox {
        background-color: #f7f7f7;
}
```

3 Apply the styles indicated in the code to the **body** and **#leftbox** selectors. We'll call this Layout Method 1.

Here the **body** has a zero margin and zero padding. The **div** is positioned relatively with a **width** of **70%**. The **margin-left**, **margin-right**, **padding-left** and **padding-right** properties are specified in percentages with the total of all of these plus the **width** adding up to 98%. This prevents the horizontal scrollbar from appearing on the browser window.

This method does not work very well in Internet Explorer version 5.0 and older browsers.

```
body {
        background: #eee url(images/bookscollage.jpg);
        margin: 0;
        padding: 0;
}
#leftbox {
position: relative;
border: 5px double #7b686a;
width: 70%;
margin-top: 30px;
margin-left: 7%;
margin-right: 7%;
margin-bottom: 30px;
padding-top: 50px;
padding-left: 7%;
padding-right: 7%;
background-color: #f7f7f7;
}
```

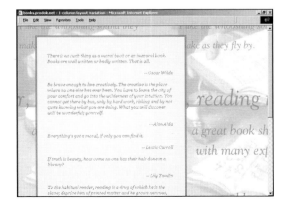

This method does not work in Internet Explorer 5.0/Windows, where the column is shifted to the left.

4 Apply the styles indicated in the code to the **body** and **#leftbox** selectors. We'll call this Layout Method 2.

Again, the **body** has a zero margin and zero padding. The **div** is positioned relatively, with a **width** of **70%**. The **margin-left** and **margin-right** property values are specified as **auto**. This means that the browser decides automatically what the margins should be, based on the other specified values.

The advantage of this method is that it's straightforward and easy to implement. In addition, the **padding** values can be specified as absolute units (pixels) because the browser will calculate the needed margins. However, this method only works in the latest browsers that support the **auto** value—Internet Explorer 6.0/Windows, Internet Explorer 5.x/Mac, and Netscape 6.x.

```
body {
        background: #eee url(images/bookscollage.jpg);
        margin: 0;
}

#leftbox {
        position: relative;
        width: 80%;
        margin-top: 50px;
        margin-bottom: 30px;
        margin-left: auto;
        margin-right: auto;
        border: 5px double #7b686a;
        padding-top: 50px;
        padding-left: 50px;
        padding-right: 50px;
        background-color: #f7f7f7;
        }
```

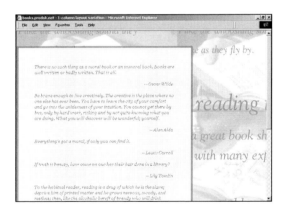

This method does not work in Internet Explorer 5.0/Windows, where the column is stuck to the left.

5 Apply the styles indicated in the code to the **body** and **#leftbox** selectors. We'll call this Layout Method 3.

For this method, an inverse kind of thinking is applied by specifying **padding** styles for the **body**. This offsets any element contained within the **body** by the specified **padding** values from the edge of the browser window. The **padding-left** and **padding-right** values have been set to **15%**, which means that logically, the contained **div** block is always 70% wide.

Surprisingly, this method works well in Internet Explorer 5.0.

```
body {
        background: #eee url(images/bookscollage.jpg);
        margin: 0;
        padding-top: 50px;
        padding-bottom: 30px;
        padding-left: 15% ;
        padding-right: 15%;
}

#leftbox {
        position: relative;
        border: 5px double #7b686a;
        padding-top: 50px;
        padding-left: 50px;
        padding-right: 50px;
        background-color: #f7f7f7;
}
```

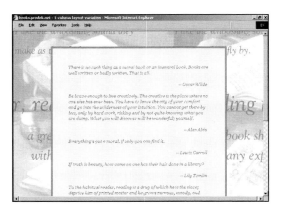

This method works well in Internet Explorer 5.0/Windows.

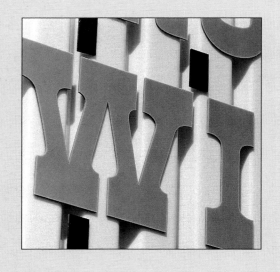

CREATING A COMPLEX
LAYOUT WITH CSS-P

"People who make no mistakes

lack boldness and the spirit of

adventure. They are the brakes

on the wheels of progress."

—DALE E. TURNER

A Page with Nested Elements

Even in the latest CSS-capable browsers, there

are bugs and pitfalls to work around. In this

project, you'll learn how to avoid the pitfalls

while creating a complex CSS-P layout with

nested elements.

Project 4

Creating a Complex Layout with CSS-P

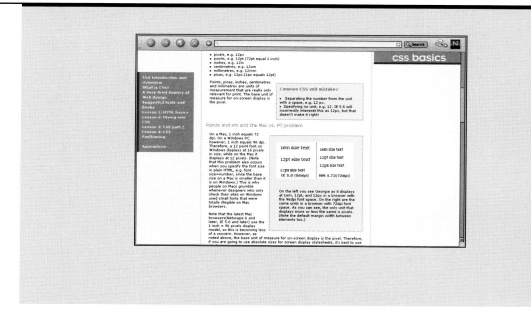

GETTING STARTED

When creating a layout with CSS-P that includes multiple nested elements, there are many bugs, omissions, and pitfalls to work around, even in the later CSS-capable browsers. We'll examine various ways of accomplishing a work around by manipulating some CSS rules to our advantage.

In this project, you will also learn about:

- The **@import** method of linking external stylesheets

- The **position: fixed** style rule

- The Cascade Order and the **!important** declaration

- The document "family" tree and inheritance

- Styling list elements with CSS

CREATING THE XHTML BASE AND LINKING AN EXTERNAL STYLE SHEET

As with previous projects, when you are creating a page that will be designed with CSS, it is crucial to have a well-formed markup document base before any styles are applied.

1 Create an external style sheet. In a text editor, open a blank document. Save the document with the name **base.css**. Note that **<style>…</style>** tags are not required.

2 Create a new XHTML page using the XHTML 1.0 Transitional **DOCTYPE** declaration.

3 Create a `<style></style>` tag within the `<head></head>` section of the XHTML page. Link the external style sheet, **base.css**, using the `@import` declaration. The `@import` method is an alternate way of associating an external style sheet to a page.

Note: The `@import` method is used to link the external style sheet rather than the `<link>` tag because the CSS rules used for this project will not work properly in older, partially CSS-enabled browsers such as Netscape 4.x. Because these older browsers don't recognize the `@import` declaration, the entire external stylesheet is ignored. Often this is a better option than a buggy display of CSS rules that can make a page unreadable.

---

4 Create the main **div** element "blocks": the navigation bar on the left, the logo at the top, and the main content. Assign the logo element the **id** attribute **logodiv**, the navigation bar element the **id nav**, and the main text block the **id main**. All of the content will be contained within the **main div** element.

5 Enclose all of the text content within standard HTML tags, such as `<h1>`, `<h2>`, and `<p>`. Indicate lists with `<ul>`, `<ol>`, and `<li>`.

This ensures that the content displays properly in non-CSS-capable browsers.

```
<!DOCTYPE html PUBLIC "-//W3C//DTD XHTML 1.0
Transitional//EN"
    "http://www.w3.org/TR/xhtml1/DTD/xhtml1-
    transitional.dtd">
<html xmlns="http://www.w3.org/1999/xhtml">
<head>
<meta http-equiv="content-type" content="text/html;
charset=iso-8859-1">
<title>Project 5</title>
<style type="text/css" media="Screen">
@import "base.css";
</style>
</head>
```

The **head** section of the XHTML page showing the `@import` method of associating an external stylesheet.

```
<body>

<!-- This div contains the site logo graphic  -->
<div id="logodiv">
<a href="#"><img src="logo.gif" alt="" width="271"
height="34" border="0" /></a>
</div>

<!-- This div contains the navigation  -->
<div id="nav">
<a href="#">CSS Introduction and Overview</a><br />
<a href="#">What is CSS?</a><br />
<a href="#">A Very Brief History of Web Design</a><br />
<a href="#">Suggested tools and books</a><br />
<a href="#">Lesson 1: HTML basics</a><br />
<a href="#">Lesson 2: Diving into CSS</a><br />
<a href="#">Lesson 3: CSS part 2</a><br />
<a href="#">Lesson 4: CSS Positioning</a><br />
<br />
<a href="#">Appendices</a><br />
</div>

<!-- This div contains the main content  -->
<div id="main">

<!--contents go here... -->

</div>
</body>
```

The **body** section of the XHTML page showing the major **div** elements.

6 Place the text and/or graphic elements that will be placed in sidebars and callout boxes within the main text in their own **div** elements. Assign each of these **div** elements the **class** attribute, **sidebar**.

Remember to enclose the text within the sidebar **div**s in the appropriate tags, such as **p** and **h1**.

Note: Sidebars and callout boxes are a good way of breaking up a long text document and help to highlight parts of the content.

7 Check the page in a browser before any CSS Rules are applied. Verify that the contents are readable and understandable.

```
<!-- This div contains the main content  -->
<div id="main">
<h1>CSS Sizing issues</h1>

<p>CSS gives us a much wider choice of sizing units to work with.
However, with this wider choice come more questions and problems
for the web designer to work with.</p>

<h2>Absolute units of measurement, in numbers</h2>

<p>Elements with an absolute unit value do not scale: they are
fixed in size. The absolute units you can use in CSS are as
follows:</p>

<ul>
<li>pixels</li>
<li>points (72pt equal 1 inch)</li>
<li>inches</li>
<li>centimeters</li>
<li>millimeters</li>
<li>picas</li>
</ul>

<div class="sidebar">
<h4>Common CSS unit mistakes:</h4>
<ul>
<li>
Separating the number from the unit with a space, e.g. 12 px.</li>
<li>Specifying no unit, e.g. 12. IE 5.5 will incorrectly interpret
this as 12px, but that doesn't make it right!</li>
</ul>
</div>

<div class="sidebar">
<img src="96-72.gif" alt="" width="242" height="120"
➥border="0" /><br />
<br />
<p>On the left you see Georgia as it displays at 1em, 12pt, and
12px in a browser with the 96dpi font space. On the right are the
same units in a browser with 72dpi font space. As you can see,
the only unit that displays more or less the same is pixels. (Note
the default margin width between elements too.)</p>
</div>

<!-- more content here... -->

</div>
</body>
```

Some of the contents of the **main div** element. The nested **div** elements are the sidebars and callout boxes. All of these **div**s have a **class** attribute of **sidebar**.

APPLYING STYLE RULES TO THE MAJOR PAGE ELEMENTS

The basic layout of the page is created by applying CSS style rules to the major page elements: the **body** and the **logodiv**, **nav**, and **main div** elements.

Tip: In IE 5.0/Mac, loading the edited style sheet itself in a browser window and then reloading the web page will display the new styles.

1 In the external style sheet, create the CSS style rules for the **body** element. Set the **margin** value to **0**. This eliminates the default browser margin. Specify a **background-color** value.

2 Create the style rules for the **#logodiv** ID selector. Specify a **position: fixed** style rule to "fix" the **div** in place. Apply the **!important** declaration to give this style rule precedence over any other **position** property rules. Specify a **right** property value of **0** so that the div is positioned in the right corner of the browser window.

At the same time, specify **position: relative** and **float: right** style rules for the **logodiv div** element. These styles are intended to compensate for browsers that don't support **position: fixed**. Use the **float: right** rule to position the **div** to the right of the page.

Note: When testing your pages in a browser, sometimes an external style sheet will be "stuck" in the cache so that you do not see the changes you have made. This can happen even if you have set your browser cache value to zero. Sometimes selecting Refresh from the browser menu while pressing the Shift key will clear the cache—but this does not always work. Internet Explorer/Windows seems to have a particularly persistent cache. If you still cannot see your style edits, quit the browser and reload the page.

```
body {
    background-color: #eeffee;
    margin: 0;
    }
```

position: fixed RULE

The **position: fixed** style rule is rarely used because it's only supported in a few browsers: Internet Explorer 5.0 and later for the Macintosh and Mozilla 0.91/Netscape 6.1+ on Windows and Macintosh. However, it is a very useful style rule that allows elements to stay "fixed" and visible at a certain position on the page, such as a logo or a navigation bar. I've used this style rule in this way on this page to keep the site logo and the navigation visible at all times. This mimics the functionality of a frameset without any of the disadvantages of using frames.

To compensate for browsers that do not support the **position: fixed** style rule (most notably, Internet Explorer 5.0, 5.5, and 6.0 on Windows), specify an alternate **position** value, and place an **!important** next to the **fixed** style rule. Browsers that do not recognize **position: fixed** will skip over the **fixed** rule, while browsers that do support it also will recognize the **!important** declaration and take this rule over any other rules specified for the **position** property. When **!important** is applied to any style specification, that supercedes any other value for that particular property.

Note that the **float** property only applies to relatively positioned elements, while the **right** property only applies to fixed or absolutely positioned elements, so both style rules need to be specified to make the **logodiv div** stay to the right of the browser window. (As with absolutely positioned elements, a fixed position element is taken out of the normal flow of the page. Therefore, you can specify the exact position coordinates for the element using the **left**, **right**, **top**, and **bottom** properties).

3 Continue to specify the style rules for the **#logodiv** selector. Specify a **z-index** value of **100** to ensure that the **div** will always stay on "top" of other elements.

The **z-index** style property is used to indicate the 3-dimensional placement of an element. The higher the **z-index** property value is, the higher up it is in the "stack" of elements.

4 Finally, specify **background-color**, **width**, **height** and **border-bottom** values for the element. The height and width match the dimensions of the graphic that is contained in this **div**.

5 Create the style rules for the **#nav id** selector. Specify a **position** value of **fixed** with the **!important** declaration. At the same time, specify **position: absolute**, to compensate for browsers that don't support the **fixed position** value.

Specify a **width** value of **150px**, and a **top** value of **70px**. This positions the **nav** element 70 pixels from the top of the page with a width of 150 pixels. Specify a **left** value of **0**.

Apply **background-color** and **color** styles, as well as a **border-left** value. Note that this border matches the **border-bottom** on the **logodiv** element.

Add some padding to the element and specify the default font style. The padding is added so that the text does not bump directly against the edges of the **div** box.

```
#logodiv {
        position: fixed !important;
        right: 0;
        position: relative;
        float: right;
        z-index: 100;
        background-color: #339966;
        width: 271px;
        height: 34px;
        border-bottom: 6px solid #333333;
}
```

The style rules for the **logodiv** element. Two values for the **position** property are specified, with the **fixed** rule declared as **!important**.

```
#nav {
        position: fixed !important;
        position: absolute;
        font: 11px/16px verdana, sans-serif;
        background-color: #339966;
        color: #ffff99;
        top: 70px;
        left: 0;
        padding: 10px;
        width: 150px;
        border-left: 6px solid #333333;
}
```

The style rules for the **nav** (navigation bar) element. Two values for the **position** property are specified— with **fixed** being more **!important**.

Note: This is a Bug Alert. Although Internet Explorer 5.x on the Macintosh does support **position: fixed**, the support is buggy: the cursor shape does not change to the "pointer" over **a** (link) elements within a **fixed** position element in this browser. Unfortunately, there's no way to compensate for this bug given that even explicitly specifying a **cursor** style doesn't work. Therefore, you might want to avoid using **position: fixed** for elements containing critical links, such as the navigation bar, on this page.

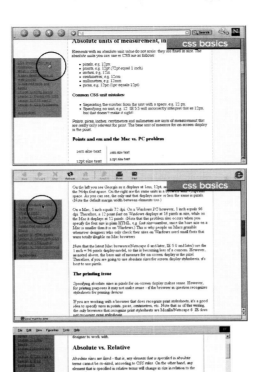

The **logodiv** and **nav div** elements stay "fixed" on the page in Netscape 6.2 (top) and Internet Explorer 5.1 for the Macintosh (middle), even when the window is scrolled. However, the cursor shape doesn't change properly over a link element in Internet Explorer 5.x for the Macintosh. In Internet Explorer 6.0 for Windows (bottom), the **logodiv** and **nav** elements scroll with the page.

6 Create the style rules for the **main div** element. Specify a **position** value of **absolute**.

An **absolute** position value is used to avoid problems with nested (child) elements. When a **relative** or other position value is specified, nested elements may behave unpredictably.

The style rules for the main element.

```
#main {
        position: absolute;
        background-color: #ffffff;
        border: 1px dashed #666666;
        width: 500px;
        padding: 15px;
        top: 70px;
        left: 200px;
        z-index: 1;
}
```

7 Continue to specify the style rules for the **main div** element. Specify a **width** value of **500px**. Specify a **left** value of **200px**. This value is the width of the **nav** (navigation bar) **div** plus 40 pixels.

Specify a **top** position value of **70px** to top align the **div** with the navigation **div**.

8 Set the **z-index** value of the **main div** to a lower number than the **z-index** value of the **logodiv div**. Finally, specify a **background-color** value for the **main div** that differs from the background color of the **body** and add a decorative **border**. This lets you see exactly where the **div** is located on the page.

Note: While many designers like to keep all the columns on a page "liquid" and resizeable, on this page the width of the **main** (content) **div** has been set to a fixed size of 500 pixels. Various studies have shown that a long text column is hard to read when it's too wide. Five hundred pixels is an arbitrary number that seems to fit comfortably in a typical browser window on an 800×600 pixel or 1028×768 pixel-size monitor.

Because the main content is "frozen" in place, the page is made to look more balanced and "liquid" by positioning the **logodiv div** on the right side.

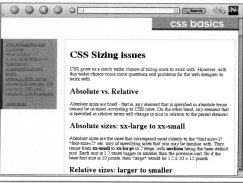

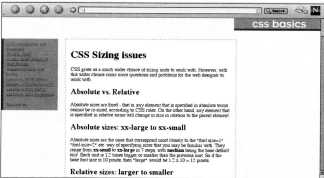

The basic page layout is set at this stage. While the **main** content **div** is a set size and absolutely positioned, the page has a "liquid" quality because the logo element is positioned on the right side of the page.

APPLYING STYLES TO THE a ELEMENTS WITHIN THE nav ELEMENT

For this page, we will use a different method for applying styles that are specific to a given parent element. Rather than specifying a **class** selector for the **a** elements, we will indicate that any **a** element within the **nav** element will be styled a certain way.

1 Apply a style to all **a** elements within the **nav id** with this syntax:

```
#nav a {
        ...style rules
        }
```

2 Apply a basic style to all **a** elements within the **nav** element and then apply different styles for the psuedo-styles **:visited**, **:link**, **:hover**, and **:hover:visited**.

Note the syntax used in the code.

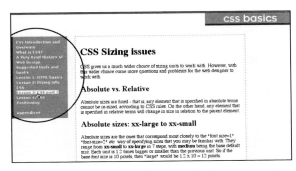

Styles applied to the navigation link text within the **nav** element.

```
#nav a {
        color: #ffff99;
        background-color: #339966;
        text-decoration: none;
        }
#nav a:visited {
        font-weight: bold;
        color: #ffff99;
        background-color: #339966;
        text-decoration: none;
        }
#nav a:link {
        font-weight: bold;
        color: #ffff99;
        background-color: #339966;
        text-decoration: none;
        }
#nav a:hover {
        color: #009966;
        background-color: #ffff99;
        text-decoration: underline;
        }
#nav a:hover:visited {
        color: #009966;
        background-color: #ffff99;
        text-decoration: underline;
        }
```

CREATING STYLES FOR THE FLOATING SIDEBAR divS

In this section, we will build the CSS styles for the sidebars or callout boxes. These boxes will "float" within the flow of the **main div** content.

1 Create a **class** selector called **.sidebar** in the stylesheet. Give it a **float** value of **right** so that all elements with this class float to the right of the parent element (the **main div**).

2 Specify a **width** for the **div**s.

In this case the **width** is set to **40%**. This is 40% of the width of the parent element (the **main div** element). If a **width** is not specified, the text will stretch out to fill the parent element.

3 Specify the **padding** and **margin** values. Each is set to **10px** on each side.

Note: Remember that **padding** means the space from the edge of the element inwards, and **margin** is the space outside the edge of the element to the parent element.

4 Specify the other style rules for the **.sidebar** class.

```
.sidebar {
        float: right;
        width: 40%;
        padding: 10px;
        margin: 10px;
        border: 1px dotted #333333;
        background-color: #ccffcc;
        color: black;
        }
```

The style rules for the **.sidebar** class.

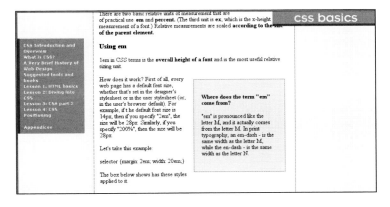

The floating sidebar (callout) box.

CREATING THE MAIN TEXT STYLES

The page design comes together when the styles for the main text are specified. As we have done in previous projects, we will stay away from using **class** or **id** selectors for elements within the main content area.

1 Create a base **font-family** style specification for the text.

```
body, h1, h2, h3, h4, p, ul, ol, li {
        font-family: verdana, helvetica, arial, sans-serif;
        }
```

Note: Specifying the style rules for several elements simultaneously is a good way of streamlining the style sheet. It makes it easier to make quick style changes later.

2 Specify a text (foreground) **color**, **font-size**, and **left** and **right** margin values for the **ul** and **ol** elements. Specify a **padding** value of **0**, to compensate for a rather large default padding value that's applied to list items in Netscape 6.x.

In addition, specify the bullet styles for each using the **list-style-type** property and the position of the bullets with **the list-style-position** property.

```
ul {
        list-style-type: square;
        list-style-position: outside;
        }
ol {
        list-style-type: lower-roman;
        list-style-position: outside;
        }
ul,ol {
        font-size: 11px;
        color: #000000;
        margin-left : 2em;
        margin-left: 1em;
        }
```

i. When you want the finest degree of control over the layout of your web page, there's really no other choice than pixels.
ii. If you're designing for NN 4.x compatibility, be careful of using anything **but** pixels. In particular, stay away from percent.
iii. In NN 4.x, mixing relative and absolute units together, e.g. font-size: 12px, line-height: 3em; can cause some serious problems.
iv. To be kind to users who are using older browsers on the Mac, avoid using too-small font sizes in points or em.
v. If you want your pages to be size-scaleable, try to plan your layout accordingly. Try testing it out in various browsers with various font sizes. Check the reflow of the text vis-a-vis the graphics.
vi. If you think most of your users will in all likelihood not be browser-savvy enough to be re-sizing the browser default font size, then stick to an acceptable absolute size, or just use 1em as your base size.
vii. If you must meet accessiblity guidelines, stick to relative sizes and use 1em as your base, being careful not to go much smaller. You may sacrifice some aesthetic value but it is the best method.
viii. Finally, there is a cop-out: some of the more modern browsers allow for resizing of the text even if the stylesheet specifies absolute sizes.

i. When you want the finest degree of control over the layout of your web page, there's really no other choice than pixels.
ii. If you're designing for NN 4.x compatibility, be careful of using anything **but** pixels. In particular, stay away from percent.
iii. In NN 4.x, mixing relative and absolute units together, e.g. font-size: 12px, line-height: 3em; can cause some serious problems.
iv. To be kind to users who are using older browsers on the Mac, avoid using too-small font sizes in points or em.
v. If you want your pages to be size-scaleable, try to plan your layout accordingly. Try testing it out in various browsers with various font sizes. Check the reflow of the text vis-a-vis the graphics.
vi. If you think most of your users will in all likelihood not be browser-savvy enough to be re-sizing the browser default font size, then stick to an acceptable absolute size, or just use 1em as your base size.
vii. If you must meet accessiblity guidelines, stick to relative sizes and use 1em as your base, being careful not to go much smaller. You may sacrifice some aesthetic value but it is the best method.
viii. Finally, there is a cop-out: some of the more modern browsers allow for resizing of the text even if the stylesheet specifies absolute sizes.

The **list-style-position: outside** style (left) versus **list-style-position: inside** (right).

3 Specify a text (foreground) **color**, **font-size**, and **left** margin for the **p** element.

```
p {
        font-size: 11px;
        color: #000000;
        margin-left: 2em;
        }
```

4 Set the **clear** attribute value of the header (**h1**, **h2**, **h3**, and **h4**) elements to **both**. This prevents the headers from wrapping around the sidebar boxes.

Specify a uniform text (foreground) **color** for all of the header elements.

```
h1, h2, h3, h4 {
        color: #006633;
        clear: both;
        }
```

74

STYLING LISTS

The **list-style-type** rule is used to specify the style of the bullet (in the case of **ul** list items) or number (in the case of **ol** list items). Several bullet and number styles are listed in the CSS2 specifications for the **list-style-type** property (see **http://www.w3.org/TR/REC-CSS2/generate.html#propdef-list-style-type**), although browser support for these styles varies. It's also possible to use a graphic as the bullet instead. See **http://www.w3.org/TR/REC-CSS2/generate.html#propdef-list-style-image**.

The **list-style-position** is used to indicate whether the bullet or number is outside of the list or inside it. Usually, choosing an outside style creates a neater looking list.

5 Fine-tune the margins between the headers. Often, the margin or gap beneath a header line is too wide; by setting this to **0**, it's possible to make the text more compact.

6 Add the **font-size** and **font-weight** style rules for the header text.

Here we have used numbers for the **font-weight** property—for the maximum amount of control. The heaviest or boldest weight is **900**, while **100** is the lightest weight. Note that not all fonts can be finely controlled this way—and not all browsers display this in the same way. The value, **400**, is equivalent to "normal" weight.

```
h4 {
    font-size: 12px;
    font-weight: 900;
    margin-top: 0;
}
h3 {
    font-size: 14px;
    font-weight: 600;
    margin-top: 0;
}
h2 {
    font-size: 16px;
    font-weight: 600;
    margin-top: 0;
}
h1 {
    font-size: 18px;
    font-weight: 600;
    margin-top: 0;
}
```

COMPLETING THE EXTERNAL STYLESHEET

In this section we will finish the external stylesheet by adding styles for the **main div** and **logodiv div a** (link) elements.

1 Set the style rules for the basic **a** elements. The base style rules for all **a** elements are specified, and then the styles for the pseudo-elements are created.

```
a {
        color: #339966;
        background-color: transparent;
        text-decoration: underline;
        }

a:visited {
        color: #339966;
        background-color: transparent;
        }
a:link {
        color: #339966;
        background-color: transparent;
        text-decoration: underline;
        }
a:hover {
        background-color: #ffff99;
        }
a:visited:hover {
        background-color: #cccccc;
        color: #339966;
        }
```

2 Create a style rule for the **a:hover** pseudo-element for the **a** element contained within the **logodiv div** element, specifying a **transparent background-color**. This is necessary to override the **background-color** style specified for the basic **a:hover** pseudo-element. Use the same syntax used to specify the styles for the **a** elements within the **nav div** element.

```
/* this style is used to prevent a background color from
appearing behind the logo GIF when the mouse passes over it.
*/

#logodiv a:hover {
        background: transparent;
        }
```

The "default" **a:hover** style puts a yellow background color behind the logo gif when the user mouses over the image link (left). To override this, specify a **background-color** value of **transparent**.

REFINING THE DESIGN WITH INLINE STYLES

As a final step, we'll fine-tune the design with inline styles. *Inline styles* are the style rules that are directly inserted into the tag with the **style** attribute.

Inline styles override all style rules that are in an external stylesheet or within **<style></style>** tags in the **<head>** section of the page, except for rules with the **!important** declaration.

1 Change the look of the list items in the first sidebar by adding some inline styles to the **ul** element tag. We've specified **margin-left** and **margin-right** rules, **padding**, a different **list-style-type**, and **list-style-position**. These inline styles supercede the style rules specified for these properties in the external stylesheet.

```
<div class="sidebar">
<h4>Common CSS unit mistakes:</h4>
<ul style="margin-left: 10px; margin-right: 10px;
padding: 0;0list-style-type: disc; list-style-position: inside;">
<li>
Separating the number from the unit with a space, e.g. 12 px.
</li>
<li>Specifying no unit, e.g. 12. IE 5.5 will incorrectly
interpret this as 12px, but that doesn't make it right!</li>
</ul>
</div>
```

The sidebar before the inline styles are applied before (left) and after (right).

2 Change the width of the second sidebar by adding an inline style rule. Because this sidebar contains a graphic that is 242px wide, the new width value is set slightly wider than that—to 250px.

```
<div class="sidebar" style="width: 250px">
<img src="96-72.gif" alt="" width="242" height="120" border="0" /><br />
......
</div>
```

This sidebar is too narrow at the **width** value of **40%** specified for the **.sidebar** class (left). Therefore, the **width** is changed with an inline style to **250** pixels to accommodate the graphic (right).

Cascade Order Basics

In CSS, the order in which style rules take precedence is called the *Cascade Order*. It's important to understand the cascade order so that you can master the use of stylesheets.

As we've seen so far, there are three ways to specify CSS style rules: in an external stylesheet; in a local stylesheet which is located in the **head** section of an HTML or XHTML document within **<style></style>** tags; and inline, within the element tag itself using the **style** attribute. In this project we've specified CSS style rules both in an external stylesheet and inline.

Generally speaking, the most recently or locally specified styles take the highest precedence in the cascade order. Therefore, inline styles take precedence over styles specified in the head section of the document, which in turn take precedence over styles specified in an external stylesheet.

To override the cascade order, use the **!important** declaration. Any style that is declared **!important** takes precedence over other rules, regardless of the order in which the styles are specified. We've used the **!important** declaration in this project to make one **position** property value supercede another.

We'll be revisiting the cascade order again in later projects.

MODIFICATION: A 3-COLUMN LAYOUT

The layout of this page can be converted to a 3-column layout that displays well in version 5 and later browsers.

1 In the XHTML document, create a new **div** element with the **id rightcol** after the end of the **main div**. Place some text content into this div. Here, we've just moved a section of the **main div** content into this new **div**.

```
<div id="main">
....contents of the main div.
</div>
<div id="rightcol">
....contents of the rightcol div.
</div>
```

2 In the external stylesheet, modify the style rules for the **#main id** selector. Make the **width** narrower (350px) and the **left** position slightly smaller (190px versus 200px). The **padding** value also has been made smaller to adjust for the narrower width of the **div** element.

```
#main {
        position: absolute;
        width: 350px;
        top: 70px;
        left: 190px;
        padding: 10px;
        z-index: 1;
        background-color: #ffffff;
        border: 1px dotted #666666;
        }
```

3 In the external stylesheet, create the style rules for a new **#rightcol id** selector. The **position** value is set to **absolute**. Note that the **left** position value equals the sum of the width of the **nav div** element (150px), the width of the **main div** element (350px), plus an extra 100px. This makes allowances for gutters (white space) between the columns of text.

The total width of the three **div** elements plus any gutter allowance should not exceed 750px—the inner width of a browser window when maximized on an 800×600-pixel monitor.

> **Note:** The three **div** elements that make up this page have a **position: absolute** value. This means that the page itself is not "liquid" (the columns are frozen in place). As noted previously, absolutely positioned elements display with fewer problems in the rather less CSS-capable browsers such as Internet Explorer 5.0 for Windows. We'll be exploring other ways of creating multiple column layouts with CSS-P in later projects.

> **Note:** The page used in this project isn't just a demonstration of CSS Style rules, but it also serves as an article that explores the issues involved when using absolute or relative size units in CSS.

```
#rightcol {
        position: absolute;
        width: 170px;
        padding: 10px;
        top: 70px;
        left: 600px;
        z-index: 1;
        background-color: #ffffff;
        border: 1px dotted #666666;
        }
```

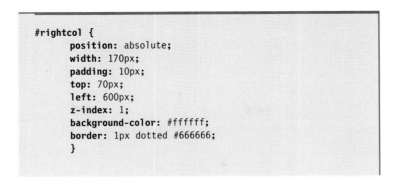

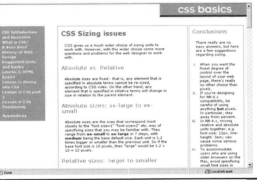

The 3-column layout with 3 **absolute position div** elements. Viewed on an 800×600-pixel monitor, the columns fill the browser window nicely. In a wider browser window, there is a gap on the left side, but the logo element helps to balance the page.

"One of the greatest joys known to

man is to take a flight into ignorance

in search of knowledge."

—ROBERT LYND

JAVASCRIPT
ROLLOVERS

MANIPULATING THE img OBJECT

Image rollovers are one of the most common

uses for JavaScript. It's also one of the few

JavaScript methods that can be safely used in

older JavaScript-capable browsers. This

project examines how IMG SRC swapping

works when used in conjunction with basic

JavaScript events.

Project 5

JavaScript Rollovers

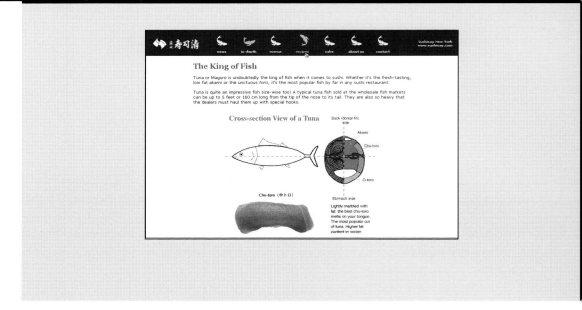

GETTING STARTED

The **img** object is one of the basic objects on a web page. A *"rollover"* script basically swaps the **src** graphic of an **img** object.

The **img src** swapping method is used in two ways in this project: for the navigation bar buttons and for the tuna "map" lower down on the page. On the navigation bar, the fish motif is used to indicate which page the view is on, as well as provide visual feedback when the user passes the mouse over each fish button. On the tuna "map," the user can mouse over the name of each section to see how the sushi created from that part of the fish looks.

If you are new to JavaScript, follow this project carefully. In this project, you will learn about

- Creating a sound, JavaScript-ready HTML markup base
- Identifying elements on the page for scripting
- Addressing **img** objects with JavaScript
- Creating a basic rollover script
- Creating more complex rollover scripts

For this project, a **table**-based layout is used instead of **div** elements positioned with CSS-P, and HTML is used instead of XHTML. This is for the sake of backward compatibility with older browsers that also can handle basic JavaScript but have problems rendering CSS or XHTML properly.

CREATING THE BASE GRAPHICS FOR THE NAVIGATION BAR BUTTONS

The navigation bar button has three states—the default state, or the off state; the over state, when the user mouses over the button; and the on state to indicate the section the user is in.

Note that I have used the same three buttons for all sections, but you may choose to create a unique set of buttons for each section.

1 Create the base static button.

I used a clipart fish and modified it in Adobe Illustrator.

2 Color the base fish button white. Color the fish button image to be used for the "on" and "section indicator" states blue. Rotate one copy of the blue fish slightly to make the section indicator version of the button.

3 Import the base white fish button into a program, such as Adobe Photoshop, and save it as a web graphic with the matte color set to the same color as the intended background color of the navigation bar. Save this with the file name `lilfish0.gif`. Save the flipped blue fish in the same way with the file name `lilfish1.gif`.

4 Import another copy of the blue fish into a program such as Adobe ImageReady or Macromedia Fireworks, and create a rotating animated gif version.

This will be the "mouse over" state of the button. Save this with the file name `lilfish2.gif`. Note that the file names are critical for the script. Each file name starts with "lilfish" followed by the number 0, 1, or 2.

The three versions of the fish button are off or static, the page indicator, and the animated version. All three graphics must be of the same dimensions.

Note: It is much easier to quickly change the color of clipart in a vector graphics application, such as Adobe Illustrator or Macromedia Freehand. Alternatively, use the vector features of a program, such as Macromedia Fireworks or Photoshop, before "fixing" the image as a bitmap graphic.

The animated rotating fish button created in ImageReady.

CREATING NAVIGATION BUTTON GRAPHICS

When creating a set of navigation button graphics, remember that they must be the same dimensions. For example, if the default state graphic is 100 pixels by 150 pixels, the "mouse over" and any other graphics must also be 100 pixels by 150 pixels.

It's not necessary to use the same graphic format for all of the buttons. You may mix GIFs, JPEGs, and PNGs, as long as they have the same dimensions.

When creating an animated GIF that will be associated with a JavaScript event, make one that will have continuous looping animation. Otherwise, the animation might appear to get "stuck" in mid-motion. Also be aware that the speed of the animation is different according to the browser—in Netscape, the animation is much faster than it is in Internet Explorer.

CREATING THE HTML LAYOUT AND CSS FOR THE NAVIGATION BAR

When creating complicated table-based layouts, it's often more convenient to build the page in small sections or blocks that are assembled at the end. Each "building block" will be a self-contained table. The first "building block" we will build is the navigation button bar.

1 Create the HTML for the navigation button section of the navigation bar.

Note that the same base graphic (**lilfish0.gif**) is used repeatedly—with descriptive text underneath each. Both the graphic and the text are made into links so that the user can click either one to navigate the site.

The navigation button **table** with no background color yet and with borders "turned on."

Note: When creating a **table** layout, it's useful to turn on the borders to see any problems right away.

The entire navigation button section is created as a single table. The table will be nested within the table row that will make up the navigation bar.

2 For each **img** object, assign a unique **name** and **id** attribute. In addition, assign each **img** object an appropriate **alt** attribute.

The **name** and **id** attributes are used to identify elements uniquely so that they can be addressed with JavaScript. Each **img** element must have a unique **id/name** so that it can be addressed with JavaScript.

```
<!-- the HTML base for the navigation buttons, with the
border turned on -->
<table border="1" cellpadding="0"
cellspacing="0" align="center">
<tr>
<td align="center" height="60" width="100">
<a href="#"><img src="images/lilfish0.gif" width="46"
height="44" border="0" alt="news" id="news" name="news"></a></td>
```

84

continues

The **alt** attribute is used so that the navigation functions in text-only browsers. See Project 4, "Creating a Complex Layout with CSS-P," for more information on the **alt** attribute.

Note: Even if each graphic looks the same, it's important to remember that each **img** object must be treated as separate and unique for scripting purposes. This is a point that often confuses designers, who are very visually oriented. Both a **name** and **id** attribute are assigned for browser compatibility. Older browsers do not recognize the **id** attribute, while newer browsers such as Netscape 6 use the **id** attribute. The **id** attribute also is recommended by the World Wide Web Consortium (W3C). Use both for backward and forward compatibility.

continued

```
<td align="center" height="60" width="100">
<a href="#"><img src="images/lilfish0.gif" width="46"
height="44" border="0" alt="indepth" id="indepth" name="indepth"></a></td>
<td align="center" height="60" width="100">
<a href="#"><img src="images/lilfish0.gif" width="46"
height="44" border="0" alt="menus" id="menus" name="menus"></a></td>
<td align="center" height="60" width="100">
<a href="#"><img src="images/lilfish0.gif" width="46"
height="44" border="0" alt="recipes" id="recipes" name="recipes"></a></td>
<td align="center" height="60" width="100">
<a href="#"><img src="images/lilfish0.gif" width="46"
height="44" border="0" alt="sake" id="sake" name="sake"></a></td>
<td align="center" height="60" width="100">
<a href="#"><img src="images/lilfish0.gif" width="46"
height="44" border="0" alt="about" id="about" name="about"></a></td>
<td align="center" height="60" width="100">
<a href="#"><img src="images/lilfish0.gif" width="46"
height="44" border="0" alt="contact" id="contact" name="contact"></a></td>
</tr>
<tr>
<td align="center" height="20" valign="top">
<span  class="navlink"><a class="navlinktext" href="#">news</a></span></td>
<td align="center" height="20" valign="top">
<span  class="navlink"><a class="navlinktext"href="#">
in-depth</a></span></td>
<td align="center" height="20" valign="top">
<span  class="navlink"><a class="navlinktext"
href="#">menus</a></span></td>
<td align="center" height="20" valign="top">
<span class="navlink"><a class="navlinktext"
href="#">recipes</a></span></td>
<td align="center" height="20" valign="top">
<span class="navlink"><a class="navlinktext"
href="#"><span sake</a></span></td>
<td align="center" height="20" valign="top">
<span class="navlink"><a class="navlinktext" href="#">about us
</a></span></td>
<td align="center" height="20" valign="top">
<span  class="navlink"><a class="navlinktext" href="#">contact
</a></span></td>
</tr>
</table>
```

3 Assign the appropriate **class** attributes to the link text **<span>** and **<a>** tags. The link text **span** class is **navlink**, and the link text **a** class is **navlinktext**.

Class attributes are added so that CSS styles can be applied to these elements.

4 Create the HTML for the rest of the navigation bar.

The navigation bar consists of three table cells. The button bar table we created in the previous step will be nested in the middle table cell of the navigation bar. The left table cell holds a **div** element with the class **bannerleft**; the div holds an **img** object. The right table cells holds a **p** element with the class **bannerright**. Classes are applied to both of these elements so that CSS styles can be applied to them.

Note: The navigation link text is enclosed within **<span>** tags because of a CSS bug in Netscape 4.x. Styles that are applied to **td** elements are not inherited properly by nested elements in this browser. If supporting Netscape 4.x is not an issue, apply the class **linktext** to the **td** element that encloses the link text instead and omit the **<span>** tags.

```
<!-- The HTML for the navigation bar -->
<table border="0" width="100%" cellpadding="0" cellspacing="0">
<tr>
<td bgcolor="#000066" width="20%" align="left">
<div class="bannerleft"><img id="top" src="images/logowonbl.gif"
alt="Sushisay logo" width="148" height="44" border="0"></div>
</td>

<td bgcolor="#000066" width="60%" align="center">

<!-- The navigation button table goes here -->

</td>
<td bgcolor="#000066" width="20%">
<p class="bannerright">
Sushisay New York<br>
www.sushisay.com
</p>
</td>
</tr>
</table>
<!-- end navigation bar -->
```

5 Create the appropriate CSS styles for the navigation bar text and links. Make the default appearance of the text link white with no underline and the hover or mouse over appearance blue (hex number **#99ccff**) to match the color of the mouse-over fish graphic color (lilfish1.gif).

The completed navigation bar with the borders "on" (top) and "off" (bottom).

```
/* CSS styles for the navigation bar text */

.navlink {
    font-family: verdana, sans-serif;
    font-size: 10px;
    color: white;
```

continues

Because the links in the main body should not be white (against a white background), it's necessary to use a **class** selector for the navigation links. I have used the **class** name, **fish**. Each **a** link element in the navigation bar HTML should have the appropriate **class** attribute declared, that is, **<a class="fish" href=……>**.

Apply the appropriate margin and padding values to each element.

Note: Class selectors are used for the navigation **a** link elements rather than contextual selectors because older browsers such as Netscape 4.x don't handle contextual selectors well.

continued

```
        font-weight: bold;
        }

.bannerright {
        font-family: verdana, sans-serif;
        font-size: 10px;
        font-weight: bold;
        color: white;
        text-align: right;
        padding-right: 20px;
        }

/* CSS styles for the div in the left
side cell of  the navigation bar */

.bannerleft { margin-left: 20px; }

/* CSS styles for the navigation bar links */
a.fish:link  {
        color: white;
        text-decoration: none;
        }
a.fish:visited  {
        color: white;
        text-decoration: none;
        }
a.fish:hover {
        color: #99ccff;
        text-decoration: none;
        }
/* CSS styles for the main body text links */
a:link {
        color: #990000;
        text-decoration: none;
        font-weight: bold;
        }
a:visited {
        color: #666666;
        }
a:hover {
        color: #990000;
        text-decoration: underline;
        }
```

PRELOADING GRAPHICS

When creating any kind of image swapping or rollover function, it is necessary to pre-load the graphics being used into the browser's memory. If this is not done, there will be a slight hesitation before the image actually changes. With slower connections or computers, the image change might not work at all.

1 Create a section within the **<head>...</head>** tags of the HTML document that will hold the JavaScript. Include the **type="text/javascript"** and the **language="javascript"** attributes.

```
<head>
<script type="text/javascript" language="javascript">
<!--
/* all the JavaScript for this page appears here. */
/* comments should be contained within /* */, or
one line comments can be prefaced with //. */
//-->
</script>
</head>
```

Note: When JavaScript is included directly on the HTML page, the syntax is similar to when CSS is included. Instead of using **<style>...</style>** tags, use **<script>...</script>** tags. No matter how many JavaScript functions or declarations you have on a page, it's only necessary to have one pair of **<script>...</script>** tags enclosing all of them.

The comment tags **<!-- ....//-->** within the **<script>...</script>** tags are used so that the actual text of your scripts will not be visible in older, non-JavaScript-capable browsers. If you think that the target audience for the site will not be using such browsers, it's not necessary to include the comment tags.

To insert comments within a script, use **/* ... */** tags. If it's just a single comment line, you also can precede it with two slashes (**//**). In the example code for this project, you will see both types of comments.

2 Create the lines that will preload the images to be used in the rollover functions.

```
<script type="text/javascript" language="Javascript">
<!--
// preload the navigation fish
lilfishPic0 = new Image;
lilfishPic0.src = "images/lilfish0.gif";
lilfishPic1 = new Image;
lilfishPic1.src = "images/lilfish1.gif";
lilfishPic2 = new Image;
```

continues

Each preloaded declaration looks like this:

```
var variable_name = new Image;
   variable_name.src =
"path/to/images/imagename.ext";
```

The first line defines the variable to be a new **Image** object. The second line then defines the **src** (source) of the **Image** object by specifying where in the web site directory the source graphic is located so that the script can find it and call it. Note that the directory path to the image file is within quotation marks.

This is a basic preload definition, which works well when there aren't that many image objects to define.

Note that the variable names are defined as **lilfishPic0**, **lilfishPic1**, and **lilfishPic2**, ending in numbers. **lilfishPic0** is the "off" state of the fish button, **lilfishPic1** is the "over" state, and **lilfishPic2** is the "you are here" state. (Note that these variable names correspond to the filenames of the graphics used.)

continued

```
lilfishPic2.src = "images/lilfish2.gif";

// end preload
//-->
</script>
```

Note: Think of a variable as a container that represents a piece of data. For example, if you define a variable named **dog** and want **dog** to hold a value of **Rover**, you would declare it like this:

```
var dog = "Rover";
```

In JavaScript, a variable is defined with **var** or simply by declaring a variable name and assigning an initial value to it, for example:

```
dog = "Rover";
```

When creating variable names, make sure they do not start with a number. The name also cannot contain any extra characters other than the underscore (_). Additionally, try to avoid names that are the same as those built in JavaScript functions or objects.

One good rule of thumb—always use and define variable names that will make sense to you later. If you use cryptic variable names, it will always be harder to fix or change something later when you have forgotten what it means.

DEFINING THE DOCUMENT OBJECT AND CREATING THE ROLLOVER FUNCTION

Put simply, a document's object model (or DOM) is the way that elements or objects on the page are addressed in scripting. For any script, it is essential to properly define the DOM; otherwise, the functions simply won't work.

While there are many ways of defining a rollover, using the built-in JavaScript **eval** method is very handy and creates a compact function that can be used for more than one JavaScript event.

1 Create a variable named **doc** and assign it a string value of **"document."**.

```
// define the base document object
var doc = "document.";
```

2 Begin to define the rollover function (function **flipfish**).

```
function flipfish(num,obj) {
// the function declarations go here
// between the curly brackets
}
```

3 Declare a variable called **fishobj**. Assign it a value that is derived by evaluating the concatenated string of the string value of **doc** and the string value of **obj**.

```
var fishObj = eval(doc + obj);
```

> **Note: eval** is a built-in (predefined) JavaScript method that evaluates whatever is contained within the parentheses, whether they are variables, text strings, or properties of existing objects.
>
> In this case, **eval** returns the string value of whatever is passed to the variables **doc** and **obj** when the **function** is called. **doc** is always assigned a value of "document," which defines the beginning of the DOM address. The **+** sign in between each variable concatenates (puts together) the two values. When this string is evaluated, the script understands which object on the page is being addressed.

4 Assign a value to the **.src** (image source) of the variable **fishobj** using the **eval** function again.

This creates the basic rollover (image swap) function. In the next section, you will see how this is implemented.

```
fishObj.src = 'lilfishPic' + num + '.src';
```

> **Note:** For this line, we calculate the string value of **lilfishPic** plus whatever value is passed to the argument **num**, plus the string **.src**.

CALLING FUNCTIONS TO ACTIVATE ROLLOVERS

In this section, you will attach the functions to the navigation bar **<a>** tags so that they are called when a user moves the mouse over them or clicks them. A basic rollover such as this one calls the function by associating a mouse event to an **a** link element.

1 Call the first rollover by associating it with an **onmouseover** event and then an **onmouseout** event in the **a** element that surrounds the first fish button.

```
<!---the HTML for the first fish button -->
<a href="#" onmouseover="flipfish(2,'news')"
onmouseout="flipfish(0,'news')">
<img src="images/lilfish0.gif" width="46" height="44"
border="0" alt="news" id="news" name="news">
</a>
```

Let's examine exactly what happens when the function is called. On the **onmouseover** event, the **flipfish** function is called with the value "**2**" passed to the **doc** variable and the value "**news**" passed to the **obj** variable.

This is what happens when these values, together with the predefined strings, are evaluated.

Let's look at the first **onmouseover** call:

onmouseover="flipfish(2,'news')"

Now we'll examine how this function call is executed:

var fishObj = eval(doc + obj);

The first line evaluates the string of "**document.news**" or the object identified on the page with the **name** (and/or **id**) "news," and assigns this to the variable **fishobj**.

Look at the second line:

fishObj.src = 'lilfishPic' + num + '.src';

The string of "**lilfishPic2.src**" is evaluated and assigned to the **src** of the variable **fishObj**.

The result of this is the following:

document.news.src = **lilfishPic2.src;**

If you look at the list of predefined and preloaded image objects created previously, you will see that **lilfishPic2.src** is defined as **"images/ lilfish2.gif"**.

When the user mouses over the **img** object named **news**, the graphic is swapped for **lilfish2.gif**.

Similarly, when the user mouses out of the **img** object named **news** (with the **onmouseout** event), the graphic is swapped for **lilfish0.gif**.

Note: An event is when something happens to or on the web page in question. The events we are using here are two mouse events (mouse actions): **mouseover** and **mouseout**. The **flipfish** function is called **onmouseover** (or when the mouse cursor passes over the object in question) and **onmouseout** (when the mouse cursor leaves the object).

The **mouseout** or "off" state of the button on the left and the "on" state of the button on the right.

2 Associate the rollover function with the **a** link text under the fish button so that it will be triggered when the user mouses over the text.

3 Call the function from all the other fish buttons and corresponding text links, using the appropriate arguments.

Note: The same function can be triggered more than once on a page from different objects.

```html
<!-- start the button bar table -->

<table border="0" cellpadding="0" cellspacing="0" align="center">
<tr>
<td align="center" height="60" width="100">
<a href="#" onmouseover="flipfish(2,'news')"
onmouseout="flipfish(0,'news')" >
<img src="images/lilfish0.gif" width="46" height="44" border="0"
alt="news" id="news" name="news"></a></td>
<td align="center" height="60" width="100">
<a href="#" onmouseover="flipfish(2,'indepth')"
onmouseout="flipfish(0,'indepth')" >
<img src="images/lilfish0.gif" width="46" height="44" border="0"
alt="indepth" id="indepth" name="indepth"></a></td>
<td align="center" height="60" width="100">
<a href="#" onmouseover="flipfish(2,'menus')"
onmouseout="flipfish(0,'menus')" >
<img src="images/lilfish0.gif" width="46" height="44" border="0"
alt="menus" id="menus" name="menus"></a></td>
<td align="center" height="60" width="100">
<a href="#" onmouseover="flipfish(2,'recipes')"
onmouseout="flipfish(0,'recipes')" ><img src="images/lilfish0.gif"
width="46" height="44" border="0" alt="recipes" id="recipes"
name="recipes"></a></td>
<td align="center" height="60" width="100">
<a href="#" onmouseover="flipfish(2,'sake')"
onmouseout="flipfish(0,'sake')" ><img src="images/lilfish0.gif"
width="46" height="44" border="0" alt="sake" id="sake"
name="sake"></a></td>
<td align="center" height="60" width="100">
<a href="#" onmouseover="flipfish(2,'about')"
onmouseout="flipfish(0,'about')" ><img src="images/lilfish0.gif"
width="46" height="44" border="0" alt="about" id="about"
name="about"></a></td>
<td align="center" height="60" width="100">
<a href="#" onmouseover="flipfish(2,'contact')"
onmouseout="flipfish(0,'contact')" ><img src="images/lilfish0.gif"
width="46" height="44" border="0" alt="contact" id="contact"
name="contact"></a></td>
</tr>
<tr>
<td align="center" height="20" valign="top">
<span class="navlink"><a class="navlinktext" href="#"
onmouseover="flipfish(2,'news')"
onmouseout="flipfish(0,'news')">news</a></span></td>
<td align="center" height="20" valign="top">
<span class="navlink"><a class="navlinktext" href="#"
onmouseover="flipfish(2,'indepth')"
onmouseout="flipfish(0,'indepth')">in-depth</a></span></td>
<td align="center" height="20" valign="top">
<span class="navlink"><a class="navlinktext" href="#"
onmouseover="flipfish(2,'menus')"
onmouseout="flipfish(0,'menus')">menus</a></span></td>
<td align="center" height="20" valign="top">
<span class="navlink"><a class="navlinktext" href="#"
onmouseover="flipfish(2,'recipes')"
onmouseout="flipfish(0,'recipes')">recipes</a></span></td>
<td align="center" height="20" valign="top">
<span class="navlink"><a class="navlinktext" href="#"
onmouseover="flipfish(2,'sake')"
onmouseout="flipfish(0,'sake')">sake</a></span></td>
<td align="center" height="20" valign="top">
<span class="navlink"><a class="navlinktext" href="#"
onmouseover="flipfish(2,'about')"
onmouseout="flipfish(0,'about')">about us</a></span></td>
<td align="center" height="20" valign="top">
<span class="navlink"><a class="navlinktext" href="#"
onmouseover="flipfish(2,'contact')"
onmouseout="flipfish(0,'contact')">contact</a></span></td>
</tr>
</table>
```

CREATING A "SECTION INDICATOR" FUNCTION

It is often a good idea to show the user which page he is on by indicating this on the navigation bar. This can be easily achieved with JavaScript.

The basic rollover function used for the mouse-over effect can be modified to create a "you are here" indicator. The combination of the basic rollover plus the section indicator is commonly called a *3-state rollover*.

1 Copy the existing **flipfish** function but give it another name. I have called it **hereIam** here, but use any name that seems logical to you.

```
// the "I am here" function
function hereIam(num,obj) {
var fishObj = eval(doc + obj);
        fishObj.src = 'lilfishPic' + num + '.src';
        }
```

2 Create a new variable called **section**. Give it the appropriate section name, corresponding to the **name** (**id**) of the navigation button that shows which page/section the user is on. In this case, the section/page name value is **indepth**.

```
// define the variable for the section
var section = "indepth";
```

3 Activate this function when the page loads by calling it as an **onload** function in the HTML **body** tag.

When the page loads, the **indepth** navigation button **img** src will change to **lilfish1.gif** to indicate that the user is on that page.

```
<body onload="hereIam(1,section)">
```

MODIFYING THE ORIGINAL FUNCTION WITH A CONDITIONAL STATEMENT

You might ask yourself why the identical function is being used for the section indicator as well as the basic mouse over or rollover. While this works well when the page is initially loaded, when the user mouses over the **indepth** button again, for example, the rollover function is activated so that when the mouse cursor leaves the triggering element, the **img** src reverts back to the "off" state. What we want to happen is for the button for that particular section to "stick." To accomplish this, we will modify the original **flipfish** function with a conditional statement.

1 Add the highlighted conditional statement to the function. Enclose the code in brackets **{}**.

> **Note:** A conditional statement is one that only executes if certain criteria are met. In this case, the script within the enclosing brackets will only happen if the value for the variable, **obj**, does not match the value of the variable, **section**.
>
> When creating any kind of nested conditional statement such as this, be careful that the curly brackets match; otherwise, there will be a JavaScript error.

2 Check the resulting effect in a browser.

Now, when the user mouses over the in-depth button or link, the fish does not spin but stays stuck in the "you are here" position.

> **Note:** Another way of making a 3-state button "stick" is to simply not call the mouseover rollover function for the appropriate navigation **img** in the HTML. However, this means that you must create different HTML for each page or section. By using the conditional statement, it's possible to reuse the same HTML for all pages on a site, needing only to change one variable on each page. This is particularly useful if you are assembling pages with server-side includes, as it streamlines the page production process.

```
function flipfish(num,obj) {
    var fishObj = eval(doc + obj);
    if (obj != section) {
        fishObj.src = 'lilfishPic' + num + '.src';
    }
}
```

The "your are here" indicator in action. Even if the user mouses over the in-depth button or text link, the button does not change in appearance.

HOW IT WORKS: THE BASIC DOCUMENT OBJECT MODEL, OR DOM 0

A document's "object model" simply reflects the way in which elements, or objects on the page, are addressed in scripting.

One of the biggest stumbling blocks when writing a script is how to properly address a particular object on the page. In later browser versions, it is possible to address every single tagged element on an HTML page. However, in earlier JavaScript-capable browsers, it was only possible to address a limited set of elements, such as **body**, **img**, and **form**. This is informally called the *DOM level 0*.

This page uses a very conservative approach in that it does not contain any elements that are nested within **div**, **layer**, or **span** tags, thus allowing you to address the image object directly. Later projects describe how the addressing method changes with more complicated pages.

If you only wish to create pages that have basic rollover effects such as the one used here, avoid nesting the relevant **img** objects within **div**, **layer**, or **span** tags.

DYNAMIC FRAMES

"That which we call a rose

By any other name would smell as sweet"

—WILLIAM SHAKESPEARE

A Photographer's Portfolio Site

Once you understand how the **img** object is

addressed on a basic web page, the next step

in conquering the basic Document Object

Model (DOM) is to understand how frames

can be addressed and manipulated.

Project 6

Dynamic Frames

GETTING STARTED

A **frameset** is a set of two or more separate web pages that are grouped together. Once they are grouped together, they become associated with each other—and it becomes possible to address objects on other pages within the **frameset** with JavaScript.

This project is a mockup of a photographer's portfolio site. The page is simple in design and consists of three frames: the top frame, which holds the photographer's name and logo in constant view; the main section in the middle where the photographs are shown; and finally the bottom navigation frame. Frames can be particularly useful for very visual sites such as this because they afford the designer a high degree of control over the size and appearance of the page being shown.

In this project, you will learn

- About frames and the Document Object Model (DOM)
- About working with external scripts
- How to address one **frame** from another
- How to keep a page framed where it should be or out of frames all together
- How to create a frameset dynamically with **document.write**
- About using conditional **if...else** statements
- How to use a **for** loop
- About accessing a **function** that is located in one frame from another
- How to read and write data from one frame to another

ORGANIZING THE WEB PAGES AND CREATING THE FRAMESET

Whenever you create a site with frames, it is particularly important to plan exactly which pages you need to create in advance. This is because each page must be a self-contained "building block." The building blocks are assembled to create the **frameset**. We've already used this kind of building block approach to creating and assembling web pages in previous projects. Frames are perhaps the ultimate building-block assemblage method.

TO USE FRAMES OR NOT TO USE FRAMES

Frames are presented in this project as a way of expanding your understanding of the DOM.

A practical question that arises is whether it is a good idea to use frames at all. Generally speaking, the current trend in web design is to shy away from frames because they present a number of problems regarding accessibility (see Project 4, "Creating a Complex Layout with CSS-P"). Some people also dislike frames for other reasons. However, frames can still be useful for creating tightly controlled layouts that work in a wide variety of browsers, as we've done here.

1 Organize the pages that will make up the **frameset**.

Three pages make up the starting **frameset**: the top frame page, the middle frame page, and the bottom frame page.

Two additional pages are needed: an additional middle frame page and a bottom frame page.

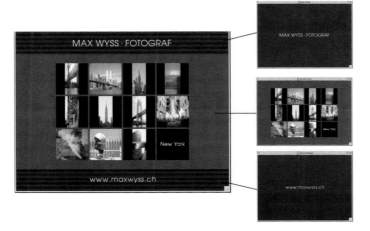

Three individual pages make up the starting frameset.

2 Create the HTML markup for the individual pages that make up the starting frameset. To keep the document structure as simple as possible, use tables to create the layouts.

As with the previous project, we've used HTML instead of XHTML markup and kept away from Cascading Style Sheet (CSS) rules that cause problems in older browsers.

```
<!-- The HTML for the top frame page -->
<!DOCTYPE HTML PUBLIC "-//W3C//DTD HTML 4.01 Transitional//EN"
        "http://www.w3.org/TR/1999/REC-html401-19991224/loose.dtd">
<html>
<head>
        <title>top frame</title>
        <style type="text/css" media="Screen">
```

continues

The top frame page is the logo centered on the page with a nested table.

The main (middle) frame page is made up of 12 table cells, each holding one of the full size photo images—but displayed at only 100×100 pixels.

The bottom frame page contains a text graphic of the site address.

Note: Once a graphic is displayed on a page, it remains in the browser cache for some time. As noted in Project 5, "JavaScript Rollovers," if a graphic file is not loaded in the cache, JavaScript actions, such as rollovers, do not work smoothly.

For this project, only one set of photographic images is used. You might wonder why we haven't created scaled-down versions of the large photos to use for the front-page "thumbnail" view, as well as the small icons on the navigation bar. While it is initially faster to load these small images, for this site the full size photos have to be loaded into the browser cache—for the photo gallery script to work in any case. Therefore, they are loaded into the cache at the start by displaying them on the starting page. This eliminates the need for a graphics preload script.

The disadvantage to this method is that the initial starting page will load rather slowly, especially on lower bandwidth connections. The main advantage of this method, besides the fact that it "preloads" the large image files, is that one set of 12 images is much easier to manage than 3 sets of 12 images each.

When using this technique, be careful to "slim down" the file size of the full size images in an editing program such as Adobe Photoshop. In this case, the file sizes of the photos are relatively small given that they are grayscale images.

continued

```
<!--
a, a:link {
     outline: none;
     }
body {
     background: #333333 url("images/stripe.gif");
     margin: 0;
     }
-->
</style>
</head>
<body>
<table border="0" width="100%" height="100%" cellspacing="0" cellpadding="0">
 <tr>
  <td align="center" valign="middle"><img src="images/logo.gif" alt="LOGO: Max Wyss,
Fotograf" width="307" height="22" border="0"></td>
 </tr>
</table>
</body>
</html>
```

```
<!-- The HTML for the starting middle (main) frame page. Note the empty a href attributes -
this is where the JavaScript triggers will be inserted. -->
<!DOCTYPE HTML PUBLIC "-//W3C//DTD HTML 4.01 Transitional//EN"
     "http://www.w3.org/TR/1999/REC-html401-19991224/loose.dtd">
<html>
<head>
     <title>main frame</title>
     <style type="text/css" media="Screen">
<!--
body {
     background-color: #333333;
     margin: 0;
     }
-->
</style>
</head>
<body>
<table border="0" width="100%" height="100%" cellspacing="0" cellpadding="0">
<tr>
<td align="center" valign="middle"><table border="0" width="200" cellspacing="5"
cellpadding="0">
     <tr>
```

continues

```
                <td width="100"><a href=""><img src="images/59thbr.jpg" alt="" width="100" height="100" border="0"></a></td>
                <td width="100"><a href=""><img src="images/brooklynb.jpg" alt="" width="100" height="100" border="0"></a></td>
                <td width="100"><a href=""><img src="images/chryslerb.jpg" alt="" width="100" height="100" border="0"></a></td>
                <td width="100"><a href=""><img src="images/eastriver.jpg" alt="" width="100" height="100" border="0"></a></td>
        </tr>
        <tr>
                <td width="100"><a href=""><img src="images/firestairs.jpg" alt="" width="100" height="100" border="0"></a></td>
                <td width="100"><a href=""><img src="images/empstat.jpg" alt="" width="100" height="100" border="0"></a></td>
                <td width="100"><a href=""><img src="images/gwbridge.jpg" alt="" width="100" height="100" border="0"></a></td>
                <td width="100"><a href=""><img src="images/rockf.jpg" alt="" width="100" height="100" border="0"></a></td>
        </tr>
        <tr>
                <td width="100"><a href=""><img src="images/rooftop.jpg" alt="" width="100" height="100" border="0"></a></td>
                <td width="100"><a href=""><img src="images/wtc1.jpg" alt="" width="100" height="100" border="0"></a></td>
                <td width="100"><a href=""><img src="images/wtctower.jpg" alt="" width="100" height="100" border="0"></a></td>
                <td width="100"><a href=""><img src="images/ny.gif" alt="" width="100" height="100" border="0"></a></td>
        </tr>
</table></td></tr></table>
</body>
</html>


<!-- The HTML for the starting bottom frame page. -->

<!DOCTYPE HTML PUBLIC "-//W3C//DTD HTML 4.01 Transitional//EN"
        "http://www.w3.org/TR/1999/REC-html401-19991224/loose.dtd">
<html>
<head>
        <title>base bottom frame</title>
        <style type="text/css" media="Screen">
<!--
body {background: #333 url("../images/stripe.gif"); margin: 0;}
-->
</style>
</head>
<body>
<table border="0" width="100%" height="100%" cellspacing="0" cellpadding="0">
<tr>
<td align="center" valign="middle"><img src="images/maxwyss.gif" alt="www.maxwyss.ch" width="207" height="22"></td>
</tr>
</table>
</body>
</html>
```

3 Create the HTML markup for the two other pages that will be used in this **frameset**. These are the secondary pages for the middle frame and the bottom frame.

The second, middle frame page consists of a large image that's centered on the page. The second bottom frame page consists of small graphical buttons that will be used to navigate the site. Each button uses the photo image file (see Step 2 and Sidebar).

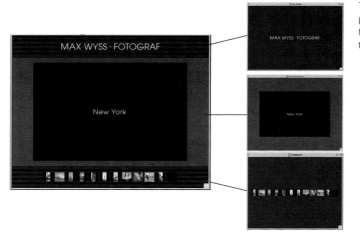

The frameset with the secondary pages in the mainframe (middle frame) and bottom frame. The top frame remains the same.

```
<!-- The HTML for the bottom frame page. Note the empty a href
attributes -  this is where the JavaScript trigger will be inserted. -->
<!DOCTYPE HTML PUBLIC "-//W3C//DTD HTML 4.01 Transitional//EN"
        "http://www.w3.org/TR/1999/REC-html401-19991224/loose.dtd">
<html>
<head>
        <title>bottom1</title>
        <style type="text/css" media="Screen">
<!--
a, img {
        border: 0;
        outline: none;
        }
body {
        background: #333333 url("images/stripe.gif");
        margin: 0;
        }
-->
</style>
</head>
<body>
<table border="0" width="100%" height="100%" cellspacing="0"
cellpadding="0">
<tr>
<td align="center" valign="middle"><table border="0" cellspacing="5"
cellpadding="0">
        <tr>
```

```
<td width="30"><a href=""><img src="images/59thbr.jpg"
alt="" width="30" height="30" border="0"></a></td>
<td width="30"><a href=""><img src="images/brooklynb.jpg"
alt="" width="30" height="30" border="0"></a></td>
<td width="30"><a href=""><img src="images/chryslerb.jpg"
alt="" width="30" height="30" border="0"></a></td>
<td width="30"><a href=""><img src="images/eastriver.jpg"
alt="" width="30" height="30" border="0"></a></td>
<td width="30"><a href=""><img src="images/firestairs.jpg"
alt="" width="30" height="30" border="0"></a></td>
<td width="30"><a href=""><img src="images/empstat.jpg"
alt="" width="30" height="30" border="0"></a></td>
<td width="30"><a href=""><img src="images/gwbridge.jpg"
alt="" width="30" height="30" border="0"></a></td>
<td width="30"><a href=""><img src="images/rockf.jpg"
alt="" width="30" height="30" border="0"></a></td>
<td width="30"><a href=""><img src="images/rooftop.jpg"
alt="" width="30" height="30" border="0"></a></td>
<td width="30"><a href=""><img src="images/wtc1.jpg" alt=""
width="30" height="30" border="0"></a></td>
<td width="30"><a href=""><img src="images/wtctower.jpg"
alt="" width="30" height="30" border="0"></a></td>
<td width="30"><a href=""><img src="images/ny.gif" alt=""
width="30" height="30" border="0"></a></td>
        </tr>
</table></td></tr></table>
</body>
```

4 Create the HTML markup for the basic **frameset**.

This is a three-frame **frameset** with fixed-size top and bottom frames and a variable size middle frame. None of the frames should have a scrollbar or a frame border.

5 Give a **name** and **id** value to all three **frames** in the **frameset**. This allows the frames to be addressed with JavaScript.

Both **id** and **name** values are given to each **frame** and the **frameset** because older browsers only recognize the **name** value—while newer and future browsers may only recognize the **id** value for identifying an object.

```
<!-- the basic frameset page code -->
<!DOCTYPE HTML PUBLIC "-//W3C//DTD HTML 4.01 Frameset//EN"
         "http://www.w3.org/TR/1999/REC-html401-19991224/frameset.dtd">
<html>
<head>
        <title>Max Wyss::Fotograf Home</title>
</head>
<!-- basic frameset -->
<frameset border="0" frameborder="0" framespacing="0" name="overall" id="overall"
rows="70,*,70">
<frame src="topframe.html" scrolling="no" frameborder="0" name="topframe" id="topframe"
noresize>
<frame src="mainframe1.html" name="mainframe" id="mainframe" frameborder="0"
scrolling="no" noresize>
<frame src="bottomframe1.html" scrolling="no" name="bottomframe" id="bottomframe"
frameborder="0" noresize>
</frameset>
</html>
```

PREVENTING THE SITE FROM BEING FRAMED

The first JavaScript script is a basic *frame controller*. It's a good idea to add this small script to any page that you want to prevent from being framed without your knowledge—for example, in a **frameset** on another site. In addition, any page that should be viewed in a **frameset** can be "forced" into the correct one.

1 Prevent the topmost page (the **frameset**) from being framed in another **frame**. This script is commonly called a *frame buster*.

Place this code within **<script....></script>** tags in the **head** section of the base **frameset** page.

Note here that **top** refers to the uppermost document that is contained within that browser window, and **self** refers to the document itself. The code looks at the **location** value (the URL) of the document. If the **location** value (the URL) of the **top** document in the browser window does not match the **location** value of **self** or this document, that means that the page has been framed. Therefore, the script forces the

```
if (top.location != self.location) {top.location = self.location};
```

top document to be the **self** document—thus preventing the page from being framed.

For example, if you've saved your **frameset** page with the filename index.html, and the page is loaded into another **frameset** named outsideframe.html, the page will "bust out" of the other **frameset** and reload as the topmost page in the browser window.

This code can be used on any page that you don't ever want to be framed.

2 Force the pages that belong in the **frameset** into the **frameset** to be displayed only in the **frameset**. Place this code within **<script....></script>** tags in the **head** sections of each page that belongs in the **frameset**.

This code works in reverse of Step 1. If the **location** value (URL) of the topmost document in the browser window matches the **location** value of the document (**self**), then it means that the page is not framed as it should be. Therefore, the proper **frameset** (in this case, the document **index.html**) is loaded into the browser window instead.

```
if (top.location == self.location) {top.location = 'index.html'};
```

Note: The statements in Steps 1 and 2 use an **if...else** conditional statement. If the conditions stated within the **( )** brackets are met, the code that is contained within the **{ }** brackets is executed.

WRITING A FRAME DYNAMICALLY

The effect that we want to achieve with this **frameset** is to have the middle section change when we click the small photo icon in the bottom frame.

For this method, the middle page is written dynamically on the fly when a link is clicked in the bottom frame—by literally writing out the HTML for the page using the **document.write** method.

Tip: Refer to the Frame Object Model diagram in the "How It Works" section to understand how each **frame** relates to the **frameset** and to other frames.

The frameset for this method is in the folder, frameset4, in the Project 6 folder on the companion CD.

1 Open a new blank text document and save it with the name **writeframe.js**.

We will be creating the function in this external document because we want to call the function on more than one page.

2 Create the base HTML for the page that will be written to the middle frame. The HTML for the page to go in the middle frame is fairly simple. This is, in fact, the code we created for the secondary middle frame page previously.

3 Begin to define the function.

The **function** that will write the dynamic page is called **writeframe**. Each time it's called, we will pass a variable to it (**picname**) that will hold the **name** of the image to be loaded.

4 Turn the HTML code into a **document.write** statement.

For multiple lines of text, it's often easier to create the **document.write** statement on multiple lines and then concatenate them. In addition, certain special characters within the string must be escaped to prevent errors.

The variable **writepage** will hold the entire string to be written.

Note: Before turning an HTML string into a document.write statement, always check it first as plain HTML in your browser to see that everything is laid out the way you intend it to be.

```
function writeframe(picname) {
    //function goes here
}
```

```
var writepage = "<html>";
writepage += "<body style=\"background: #333333; margin: 0; color: white;\">";
writepage += "<table border=\"0\" width=\"100%\" height=\"100%\"    cellspacing=\"0\"
➥cellpadding=\"0\">";
writepage += "<tr><td align=\"center\" valign=\"middle\">";
writepage += "<table border=\"0\" cellspacing=\"5\" cellpadding=\"0\">";
writepage += "<tr><td bgcolor=\"black\"><img src=\"../images\/" + picname + "\"alt=\
➥"Photos of New York\" id=\"pic\" name=\"pic\" height=\"319\" width=\"480\"></td><\
➥/tr>";
writepage += "<\/table></td></tr></table>";
writepage += "</body></html>";
```

Note: A **document.write** statement tells the browser to write out whatever is within the brackets onto a page. The basic syntax is as follows:

```
document.write("string" + variable + "string");
document.close();
```

Note that on the sixth line of the function, the variable **picname** is inserted into the string.

Certain characters within a string, in particular the slash (**/**) and quotation mark (**"** or **'**) characters, must be "escaped" with a backslash (****) in front. This is because these characters are interpreted as a closing tag. To avoid errors, be sure you are using the same quotation mark; type either **"** or **'** to open and close your string and to escape all the other incidences of **/**, **"**, and **'**.

It's quite easy to make a syntax error mistake when creating a long **document.write** statement. To avoid this, it's often a good idea to break the string apart into smaller, manageable sizes and to concatenate them.

Concatenating is a programming term that means small pieces of data are added to each other. In this case, we are assembling a longer string of text in small chunks. Note that the first line declared **writeframe = "<html>"**—this initiates the value of **writeframe**. The following lines use the operator **+=**, which tells the script that the data within the **" "** quotation marks should be added on to the previous data.

5 Create the function that will dynamically write the page and then save the document.

The complete function writes the whole HTML to the middle frame with the **document.write** statement. The address for the middle frame is **parent.mainframe**. Be sure to end the statement by closing the document with **document.close()**.

```
function writeframe(picname) {
    var writepage = "<html>";
    writepage += "<body bgcolor=\"#333333\" text=\"white\">";
    writepage += "<table border=\"0\" width=\"100%\" height=\"100%\" cellspacing=\"0\"
➡cellpadding=\"0\">";
    writepage += "<tr><td align=\"center\" valign=\"middle\">";
    writepage += "<table border=\"0\" cellspacing=\"5\" cellpadding=\"0\">";
    writepage += "<tr><td bgcolor=\"black\"><img src=\"../images/" + picname + "\"alt=\
➡"Photos of New York\" id=\"pic\" name=\"pic\" height=\"319\" width=\"480\">
➡</td></tr>";
    writepage += "</table></td></tr></table>";
    writepage += "</body></html>";
    parent.mainframe.document.write(writepage);
    parent.mainframe.document.close();
}
```

6 Call the external JavaScript in each page that you wish to execute this function in. In this case, we want to execute it from both **mainframe.html** (the starting middle page) as well as **bottomframe.html** (the bottom navigation frame).

Within the **<head>...</head>** tags of each page, place this code.

```
<script src="writeframe.js" type="text/javascript"></script>
```

Note: When calling an external script file, note that it's not necessary to put the comments tags in between the **<script>...</script>** tags.

It's possible to call several external scripts from one page or to have more than one function in a single external script document.

7 Create the HTML code that will call the function.

We want to trigger this code when the user clicks one of the thumbnail images on the starting middle frame and also when the user clicks on the icons in the bottom frame. To do this, you have to place the code in the **a** link tags surrounding each **img** object.

```
<a href="javascript:writeframe('name of graphic')">
➡<img src...></a>
<a href="javascript:writeframe('59thbr.jpg')"><img
src="../images/59thbr.jpg" alt="" width="30" height="30"
border="0"></a>
```

Note: The JavaScript function is called directly with the **javascript:** method. This is equivalent to calling a function upon an **onclick** mouse event. However, note that this method does not accommodate users of browsers with JavaScript disabled and therefore should be used only on sites or pages where JavaScript is essential—or on a site like this that is essentially graphical.

Note: Bug Alert! If this page is reloaded with the Refresh button in Internet Explorer 5.x on the Macintosh, the bottom frame page is displayed in the mainframe.

When a user clicks an icon in the bottom frame, the middle page is written dynamically, displaying the new image that corresponds to the icon. The icon gives a tiny preview of the large image.

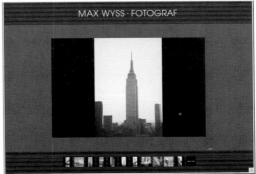

READING AND WRITING DATA FROM ONE FRAME TO ANOTHER

In this section we'll use a method that passes a piece of data from one frame to another. In addition, a function in one frame is read from another. It is a bit more complicated than the method outlined in the previous section, but it's much more flexible.

The frameset for this method is in the folder frameset5 in the Project 6 folder on the companion CD.

1 Give a **name** and **id** value to the **img** object in the HTML markup of mainframe.html.

This is necessary because we will be swapping the **src** of this **img** object.

```
<img src="../images/nybig.gif" alt="Photos of New York" id="pic"
name="pic" height="319" width="480">
```

2 Give a **name** and **id** value to each of the **img** objects in the HTML markup of bottom.html in the same way as in Step 1. Give each **img** object the following name/ids: **five**, **bkb**, **cry**, **east**, **fire**, **emp**, **gwb**, **rock**, **roof**, **wtc1**, **wtc2**, and **ny**.

Each tag should look like the tag represented in the code sample.

```
<img src="../images/wtc1.jpg" alt="" width="30" height="30"
border="0" name="wtc1" id="wtc1">
```

Tip: You may choose to give the img objects the same name/id value as the src graphic name. The only exception in the example is the file, 59thbr.jpg: you can't use 59thbr as a variable name because it begins with a number.

3 Create a hidden form field on the bottom frame page.

This hidden form field will hold a value that will be passed from one frame to another. The initial value of the form field is set to **0**.

```
<form name="theForm">
<input type="hidden" name="frameID" value="0">
</form>
```

Note: For this method, we need to be able to dynamically pass a value from one page in the **frameset** to another page in the same **frameset**. The only object that allows for such data to be passed into it in older (version 4) browsers is a **form** field.

4 Create the **function** that will set the value of the hidden **form** field. The function is placed within the **<script>...</script>** tags in the **head** section of the bottomframe.html page.

This function will be called with an **onclick** event whenever the user clicks one of the small icons in the bottom frame.

Note that the form field is addressed in the format **document.formname.formfieldname**.

```
function setpicID(picID) {
        document.theForm.frameID.value = picID;
}
```

5 Continuing within the **<script>...</script>** tags in bottomframe.html, declare the **Image** object variables that will be used in the **img src** swapping function. Assign the appropriate graphic file to the **src** of each Image object. (This is the image preload method described in Project 5.)

Note: Even though the graphic files themselves are pre-loaded into the browser cache when the thumbnails on the first page are loaded, it is still necessary to declare them as being Image objects in JavaScript to make them available to subsequent functions.

```
/* preload the images */
pic0 = new Image;
pic0.src = "images/nybig.gif";
pic1 = new Image;
pic1.src = "images/59thbr.jpg";
pic2 = new Image;
pic2.src = "images/brooklynb.jpg";
pic3 = new Image;
pic3.src = "images/chryslerb.jpg";
pic4 = new Image;
pic4.src = "images/eastriver.jpg";
pic5 = new Image;
pic5.src = "images/firestairs.jpg";
pic6 = new Image;
pic6.src = "images/empstat.jpg";
pic7 = new Image;
pic7.src = "images/gwbridge.jpg";
pic8 = new Image;
pic8.src = "images/rockf.jpg";
pic9 = new Image;
pic9.src = "images/rooftop.jpg";
pic10 = new Image;
pic10.src = "images/wtc1.jpg";
pic11 = new Image;
pic11.src = "images/wtctower.jpg";
pic12 = new Image;
pic12.src = "images/nytext.gif";
picover = new Image;
picover.src = "images/arrow.gif";
pichere = new Image;
pichere.src = "images/reddot.gif";
```

6 Continuing within the **<script>...</script>** tags in bottomframe.html, create the function that will swap the **img** object **src** in the main (middle frame) page (**function loadpic**). This function is called in the middle frame and is triggered by the **onload** event.

The function evaluates the value of **"pic"** plus the variable **picID** and returns the **newpic.src** value. For example, when it is called with a **picID** value of **"1"**, the value of **newpic1.src**, which is **"images/59thbr.jpg**," is returned.

```
/*load the pic.src, based on the value of picID.
this function is called from the middle (mainframe) frame with an onload event.
*/
function loadpic(picID) {
     var newpic = eval('pic'+picID);
     return(newpic.src);
}
```

7 Create the function that calls the **function loadPic** from the bottom frame and then triggers the image change. This function is placed within **<script>...</script>** tags in the **<head>...</head>** section of main.html.

Note that the function starts with the 'keep in frame' code. If the page is not in the right frameset, that frameset page is loaded, and the function is aborted.

The second line obtains the value that is in the **frameID** form field in the bottom frame. This is the **picnumber** that is passed to the **function**, **loadPic(picID)**, in the third line.

8 Insert the code necessary to trigger this function when the document is loaded by inserting this call to the function in the **body** tag in the HTML markup of **mainframe.html**. Call the function with a slight delay using the **setTimeout()** method.

9 In the document bottomframe.html, insert the **onclick** event in each **a** element that will trigger the **setPicID()** function. Each function should look like the example code. Insert the right value for each **picID** you wish to set with each click. For example, here it is set to **11**, so the picture that will be loaded in the main frame will be **pic11.src**, or **"images/wtctower.jpg"**.

10 Test the code at this point. The visual results are the same as with the method described in the previous section. However, you might find that the image change is slightly snappier. In addition, the page refresh bug noted for Internet Explorer 5.x for the Macintosh does not occur with this method.

```
function getPic() {
        if (top.location == self.location) {
                top.location = 'index.html';
                return;
        }
        picnumber = parent.bottomframe.document.theForm.frameID.value;
        document.pic.src = parent.bottomframe.loadpic(picnumber);
}
```

Note: To address a form field from another frame in a frame set, refer to **parent.framename.document.formname.formfieldname**. See the diagram in the *How It Works: Framesets and JavaScript* sidebar for additional information.

```
<body onload="setTimeout('getPic()',500)">
```

Note: The function is called with a delay (in this case, a delay of 500 milliseconds—or half a second) because it takes a little time for the browser to recognize that each frameset has been created. Without this delay, a JavaScript error will occur.

```
<a href="main.html" target="mainframe" onclick="setpicID(11)">
```

EXTENDING THE SCRIPT FOR MORE FUNCTIONALITY

The previous method results in a similar effect to the first one we discussed. However, it's possible to extend these methods to include a mouse-over effect as well as a "you are here" indicator.

The frameset for this method is in the folder frameset6 in the Project 6 folder on the companion CD.

All of the JavaScript in this section is created in the bottombase.html page.

1 Create a variable called **currentIconID** and give it an initial value of **0**.

```
var currentIconID = 0;
```

2 Create the basic image swapping **function**.

This function is very similar to the one used in the previous project. Note that the function is only called if the value of **picID** does not equal **0** (0 is the default value).

```
// basic image swapping function
function changeIcon(picID,picsrc_num) {
    if (picID != 0) {
        icon = eval('document.'+ picID);
        newicon = eval ('pic'+ picsrc_num);
        icon.src = newicon.src;
    }
}
```

3 Create a new array called **iconIDarray** that will hold the **name/id** values of the icon **img** objects.

Remember that an array starts with **0**, so give the first array item an empty value, or **""**.

```
/* create an array that holds the value of the iconID. */
iconIDarray = new Array('','five','bkb','cry','east','fire','emp','gwb','rock',
➥'roof','wtc1','wtc2','ny');
```

Note: An array is an object that contains a set of data. When items are put into an array, it is like placing them into a sequential list. To reference any item in the array, you can use its index number. The first item in the array is actually item number **0** (because computers start counting at **0**), the second one is number **1**, and so on. In this array, **iconIDarray[3]** for example would be '**cry**'.

4 Create the **function** called **hereIam()**. This is the "here I am" indicator function, that shows which image the user is looking at.

On the first line, the variable **hereID** is assigned the value of the array object located at the index number that is set in the **frameID** field. For example, if the value of **frameID** is 4, **hereID** equals **iconIDarray[4]**, or **"east"**.

On the next line, the **changeIcon** function is called with the value of **hereID** assigned to the first variable. If **hereID** is **"east"**, then the **src** of the **img** object **"east"** is swapped for the **"here"** image, reddot.gif.

The next section of the function checks to see if the value of **currentIconID** equals that of **hereID**. If it does not, it loops through the **iconIDarray** with the **for** loop. If the value of **iconIDarray** matches that of **currentIconID**, then the **img** object with the **currentIconID** is reverted back to the **"off"** state.

5 Insert the calls to the functions in the HTML markup and assemble the page.

Note that each **a** element surrounding each icon **img** contains the following:

- An **onmouseover** event that triggers the **changeIcon()** function. This causes the red arrow to appear.

- An **onmouseout** event that triggers the **changeIcon()** function again, to revert the icon **img src** to the 'off' state—plus the **hereIam()** function.

- An **onclick** event that triggers the **setpicID()** function plus the **hereIam()** function.

```
function hereIam() {
        var hereID = iconIDarray[document.theForm.frameID.value];
        changeIcon(hereID,'here');
        if (currentIconID != hereID) {
                for (var i = 0; i<=iconIDarray.length; i++) {
                        if (iconIDarray[i] == currentIconID) {
                                changeIcon(currentIconID,i);
                                }
                        }
                        currentIconID = hereID;
                }

}
```

Note: A **for** loop repeats an action, using a counter that counts up (or down) a specified number of times in a specified way.

In this example, the counter variable **(i)** starts at **0** **(i=0);** continues counting up until the value of **i** is less than or equal to the length of the array **iconIDarray (i<=iconIDarray.length)**, and is incremented by **1** **(i++)**.

```
<a href="main2.html" target="mainframe"
onmouseover="changeIcon('gwb','over')"
onmouseout="changeIcon('gwb','7');hereIam()"
onclick="setpicID(7);hereIam()">
```

6 Test the frameset in a browser. When a user mouses over one of the icons, the red arrow appears. When she mouses out, the red dot appears on the icon that indicates which picture she is looking at in the middle frame. When she clicks an icon, the picture above changes, and the red dot position changes.

This project is presented in different stages of development. Check the project files on the CD and the companion web site. The final version of the project is in the folder, frameset-final.

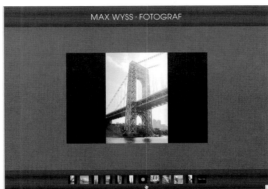

When the user mouses over one of the icon buttons, the red arrow graphic is shown (top). When the user clicks an icon, the image in the main frame changes, and the icon changes to a red dot (bottom) to indicate that this is the image being viewed.

HOW IT WORKS: FRAMESETS AND JAVASCRIPT

The illustration shows how specific objects within a frame can be addressed from another frame within the frameset.

When trying to create functions that talk from one frame in a frameset to another, there are some things to take into consideration, as noted in the following list:

- In Internet Explorer, all the pages within a frameset must be located on the same server; otherwise, a "permission denied" error results. (This is not a bug, but follows recommended specifications.)

- As shown in the preceding example, when creating scripts that must work on version 4 and older browsers, the only way to reliably pass data from one frame to another without using a browser cookie or resorting to `document.write()` is via a form field.

- In older browsers, it is not possible to directly trigger an `img src` change in another frame from a different frame. Therefore, the `function` to trigger the `img src` change must be on the same page as the `img` object.

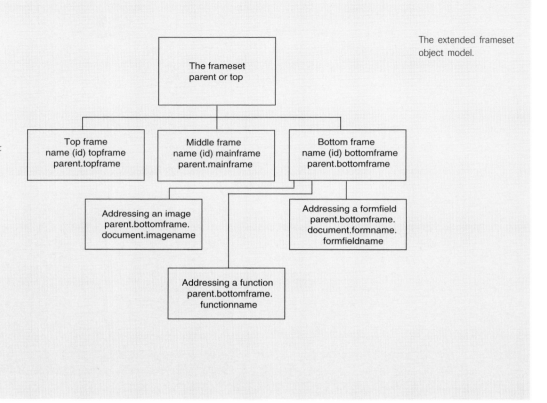

The extended frameset object model.

MODIFICATIONS

Sometimes it is not possible to use just one set of pictures for large photos, an opening page thumbnail, and small icons as we did in this project. This is especially true if the large photos are too big in file size. If that is the case, make medium-sized (thumbnail) and tiny-sized (icon) images and call them in your HTML markup or JavaScript preload code as appropriate.

In this project, we have given **name** and **id** values to each of the frames in the frameset and referred to the frames by the name and id. An alternate way of addressing frames within a frameset is by frame array number. The first frame that is loaded into a frameset is **parent.frames[0];** (the first frame in the array); the second one is **parent.frames[1]**; and so on.

Note: One final note about the photographs used in this project—the photos were taken by my partner, Max Wyss, during numerous visits to New York City. The mock site used in this project was created prior to the tragic events of September 11, 2001.

We considered pulling out the photos of the World Trade Center, but we decided to keep them in. We'll always remember the World Trade Center as a beautiful building as well as the symbol of freedom it has become.

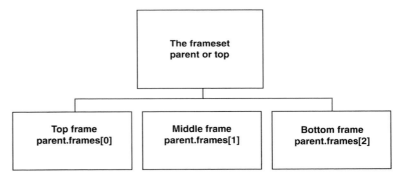

An alternate way of addressing frames.

WORKING WITH
BROWSER WINDOWS

"The hardest thing to know in life is

which bridge to cross and which to burn."

—DAVID RUSSEL

A Photo Album with Pop-up Windows

The third basic object after the **img** object

and frames that we will learn how to address

and manipulate with JavaScript is the browser

window.

Project 7

Working with Browser Windows

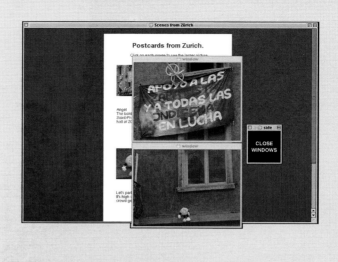

GETTING STARTED

The top-level object in a web browser is the **window** object. Every web page and frameset has as its top "parent," a corresponding **window** object.

> **Note:** In programming terms, the **object** object in JavaScript is the most basic unit or building block. In client-side JavaScript (JavaScript that is executed in a web browser), the topmost object after the **object** object is the **window** object.

> **Note:** Like frames, windows can be manipulated in many ways with JavaScript, even in version 3 browsers. Mastering control over the **window** object is yet another step toward a better understanding of the Document Object Model (DOM).

This project is a photograph album site that uses several window manipulation "tricks" depending on the image. While you may not use all of these methods on real life sites, it's useful to know just some of the things you can do when you open a new browser window with JavaScript.

In this project, you will learn about the following:

- The anatomy of a browser window
- **window** events
- **window** status messages
- How to open and close new windows with JavaScript
- How to control the appearance and position of new windows
- Talking between windows

OPENING A BASIC WINDOW

As a first step, we will create a basic function that opens a new window with JavaScript.

1 Create a basic JavaScript **function** that will open a new browser window.

```
function plainWindow() {
        var newWin = window.open();
}
```

2 Create a plain HTML page and call this function via a link. Note that we've used HTML instead of XHTML for this project to accommodate older browsers, but you may use XHTML instead.

This **function** creates a new **window** object with the name **newWin**. Note that by giving the new object a unique name, it becomes possible to address it directly with JavaScript. This is similar to giving a **frame** in a **frameset** a unique name or an **img** object a unique name.

In the function itself, a reference is made immediately to the **newWin** object by giving it **focus** (bringing it to the front) with **newWin.focus();**.

3 Try out this function in various browsers.

This will open a new blank window. You will see that in each browser, the resulting window is different. This has a lot to do with the default settings you (or the user) have set in your Preferences or Internet Options, but it also depends on how each browser interprets the command.

```
<html>
<head>
        <title>plain window tester</title>
        <script type="text/javascript">
<!--

function plainWindow() {
        var newWin = window.open();
        newWin.focus();
}

//-- >
</script>
</head>
<body>

<a href="javascript:plainWindow()">click here to open a
plain new window.</a>

</body>
</html>
```

CREATING A FUNCTION THAT CLOSES A WINDOW

If you open a new window, sooner or later you'll want to close it too.

1 Create the function that closes the window.

The **closeWindow()** function detects to see if the object **newWin** exists. If **newWin** does exist and if it is not closed, then the function closes it.

```
function closeWindow() {
      if (newWin && !newWin.closed) {
            newWin.close();
      }
}
```

2 Insert this function into your tester page. When clicking the "close window" link, if the new window exists, it is closed.

```
<html>
<head>
      <title>plain window tester</title>

      <script type="text/javascript">
<!--
function plainWindow() {
      var newWin = window.open();
}

function closeWindow() {
      if (newWin && !newWin.closed) {
            newWin.close();
      }
}
//-- >
</script>
</head>
<body>

<a href="javascript:plainWindow()">click here to open a
plain new window.</a>
<br>
<a href="javascript:closeWindow()">click here to close the
new window.</a>
</body>
</html>
```

LOADING A PAGE INTO A NEW WINDOW

When opening a new window, you will want to control its appearance and size in most cases. To do this, you use the window opening function.

1 Declare the **function basicWindow**. It will have three arguments passed to it: **url**, or the URL of the page to be loaded into the new window; **w**, or the width of the window, and **h**, the height of the window.

```
function basicWindow(url,w,h) {
```

2 Create a string that specifies the settings for the window—to control its appearance.

In this case, we want to open a very plain window with minimal chrome. The values specified for **w** and **h** are inserted into the string.

```
settings = '"toolbar=no, directories=no,
➡menubar=no,scrollbars=no,resizable=no,
➡status=no,width='+w+',height='+h+'"';
```

3 Call the **closeWindow()** function just in case **newWin** already exists.

This is not necessary, but it is good practice to avoid spawning multiple windows—something that can irritate the user.

4 Open the new window and pass it the URL, a window **name** (we have used **newWin** here), and the settings.

```
var newWin  = window.open(url,'newWin',
➡settings);
```

> **Note:** Care is needed when assembling a string in **window.open** that specifies the settings for a window because the whole string must have quotation marks around it. A good practice is to use double quotes (**"**) to enclose the string elements and single quotes (**'**) to enclose the settings themselves.
>
> In this example, if **w** is **500** and **h** is **300**, a window that is 500 pixels by 300 pixels in size will pop up. The new window will have no menu bar, scrollbars, or status bar. Also the window will not be resizable.

5 Give the new window focus (bring it to the front) and close the **function**.

```
newWin.focus();
  }
```

```
/* first, declare the variable newWin that will be used
for the new window object, so that we can refer to it later. */
var newWin;

/* the basic window opening function. */
function basicWindow(url,w,h) {
        var settings = '"toolbar=no, directories=no,menubar=no,
     ➥scrollbars=no,resizable=no,status=no,
     ➥width='+w+',height='+h+'"';
        closeWindow();
        var newWin = window.open(url,'newWin',settings);
        newWin.focus();
}


/* the closeWindow function */

function closeWindow() {
        if (newWin && !newWin.closed) {
                newWin.close();
        }
}
```

6 Call this function in your HTML in an **<a>** link.

```
<a href="javascript:basicWindow
➥('building.html',302,500)">click here to open
➥a new window</a>
```

Note: For a list of the parts of a window that can be controlled, see the section "How it Works: Anatomy of a Browser Window" at the end of this project.

Clicking the link opens a new window that is 302 pixels wide by 500 pixels high, to the left of the opening browser window or the left top corner of the screen, depending on the browser.

Note: The new window has a Close Window link. This is good practice because some users don't naturally use the Close button on the window itself, and they will search for a link within the document to close the window.

To close a window from within itself, simply insert the following into an **<a>** link:

```
<a href="javascript:window.close()">close window</a>
```

Alternatively, use the following:

```
<a href="javascript:self.close()">close window</a>
```

If the new window loads a frameset, use **parent.window.close()** or **top.window.close()** in one of the framed pages.

The link can be a simple text link or a fancy graphic.

CHANGING THE WINDOW STATUS MESSAGE

In some cases, it is useful to change the default window status message that appears at the bottom of the browser window. On the example page, the default status message when a user mouses over the image link displays the call to the JavaScript function. Because this is not very informative for the user, we are going to change the message to something more descriptive.

1 In your **<a>** link, call a window status message change with an **onmouseover** event.

```
onmouseover="window.status='a photo of a
squatter\'s building';return true"
```

Note that the single quote **'** in the message is escaped with a backslash (\). This is to tell the script that the following character should be displayed as-is, rather than being interpreted as the closing quote for the message. If you don't escape this character, you might cause JavaScript errors because the browser engine will think everything after the **"'"** is actual JavaScript code.

The **return true** statement is necessary to display the message.

2 To return the status message to a default or blank state, call another window status message change with an **onmouseout** event.

```
onmouseout="window.status='';return true"
```

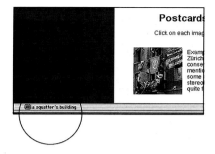

When the user mouses over the image link, the window status message changes.

OPENING A CENTERED WINDOW

It's often desirable to position a window in the center of the screen—where it's more likely to grab the user's attention. It's possible to do this by measuring the dimensions of the user's monitor screen with JavaScript.

1 Declare the **function centeredWindow**. It will have four arguments passed to it: **url**, or the URL of the page to be loaded into the new window; **winname**, or a unique name for this window; **w**, or the width of the window, and **h**, the height of the window.

```
function centeredWindow(url,winname,w,h) {
```

2 Declare two local (function-only) variables, **windowleft** and **windowtop**.

The **windowleft** variable will hold the value of **screen.width** (the width of the screen) minus the width of the element, divided by two. The **windowtop** variable will hold the value of **screen.height** (the height of the screen) minus the height of the element, divided by two. This should give us the correct **left** and **top** numbers to position the window in the center of the monitor screen.

```
windowleft = (screen.width - w)/2;
windowtop = (screen.height - h)/2;
```

Note: In many cases the result of the calculations in the code will return a number such as 350.5 rather than an integer such as 350. You usually don't have to worry about this given that most browsers will round off the number into an integer. If you do experience problems, however, you might use the JavaScript **Math.round()** method. **Math.round()** rounds off the argument within the parentheses to the nearest integer, shown here:

```
windowleft = Math.round((screen.width - w)/2);
windowtop = Math.round((screen.height - h)/2);
```

3 Create a string that specifies the settings for the window to control its appearance. The values specified for **w**, **h**, **windowleft**, and **windowtop** are inserted into the string.

```
settings = '"toolbar=no,directories=no,
➥menubar=no,scrollbars=no,resizable=no,
➥status=no,width='+w+',height='+h+',
➥left='+windowleft+',top='+windowtop+'"';
```

4 Call the **closeWindow()** function just in case **newWin** already exists.

```
closeWindow();
```

5 Open the new window and pass it the url, a window name (we have used **newWin** here), and the settings.

```
newWin   = window.open(url,winname,settings);
```

6 Give the new window **focus** (bring it to the front) and close the function.

```
newWin.focus();
}
```

```
/* first, declare the variable newWin that will be used
for the new window object, so that we can refer to it later. if you are using the
basicWindow() function on the same page, you only need to declare it once.
*/
var newWin;

/* the centered window opening function. */
function centeredWindow(url,winname,w,h) {
       windowleft = (screen.width - w)/2;
       windowtop = (screen.height - h)/2;
       settings = '"toolbar=no,directories=no,menubar=no,scrollbars=no,resizable=no,
       ➥status=no,width='+w+',height='+h+',left='+windowleft+',top='+windowtop+'"';
       closeWindow();
       newWin = window.open(url,winname,settings);
       newWin.focus();
}

/* the closeWindow function Note that this only has to appear on the same page once. */

function closeWindow() {
       if (newWin && !newWin.closed) {
              newWin.close();
       }
}
```

7 Call this **function** in your HTML in an **<a>** link. Insert the appropriate values for the **url** and **winname** arguments. In this case, the **url** is 'angel.html,' and the **winname** is 'angelWin'.

```
<a href="javascript:centeredWindow
➥('angel.html','angelWin',500,470);">
link</a>
```

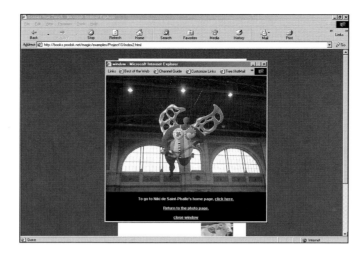

Clicking the image opens a new window that is 500 pixels wide by 470 pixels high in the center of the screen.

CHANGING THE CONTENTS OF THE PARENT WINDOW

When a new window is opened, the window from which it was opened, can be referred back to as the **opener**. Here we will use the Angel image window to load different content into the parent window.

1 In the HTML page that will be opened in the new popup window, create a function that will load different content into the **opener** window. We will pass one parameter to it, the new URL to be loaded.

```
function changeParent(url) {
```

2 Check to see if an **opener** exists. If it does, the function will continue. If not, the function will stop.

```
if (window.opener) {
```

3 Change the **location.href** (URL) of the **opener** document and then close off the function.

```
window.opener.document.location.href = url;
    }
}
```

```
function changeParent(url) {
    if (window.opener) {
        window.opener.document.location.href = url;
    }
}
```

4 Call this function in an **<a>** link on the page that is loaded in the new window. In this case the page is called angel2.html.

```
To go to the new page,
➥<a href="javascript:changeParent
➥('http://www.makikoitoh.com/')">
click here.</a><br><br>
```

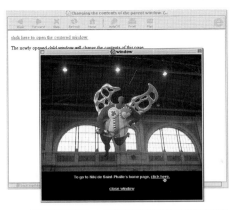

Click the link (top) to load a different web page into the parent window (bottom).

PUSHING A WINDOW TO THE BACK AND MOVING IT

When the new content is loaded into the **opener** window, you want the small window itself to be more discreet—put to the back of the stack of windows and to the left of the screen.

1 Pushing the window to the back is accomplished with the built-in JavaScript **window.blur** function. In the **<a>** link that loads the new content in the **opener** window, insert the following:

```
window.blur();
```

2 For repositioning the window, use the following:

```
window.moveTo(0,0);
```

This will move the window to the **top** and **left** coordinates **0** and **0** on the screen.

3 Create a **function** that will move the window and then push it back in the stack of windows.

4 Call this **function** in your **<a>** link on the page that is loaded in the new window (in this case, the angel3.html page).

```
To go to Maki's home page,
➡<a href="javascript:changeParent
➡('http://www.makikoitoh.com/');moveWindow(0,0)
➡">click here.</a><br><br>
```

Note: window.blur() pushes the window to the very back of the stack of windows. Therefore, if the user has a lot of windows open already, it may get lost in the pile.

Note: window.moveTo() moves a window to the specified coordinates on the screen. Another built-in function, **moveBy**, also is available: it moves a window by a specified number of pixels.

```
function moveWindow(x,y) {
      window.moveTo(x,y);
      window.blur();
}
```

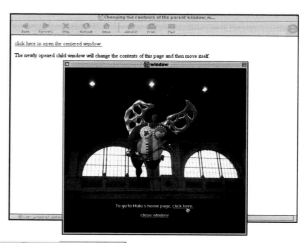

When a user clicks the appropriate link, the content in the opener window changes, and the small window itself moves to the left and back.

OPENING MORE THAN ONE WINDOW

On occasion, you might want to open more than one window at a time. When you do this, care should be taken that they are not positioned on top of each other. In this example, the new window opened from the base window spawns yet another window.

1 Create two functions that will place the windows relative to the vertical center of the monitor screen.

placeWinTop() puts the new window to the top of the vertical center, and **placedWinBottom()** puts the new window to the bottom of the vertical center.

Note that in both cases, a small adjustment has been made to the **windowtop** number to account for the width of the window chrome.

```
function placedWinTop(url,winname,w,h) {
        windowleft = (screen.width-w)/2;
        centerver = screen.height/2;
        windowtop = centerver - h-20;
        settings = '"toolbar=no, directories=no,menubar=no,scrollbars=no,resizable=no,
➥status=no,width='+w+',height='+h+',left='+windowleft+',top='+windowtop+'"';

        newWindow1 = window.open(url,winname,settings);
        newWindow1.focus();
}


function placedWinBottom(url,winname,w,h) {
        windowleft = (screen.width-w)/2;
        centerver = screen.height/2;
        windowtop = centerver+10;
        settings = '"toolbar=no, directories=no,menubar=no,scrollbars=no,resizable=no,
➥status=no,width='+w+',height='+h+',left='+windowleft+',top='+windowtop+'"';
        newWindow2 = window.open(url,winname,settings);
        newWindow2.focus();
}
```

2 Call **placeWinTop()** from a link on the base window. This will open the first (top) window.

```
<a href="javascript:placedWinTop
➥('messagetop.html','m1',333,250);">link</a>
```

3 In the HTML of the page that is loaded in the top window (in this case, messagetop1.html), place the following **onload** event call in the **<body>** tag:

```
<body onload="placedWinBottom
➥('messagebottom.html','mes2',333,250)">
```

This will open the second window as soon as the first one loads.

WRITING CONTENT TO A NEW WINDOW
ON THE FLY

The third window in this sequence is generated on the fly. It shows how you can write
the contents of a new window and pass it one or more parameters.

1 Create a new **function** that will place a small window
to the right of the two previously opened windows.

In this case, we will predefine the **w** (width) and **h**
(height) values.

```
function placedWinSide(graphic) {
w = 100;
h = 100;
centerver = screen.height/2;
windowtop = centerver -50;
```

2 To position the element to the right of the original
window, it is necessary to do a little browser
detection.

This is because while Netscape (versions 4.x, 6, and
Mozilla) recognizes the **window.outerWidth** value,
Internet Explorer does not. Therefore, we will insert
a conditional statement that sees if the browser in use
is Internet Explorer.

This sees if the text string "MSIE" exists in the
navigator.userAgent property. If it does, then
windowleft is defined as **screen.width** divided by
two (the horizontal center), plus **document.body.
clientWidth** (the inner dimensions of the opening
window) divided by two, and plus an adjustment
number.

```
if (navigator.userAgent.indexOf('MSIE') != -1){ windowleft =
➡screen.width/2 + document.body.clientWidth/2 + 25;
{else {
        windowleft = (screen.width)/2 + window.outerWidth/2 + 20;}}
```

3 Specify the settings with the values for **w**, **h**,
windowleft, and **windowtop** inserted into the string.

```
settings = '"toolbar=no, directories=no,menubar=no,scrollbars=
➡no,resizable=no,status=no,width='+w+',height='+h+',left='+
➡windowleft+',top='+windowtop+'"';
```

4 Specify a string for the contents of the new window (**sidewincontent**). Note that the value of the argument **graphic** is inserted into the string.

> **Note:** All the quotes (" or ') and slashes (/) in the string must be escaped with a backlash (\). This is because a quote or slash can be interpreted by JavaScript as an ending character. If these characters are not escaped in a string, a syntax error will be generated.

5 Create the new window.

Note that the first value where the URL will go is normally blank because no URL is present.

6 Write the text string that you previously created with the **document.write()** method. This writes the string directly into the new window, creating a page on the fly. Close the document with **document.close()** after the content is written.

7 Give **focus** (bring to the front) the new window and close the function.

```
newWindow3.focus();
}
```

```
sidewincontent = "<html><head><title>side<\/title><\/head>";
sidewincontent += "<body marginheight=\"0\" marginwidth=\"0\" style=\"margin:0\">";
sidewincontent +="<table cellpadding=\"0\" cellspacing=\"0\" border=\"0\">";
sidewincontent +="<tr><td width=\"100\">";
sidewincontent += "<a href=\"javascript:window.opener.close();self.close();\">
➡<img src=\""+graphic+"\" alt=\"close window\" width=\"100\" height=\"100\
➡"border=\"0\"><\/a><\/td>";
sidewincontent += "<\/tr><\/table><\/body><\/html>";
```

```
newWindow3 = window.open('','sidewin',settings);
```

```
newWindow3.document.write (sidewincontent);
newWindow3.document.close();
```

```
function placedWinSide(graphic) {
    w = 100;
    h = 100;
    centerver = screen.height/2;
    windowtop = centerver -50;
    settings = '"toolbar=no, directories=no,menubar=no,scrollbars=no,
    ➡resize=no,status=no,width='+w+',height='+h+',left='+
    ➡windowleft+',top='+windowtop+'"';

    if (navigator.userAgent.indexOf('MSIE') != -1) {
        windowleft = screen.width/2 + document.body.
        ➡clientWidth/2 + 25;
    } else {
        windowleft = (screen.width)/2 + window.outerWidth/2 + 20;
    }
}
```

```
sidewincontent = "<html><head><title>side<\/title><\/head>";
    sidewincontent += "<body marginheight=\"0\" marginwidth=\"0\"
    ➡style=\"margin:0\">";
    sidewincontent +="<table cellpadding=\"0\" cellspacing=\"0\"
    ➡border=\"0\">";
    sidewincontent +="<tr><td width=\"100\">";
    sidewincontent += "<a href=\"javascript:window.opener.close();
    ➡self.close();\"><img src=\""+graphic+"\" alt=\"close window\"
    ➡width=\"100\" height=\"100\"border=\"0\"><\/a><\/td>";
    sidewincontent += "<\/tr><\/table><\/body><\/html>";

    newWindow3 = window.open('','sidewin',settings);
    newWindow3.document.write (sidewincontent);
    newWindow3.document.close();
    newWindow3.focus();
}
```

131

8 Call this function with an onload event by inserting the following into the **<body>** tag of the page that is loaded in the second window (messagebottom1.html in this case).

```
<body onload="placedWinSide('images/closewin.gif')">
```

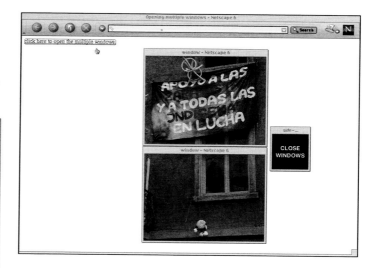

Clicking the link that opens the first window initiates a "chain reaction": first the top window is opened, then the second, and finally the third.

> **Note:** The second window is opened as soon as the first one is opened, but instead of calling the function with a link, it's called as an **onload** event in the first (top) window. Then, the second window opens the third window. This shows how you can open new windows with onload (when a document is loaded).
>
> If you have ever wondered how some sites you have visited manage to spawn window after window as soon as you close one, it's because they have been written to open a new window upon an **unload** (window closed) event in the **body** tag.

CLOSING MULTIPLE WINDOWS

Because we opened three windows as a set, we want to close them all at once too. This is done with a reverse "chain reaction" order, which closes the **self**, the **opener**, and then the **opener** of the **opener**.

1 Note that previously we inserted the following into the **<a>** link element:

```
<a href="javascript:window.opener.close();
➥window.close();>
```

2 In the **<body>** tag of the second window opened (messagebottom1.html in this case), call a function that will close the opener when the window is closed.

```
<body... onunload="if (window.opener)
➥{window.opener.close()}">
```

When the user clicks the "close window" graphic in the third window, it closes the previous window, which then closes the first window.

> **Note:** When referring to the opener of a new window, you may use either opener or window.opener. Therefore, both **opener.close()** and **window.opener.close()** are correct.

The window.history Array

Each browser window contains a **history** array, where the locations of previously visited pages within that window are stored. Here is one way in which this might be used.

1 Open a new window that is centered on the page, using the **centeredWindow()** function.

```
<a href="javascript:centeredWindow
➥('rave.html','raveWin',492,450)">link</a>
```

2 Create a link on the second and third pages to be loaded (rave2.html and rave3.html in this case) that, when clicked, goes back to the **-1** item in the **window.history** array. The method used is **history.go**.

```
<a href="javascript:history.go(-1)">go back</a>
```

Note: In the **window.history** array, **0** is the current page. **-1** is the page previously visited, **-2** is the one before that, and so on. You can move to any position in that array with the **history.go** method.

The **window.history** array is not very reliable for navigation considering that you never really know what pages the user has previously loaded into a particular browser window. However, in controlled situations it can be used.

history.go(-1) ➤

Clicking an area within the first page loads the new URL. The "go back" page returns to -1 in the window.history array (the previous page).

Scrolling a Window Automatically

On occasion, you might want to scroll a window up or down to show a particular part of the page. Here is how to do it.

1 Open a new window that is centered on the page—but with the scroll bar visible. This is the **centeredWindow()** function with the **scrollbars** value modified.

```
function centeredscrollingWindow(url,winname,w,h) {
    windowleft = (screen.width - w)/2;
    windowtop = (screen.height - h)/2;
settings='"toolbar=no,directories=no,menubar=no,scrollbars=yes,resizable=yes,status=no,
➥width='+w+',height='+h+',left='+windowleft+',top='+windowtop+'"';
```

continues

2 Create a scrolling **function**. First, define a variable called **vPos** (for vertical position) and give it an initial value of **0**.

```
var vPos=0;
```

3 Start the **function** itself. A variable of **h** for the height of the window contents is passed. The rest of the function will work if the **window.scroll()** method is recognized by the browser in use.

```
function scrollWindow(h) {
if (window.scroll) {
```

4 Add the scrolling functionality.

The scrolling function scrolls the window up and down using a **do...while** loop. The first part of the function defines what will happen while the value of **vPos** is less or equal to **h** (the height). Then, the second part of the function will scroll the window up while the value of **vPos** is more than **0**. In each case, the value of **vPos** is incremented by **1**: in the first half of the function, and the window is scrolled by an **x** value of **0** and a **y** value of **vPos**. In the second half, the window is scrolled by an **x** value of **0** and a **y** value of **-vPos**, which will make the window scroll up.

```
do {
    vPos+=1;
    window.scroll(0,vPos);
} while (vPos <= h);
do {
    vPos -= 1;
    window.scroll(0,vPos);
} while (vPos > 0);

}
}
```

continued

```
        closeWindow();
        newWin = window.open(url,winname,settings);
        newWin.focus();
}
```

```
/* Start window scrolling function. First initialize the variable
vPos to 0.
*/
var vPos=0;

/*  the scrolling up and down function */
function scrollWindow(h) {
        if (window.scroll) {
                do {
                        vPos+=1;
                        window.scroll(0,vPos);
                } while (vPos <= h);
                do {
                        vPos -= 1;
                        window.scroll(0,vPos);
                } while (vPos > 0);
        }
}
```

5 Call this code with an **onload** event in the cows1.html window.

```
<body onload="if (window.scroll)
➥{window.scroll(0,30);setTimeout('scrollWindow
➥(530)',2000)}">
```

Note that an initial **window.scroll()** is called when the page is loaded, to scroll the window down by 30 pixels. This is a little trick to hide the "close window" section of the page. Then the **scrollWindow()** function is called with a **setTimeout** delay of 2000 milliseconds, or 2 seconds.

Note: A single **window.scroll(x,y)** call will simply scroll the window down to a specified coordinate. This is useful when you wish to scroll to a precise place in a window. You also may use **window.scrollTo(x,y)** in version 4 and later browsers.

Note: The **do...while** is another conditional statement. It executes whatever is in the brackets following the **do**, while the condition specified in the **while** returns true.

The window scrolls up...then down.

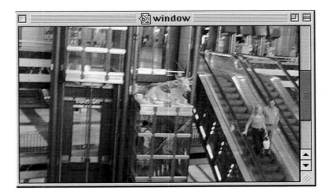

WRITING INFORMATION BACK TO THE OPENER

We have seen how it is possible to dynamically write information to a new window. In this example, we'll see how it's possible to write information back to the **opener** or opening window.

1 Create a function that will write a string into a form field.

A value for **text** is created in the child window. This value is inserted into a string (**textstring**), which is then passed back to a form field in the opener window. The function will only execute if the **opener** (opening window) exists.

When executed, the function assembles a text string.

```
function insertname(text) {
        if (window.opener) {
                textstring = " Welcome, "+text +". Please enjoy your stay.";
                opener.document.nameform.namefield.value=textstring;
        }
}
```

2 Create a form on a new page with a text field, where a user can input his name. Call the **insertname()** function on an **onsubmit** event. The value passed to the function is the value of the field name **visitorname** in this form. (**this.visitorname.value**).

```
<form name="visitorform" onsubmit="insertname(this.visitorname.
↪value);window.close();return false;">
<p>What is your name?<br><br>
<input type="text" name="visitorname">
</p>
<input type="submit" name="submitbutton" value="submit">
</form>
```

3 Create a form on the **opener** page with an empty text field. This is where the new value will be inserted.

```
<form name="nameform">
<input type="text" name="namefield" size="50">
</form>
```

Note: In older browsers such as Netscape 4.x, it is only possible to pass values into form fields in the **opener** window. In later browsers it is possible to pass values to other elements. See Part 4 of this book for more about the latest DOM methods.

Because only form fields can be used, the designer might want to control the appearance of the form fields as much as possible with CSS. Unfortunately, the older browsers don't recognize CSS style rules for form elements. It's Catch-22, isn't it?

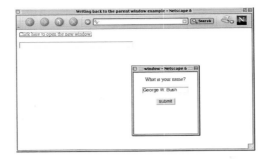

The user types in his name (top). When the form is submitted, the new text value is inserted into the text field in the opener window (bottom).

PUTTING IT ALL TOGETHER: THE PHOTO ALBUM SITE

The window manipulation functions come together to create the Photo Album mini-website. You can find all of the files used for the Photo Album in the **photoalbum** folder in the Project 7 folder on the CD and companion web site.

The scripts are described in preceding sections.

1   Place all the functions used on the pages into an external JavaScript file, windows.js. Link to this external JavaScript file from all of the HTML pages on this site by placing the following code in the **<head></head>** section of each page.

```
<script src="windows.js"
type="text/javascript"></script>
```

2 On the opening page, create the form field that will hold the text string passed to it from the small pop-up window. Call the function that opens the child window where the user will enter his name with an onload event in the **<body>** tag.

```
<body onload="centeredWindow('formwindow.html',
➥'formwin',300,100)">
```

The visitor enters his/her name into the form field, which is then entered into the form field on the parent window. Note that the borders of the form field on the parent window are made invisible with CSS.

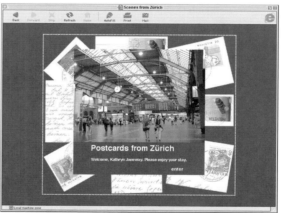

3 Create a page that calls the various window manipulation functions.

On this page, the thumbnail images are the links that open the new windows. Note that the status message at the bottom of the browser window changes appropriately when the user mouses over one of the thumbnails.

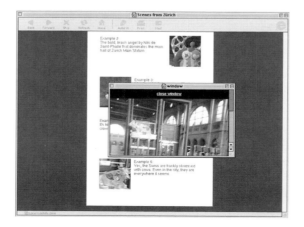

The visitor clicks the small thumbnail images, which are links that open the corresponding new windows.

How It Works: The Anatomy of a Browser Window

It is useful to know which parts of a window we can specify to show or not show when opening a new window. The following is a list of the window features that are common to the major browsers in widespread use.

Table 7.1 Common Window Features

Feature	Specify	Specifies or Displays	Default
Height	number	height of the window	See Comments
Width	number	width of the window	See Comments

> **Comments:** The default value for height and width differs from browser to browser. In Internet Explorer 5.x on Windows, the size of a second open window defaults to the same size as the first, and relaunching the browser application loads a window the same size as the window you had open before quitting the application.
>
> In Netscape 4.x, the second window is about the same size as the first window. In Internet Explorer 5.x on the Mac, it's the same size as the last window opened.

Table 7.2

Feature	Specify	Specifies or Displays	Default
Top (IE)	number	top location of the window	See Comments
ScreenY (NS)	number	top location of the window	See Comments
Left (IE)	number	the left location of the window	See Comments
ScreenX (NS)	number	the left location of the window	See Comments

> **Comments:** The default is to place the window on the upper left corner of the screen.

Table 7.3

Feature	Specify	Specifies or Displays	Default
Location	yes/no	location bar	yes
Menubar	yes/no	menu bar	yes
Resizable	yes/no	If the window can be resized	yes
Scrollbars	yes/no	vertical scrollbars	yes
Status	yes/no	status bar	yes
Toolbar	yes/no	toolbar	yes

In addition, the following can be specified for Internet Explorer 5.x and above on Windows:

Table 7.4 Specifications for Internet Explorer 5.x and Above

Feature	Specify	Specifies or Displays	Default
Channelmode	yes/no	Whether to display the window in "theater mode"	no
Directories	yes/no	Directory buttons	yes
Fullscreen	yes/no	Whether to display the window in full screen mode. Fullscreen mode eliminates all the "chrome" around the window. Therefore, this should be used with caution, if at all, because it takes away all navigation controls from the user until she closes the window with the keyboard (ALT+F4).	no

WINDOW ETIQUETTE

Unfortunately, opening new windows with JavaScript is one of the most abused functions on the web right now. You are probably familiar with the sites that open new windows periodically (usually containing ads) or continue to spawn new windows continuously once one is closed. There are even programs that specifically catch any attempt to open a new window and kill that action. When a site relies on putting information into new windows, this can cause a problem.

As with any kind of technology, the designer should use this most useful aspect of JavaScript with restraint.

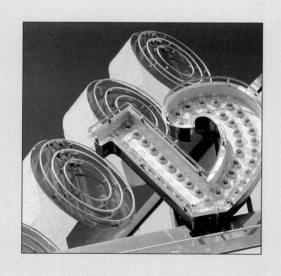

BROWSER DETECTION AND DISPLAYING ELEMENTS DYNAMICALLY

"Our inventions are wont to be pretty

toys, which distract our attention from

serious things. They are but improved

means to an unimproved end."

—HENRY DAVID THOREAU

The Daily Horoscope

In this project we delve into the different

Document Object Models (DOMs) for version 4

and later browsers, as we create a page that

displays a daily horoscope. A solid understand-

ing of the various browser-specific DOMs is

crucial when creating dynamic web pages.

Browser Detection and Displaying Elements Dynamically

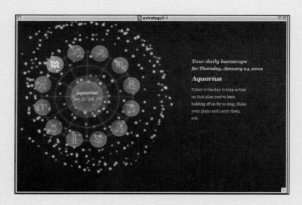

GETTING STARTED

The DOM is the term used to describe the method in which elements in a document or a web page are addressed. Currently, there are three major types of graphical browsers in use: Netscape version 4.x (4.08 and higher), Internet Explorer version 4.x and 5.x, and finally the most current browsers, which adhere more or less strictly to the Document Object Model standards set down by the W3C.

In this project, we'll see how to detect for the major graphical browsers in use and how to write scripts that accommodate the differences in each.

The example page is a daily horoscope page. The viewer can click on his astrological sign to view his horoscope for the day. The horoscopes are contained within **div** elements that are displayed "dynamically." Showing and hiding the elements according to which ones are clicked accomplishes this. This method is very useful for pages where there is a lot of text information and a less cluttered appearance is required.

In this project, you will learn how to

- Detect for the major browsers with object detection
- Create your own document object
- Branch your code according to the browser
- Address and change the **visibility** style of an element
- Create a persistent variable
- Utilize an image editor effectively to generate a large number of rollover images
- Write text onto a page dynamically

CREATING THE HTML BASE

This page is made up of three major elements: the left side **div** that encloses the sliced up horoscope graphic; the header text that shows the current date; and the horoscope text itself. The horoscope text is actually contained in 13 different **div** elements. First, we'll create the HTML.

1 Give a **name** and **id** attribute value to each of the **img** elements that will have their **src** graphic swapped. The **img** elements that this applies to are the 12 zodiac signs and the center graphic that indicates the astrological sign name and the date range for each.

The **name** and **id** should correspond to the astrological sign, for example, **sag** (for Sagittarius), **lib** (for Libra), and so on. Name the middle circle **img** element **mid**.

2 Surround each of the horoscope sign **img** objects with an **<a>** (link) tag.

3 Put the table containing the sliced up horoscope graphic in a **div** element with the **id** value of **chart**.

4 Create an empty **div** element named **header**. This will hold the current date text, which is generated dynamically.

5 Create 13 **div** elements that hold the text for each horoscope (plus the default text). Give all of these **div** elements a **class** value of **horoscope**.

6 Give each of the horoscope **div** elements a unique **id**, corresponding to the astrological sign. Here they have been named **saghoroscope** (for Sagittarius), **libhoroscope** (for Libra), and so on.

```
<!-- the IMG tags for each horoscope sign graphic should look
like this. -->

<a href=""><img border="0" name="can" id="can" alt="Cancer"
src="images/can.jpg" width="73" height="59"></a>

<a href=""><img border="0" name="gem" id="gem" alt="Gemini"
src="images/gem.jpg" width="73" height="59"></a>

<!-- etc. The middle circle graphic IMG tag should be: -->

<img border="0" name="mid" id="mid" alt="What's your sign?"
src="images/mid.jpg" width="146" height="144">
```

The **img** tags for each astrological sign should look like this. Note the appropriate **name** and **id** values and the **alt tags.**

```
<!-- the DIV elements -->

<div id="chart">
<!-- holds the horoscope graphic table Omitted for clarity -->
</div>

<div id="header">
<!-- empty. Will hold the dynamically generated current date
text. -->
</div>


<div class="horoscope" id="defhoroscope"> <!-- the default
horoscope text -->
```

The HTML code for the **div** elements make up this page.

continues

```
<h1>What is in the stars today?</h1>
<p>What is awaiting you today? Is it wealth, health, love,
good or bad luck? Just click on your astrological symbol to
read your horoscope.</p>
</div>

<div class="horoscope" id="saghoroscope">
<h1>Sagittarius</h1>
<p>You will meet a mysterious dark stranger today. You
never know what will happen! Carry a red rose with you.</p>
</div>

<div class="horoscope" id="scohoroscope">
<h1>Scorpio</h1>
<p>Invite some friends over today for dinner and show off
your cooking skills. Someone will come with one of your
friends and that someone will be your future spouse.</p>
</div>

<div class="horoscope" id="libhoroscope">
<h1>Libra</h1>
<p>If you are looking for a new job, today is a good day to
peruse the want ads. Your next phone call will lead to the
job of your dreams.</p>
</div>

<div class="horoscope" id="virhoroscope">
<h1>Virgo</h1>
<p>Your financial luck is very good today to buy a lottery
ticket. Who knows, you could win!</p>
</div>

<div class="horoscope" id="leohoroscope">
<h1>Leo</h1>
<p>Someone close to you wants you to contact them. They are
missing you a lot. Give them a call.</p>
</div>

<div class="horoscope" id="canhoroscope">
<h1>Cancer</h1>
<p>You might get into an argument with a coworker today, so
watch out for any temper tantrums. Today is a good day to
lay low.</p>
</div>

<div class="horoscope" id="gemhoroscope">
<h1>Gemini</h1>
<p>You'll have a good day. A good day. A really really good
day. You'll find love, wealth, a good job, and $50 under
your sofa cushions.</p>
</div>

<div class="horoscope" id="tauhoroscope">
<h1>Taurus</h1>
<p>You must call your mom. And call your dad too. Be nice
to your dog. Stroke your cat. Smile politely to your
neighbors. Watch out for oncoming traffic. Kiss your
spouse.</p>
</div>

<div class="horoscope" id="arihoroscope">
<h1>Aries</h1>
<p>Someone that you now only think of as a friend may soon
become something more. Do you know who that person is? If
you do, invite them out for coffee.</p>
</div>

<div class="horoscope" id="pishoroscope">
<h1>Pisces</h1>
<p>Look out when you cross the street today because if you
are not careful, you might get hit by a car.</p>
</div>

<div class="horoscope" id="aquhoroscope">
<h1>Aquarius</h1>
<p>Today is the day to take action on that plan you've been
holding off on for so long. Make your plans and carry them
out.</p>
</div>

<div class="horoscope" id="caphoroscope">
<h1>Capricorn</h1>
<p>You are working too hard and you feel tired and worn
out. Take a break and plan for a vacation.</p>
</div>
```

CREATING THE CASCADING STYLE SHEET (CSS)

In a layout such as this one with a prominent graphic that also features graphical text, it's a good idea to specify element sizes in absolute terms (pixels). The CSS-controlled font sizes and typefaces should be a good match for the graphical text.

1 Create the CSS that controls the font and appearance. Note that **font-size** and **line-height** are specified in pixels.

```css
/* the CSS to control appearance */
img {
        border: 0;
        display: block;
        }

a {
        outline: none;
        }

h1,h2 {
        color: #ffff33;
        background: transparent;
        font-family: georgia, serif;
        font-style: italic;
        }

h1 {
        font-size: 20px;
        }

h2 {
        font-size: 16px;
        line-height: 24px;
        }

p {
        font-family: georgia, serif;
        color: #ffffff;
        background: transparent;
        font-size: 12px;
        line-height: 24px;
        }

body {
        background: #000066;
        color: #ffffff;
        margin: 0px;
        }
```

Note: There are two CSS rules here that deal with particular CSS display problems.

The **display: block** rule given to the **img** selector specifies that all **img** elements should be displayed as block style instead of inline (which is the default value). This is necessary for displaying graphics that have been sliced up and reassembled into a table—in some of the newer browsers such as Netscape 6.x or Mozilla. If you see ugly "gaps" in your sliced graphics when viewed in these browsers, this is because the default display behavior of **img** elements according to the W3C specifications is inline. The display: block style rule will eliminate the gaps. (Note that the "gaps" will only show if you declare a Strict HTML or an XHTML DOCTYPE.)

The **outline: none** rule given to the **a** element is specifically for Internet Explorer 5 on the Mac. The default behavior in that browser is to give a thick, colored outline to any clickable element (such as **a** or **area**). Because this is not desirable on this page, the outline is eliminated. Unfortunately, the **outline: none** rule does not get rid of the dotted outline in other browsers.

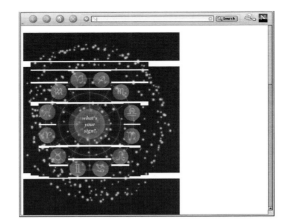

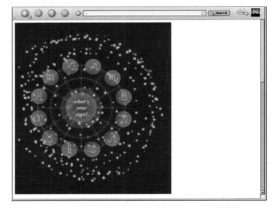

When viewed in Netscape 6, the table slices show gaps (top). Applying the **display: block** rule to **img** elements fixes this (bottom).

2 Create the CSS for the **div** elements.

Note that the horoscope text **div**s are given a **visibility** value of **hidden**. For the sake of browser compatibility, they are given a **position: absolute** value.

The **chart div** is given a negative **top** value simply because design-wise, the graphic seemed to fit better when positioned slightly higher. Rather than re-create a complicated sliced graphic, it was simply repositioned with CSS.

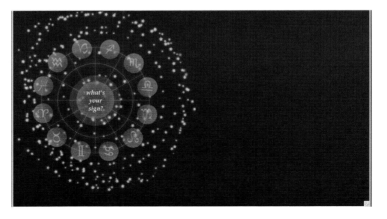

The page with all the CSS style rules defined. The text elements are invisible at this point.

The horoscope text **div**s (with the **class** selector **horoscope**) are given a **left** value of **65%**. This means that the **div**s will reposition themselves according to the browser window width, but if the window is resized to a narrow width, the text will overlap the graphic. (For this reason, give the text **div**s a higher **z-index** value than the **chart div**.) If this behavior is not desired, give a **left** value in absolute terms, that is, **500px**—so that the text never overlaps.

```
/* the DIV CSS */

#chart {
        position: absolute;
        top: -50px;
        left: 0px;
        z-index: 0;
        }

#header {
        position: absolute;
        z-index: 1;
        left: 510px;
        width: 200px;
        top: 110px;
        vertical-align: top;
        background: transparent;
        }

.horoscope {
        position: absolute;
        z-index: 2;
        left: 65%;
        width: 180px;
        top: 180px;
        visibility: hidden;
        background: transparent;
        }
```

DETECTING FOR OBJECT SUPPORT IN BROWSERS

Because of the different JavaScript implementations in each of the major browsers, it is necessary to do some browser detection for our scripts to work properly. The method used here shows how a browser supports a particular object. This method works well for most cases.

1 Detect for Netscape Navigator version 4.x.

Netscape Navigator 4.x supports a proprietary object called the **layer** object. Therefore, to see if a browser is Netscape Navigator 4.x or not, use this **if**…conditional statement:

```
if (document.layers) {.....statements that will
only be executed in NN 4.x }
```

2 Detect for Internet Explorer 4.x through 6.x.

Internet Explorer 4.x through 6.x uses a proprietary property to access the DOM called **document.all**. Therefore, to see if a browser is Internet Explorer 4.x or not, use this **if**...conditional statement:

```
if (document.all) {....statements that will
only be executed in IE 4.x and 5.x.}
```

3 Detect for W3C DOM-compliant browsers such as Netscape 6.

The newer W3C DOM compliant browsers support the **document.getElementById()** method to access the DOM. To see if a browser is W3C DOM compliant, use this **if**...conditional statement:

```
if (document.getElementById) {....statements
that will be executed in W3C DOM compliant
browsers... }
```

> **Note:** Although version 5.x and later versions of Internet Explorer also support the W3C DOM in large part, often the methods used by IE are proprietary and/or differ from those used in Netscape 6 and other Mozilla-based browsers. Therefore, in many cases it is more practical to use the **document.all** object model for Internet Explorer 4.x and above, as opposed to **document.getElementById()**—unless you are using a W3C DOM specific method.

CREATING YOUR OWN DOCUMENT OBJECT

It's often convenient to assemble your own document object rather than type the proprietary document objects over and over again for each browser. This object can be reused repeatedly for addressing elements on the page correctly.

1 Declare the global variables, which will be used as pieces of the document object.

```
var doc, doc2;
```

> **Note:** A global or page-wide variable is one that is available to all functions on the page. To declare a global variable, place the **var** statement outside of a **function**.

2 Detect for Netscape Navigator 4.x, Internet Explorer 4.x/5.x, and W3C DOM-compliant browsers and assign the appropriate values to the variables—with a series of **if…else if** statements.

We just created four global variables that contain the correct code for each browser to access objects in the page.

The values assigned to the variables **doc**, **doc2**, **doc3**, and **sty** will be used in many of the functions on this page.

Note: The **if…else if** conditional statements are executed in sequence. This script only detects for the major version 4 and older browsers.

```javascript
var doc, doc2,doc3,sty;
        if (document.layers) {
                // if Netscape 4
                doc = "document.";
                doc2 = "";
                doc3 = "";
                sty = "";
        } else if (document.all) {
                // if IE
                doc = "document.all.";
                doc2 = "";
                doc3 = "";
                sty = ".style";

        } else if (document.getElementById) {
                // if DOM compliant
                doc = "document.getElementById('";
                doc2 = "')";
                doc3 = "')";
                sty = ".style";
        }
```

CREATING A FUNCTION THAT LOADS IMAGE OBJECTS AND RETURNS A LOADED FLAG

In this step we will create a function that loads the image objects and once the images are loaded, sets a "loaded" flag.

1 Define two global variables that will be used for the image loading function. The **loaded variable** value (the "are the images loaded or not?" flag) is set to **false** initially.

The **imagedir** variable is assigned the **string** value of the path to the **images** directory. This is handy for cases where you might be moving pages around within your site or using the same function on pages in different directories. By simply changing this one value, you can change the path for all the images loaded on your page.

2 Start the function and check for the existence of the **document.images** object. If the browser in use does not support this object, the whole script will not execute.

The images that will be swapped in and out of the **src** of the **mid** (middle circle) image element are loaded into an array. Each item in the array is an **Image** object with an **src** assigned. Note that the **src** value is the string of **imagedir**, plus the graphic name.

> **Note:** Given that all version 4 and later browsers support the **document.images** object, it is not always necessary to check for this object anymore for the graphical JavaScript-capable browsers in current use. However, if you wish to allow for version 3 browser users, check for the existence of the images object this way.
>
> Note that text-only and other non-JavaScript browsers will simply skip over any scripts.

3 At the end of the function, set the value of the loaded variable to **true**.

When the loaded variable value is **true**, it means that all the **image** objects have been loaded into the browser cache.

4 Invoke the **preload()** script by calling it.

> **Note:** When creating and saving your graphics with a graphics program, it's important to name the files in a way that makes them easier to address in your scripts. The images that make up the horoscope sign "rollovers" are given logical names according to what state they will represent, that is, "**off**" (for the off state image), "**over**" for the mouse over state, and "**click**" for the mouse click state.

The graphics used in this project were created in Adobe Photoshop and ImageReady. The large graphic was sliced up in ImageReady, carefully isolating the graphics that would "roll over"—the 12 star sign buttons and the central circle. The table slices were generated by ImageReady, as were the rollover graphics. The graphic files that were used for the rollovers were named appropriately and logically within ImageReady, instead of relying on the program defaults. (Note that the naming of the filenames of the unscripted graphics in the table is left up to the program's defaults because they won't be addressed with JavaScript.)

```
/* define some global variables for the image loading
function */
var imgdir = "images/";
var loaded = false;

//preload images
function preload() {
if (document.images) {
```

```
midImg = new Array();
midImg[0] = new Image;
midImg[0].src = imgdir + "mid.jpg";
midImg[1] = new Image;
midImg[1].src = imgdir + "mid-sag.jpg";
midImg[2] = new Image;
midImg[2].src = imgdir + "mid-sco.jpg";
midImg[3] = new Image;
```

continues

```
midImg[3].src = imgdir + "mid-lib.jpg";          vir_over.src = imgdir + "vir-over.jpg";
midImg[4] = new Image;                           vir_click.src = imgdir + "vir-down.jpg";
midImg[4].src = imgdir + "mid-vir.jpg";
midImg[5] = new Image;                           leo_off = new Image;
midImg[5].src = imgdir + "mid-leo.jpg";          leo_over = new Image;
midImg[6] = new Image;                           leo_click = new Image;
midImg[6].src = imgdir + "mid-can.jpg";          leo_off.src = imgdir + "leo.jpg";
midImg[7] = new Image;                           leo_over.src = imgdir + "leo-over.jpg";
midImg[7].src = imgdir + "mid-gem.jpg";          leo_click.src = imgdir + "leo-down.jpg";
midImg[8] = new Image;
midImg[8].src = imgdir + "mid-tau.jpg";          can_off = new Image;
midImg[9] = new Image;                           can_over = new Image;
midImg[9].src = imgdir + "mid-ari.jpg";          can_click = new Image;
midImg[10] = new Image;                          can_off.src = imgdir + "can.jpg";
midImg[10].src = imgdir + "mid-pis.jpg";         can_over.src = imgdir + "can-over.jpg";
midImg[11] = new Image;                          can_click.src = imgdir + "can-down.jpg";
midImg[11].src = imgdir + "mid-aqu.jpg";
midImg[12] = new Image;                          gem_off = new Image;
midImg[12].src = imgdir + "mid-cap.jpg";         gem_over = new Image;
                                                 gem_click = new Image;
sag_off = new Image;                             gem_off.src = imgdir + "gem.jpg";
sag_over = new Image;                            gem_over.src = imgdir + "gem-over.jpg";
sag_click = new Image;                           gem_click.src = imgdir + "gem-down.jpg";
sag_off.src = imgdir + "sag.jpg";
sag_over.src = imgdir + "sag-over.jpg";          tau_off = new Image;
sag_click.src = imgdir + "sag-down.jpg";         tau_over = new Image;
                                                 tau_click = new Image;
sco_off = new Image;                             tau_off.src = imgdir + "tau.jpg";
sco_over = new Image;                            tau_over.src = imgdir + "tau-over.jpg";
sco_click = new Image;                           tau_click.src = imgdir + "tau-down.jpg";
sco_off.src = imgdir + "sco.jpg";
sco_over.src = imgdir + "sco-over.jpg";          ari_off = new Image;
sco_click.src = imgdir + "sco-down.jpg";         ari_over = new Image;
                                                 ari_click = new Image;
lib_off = new Image;                             ari_off.src = imgdir + "ari.jpg";
lib_over = new Image;                            ari_over.src = imgdir + "ari-over.jpg";
lib_click = new Image;                           ari_click.src = imgdir + "ari-down.jpg";
lib_off.src = imgdir + "lib.jpg";
lib_over.src = imgdir + "lib-over.jpg";          pis_off = new Image;
lib_click.src = imgdir + "lib-down.jpg";         pis_over = new Image;
                                                 pis_click = new Image;
vir_off = new Image;                             pis_off.src = imgdir + "pis.jpg";
vir_over = new Image;                            pis_over.src = imgdir + "pis-over.jpg";
vir_click = new Image;                           pis_click.src = imgdir + "pis-down.jpg";
vir_off.src = imgdir + "vir.jpg";
```

continues

continued

```
aqu_off = new Image;
aqu_over = new Image;
aqu_click = new Image;
aqu_off.src = imgdir + "aqu.jpg";
aqu_over.src = imgdir + "aqu-over.jpg";
aqu_click.src = imgdir + "aqu-down.jpg";

cap_off = new Image;
cap_over = new Image;
cap_click = new Image;
```

```
cap_off.src = imgdir + "cap.jpg";
cap_over.src = imgdir + "cap-over.jpg";
cap_click.src = imgdir + "cap-down.jpg";

loaded = true;
 }
}

//invoke the preload script
preload();
```

CREATING THE IMAGE ROLLOVER SCRIPTS

The image objects with rollovers are nested within a **div** element. Therefore, it is necessary to address them in a different way in Netscape 4.x, which handles nested objects differently from our other target browsers.

1 Create the rollover script for the horoscope images.

Two arguments are passed to the function: **obj** (for object **id/name**) and **state** (for the desired rollover state). The function first checks to see if the value of **loaded** is **true** (that is, if all the image objects have loaded).

The first line of the function checks the value of the variable **loaded**. If this is **true**, it means that the **image** objects have been preloaded, and so the function will execute. This prevents the function from executing if the user clicks a graphic prematurely before the page has finished loading.

The next section of the script assembles a different document object depending on the browser in use with the **eval()** method. If the browser is Netscape 4.x, the variable source is assigned the evaluated value of the string **doc + 'chart' + doc2 + obj**. We've declared these variables earlier, so the string is **document.chart.document.objectID**.

```
function rollit(obj,state) {
        if (loaded == true) {
                // if all image objects have loaded
                if (document.layers) {
                        source = eval(doc + 'chart'
                        ➡+doc2+obj);
                } else {
                        source = eval(doc + obj+doc2);
                }
                newpic = eval(obj + '_'+ state);
                source.src = newpic.src;
        }
}
```

154

If the browser is Internet Explorer 4.x and above or a W3C DOM-compliant browser, the string **doc + obj + doc2** is evaluated. If the browser is Internet Explorer, the string is **document.all.objectID**; if the browser is Netscape 6, the string is **document.getElementById('objectID')**. This creates the correct document object, or "pointer," to the right object on the page for each browser.

Finally, the script evaluates the string of **obj + "_" + state** and assigns this to the variable, newpic. The **src** graphic of **source** (the document object) is switched to the **src** graphic of **newpic**.

ADDRESSING PAGE ELEMENTS CORRECTLY

Using the correct DOM, or the right "address," for the objects on the page is critical to successful scripting.

The method we've used here assembles the "address" on the fly, depending on the browser that's being used to access the page. For Internet Explorer and Netscape 6, the "address" is fairly straightforward. When an element on the page has a unique id, all you have to do to point to it properly in your script is to address it by its id value. Internet Explorer 4.x and above use the **document.all.objectID** method, and W3C DOM-compliant browsers such as Netscape 6 use **document.getElementById('objectID')**.

In Netscape 4.x, it's a bit more complicated. To address an element that is not nested within a **div** or **span** element, you can address it with the **document.objectID** method. This is what we did in the previous section—where we didn't use nested elements. (Elements that are contained within table cells are not considered to be nested.) However, when an element is nested within a div element, it's necessary to start the "address" with the outermost element and work inward. On our page, the **img** elements are nested within the **div** element, **chart**. Therefore, we must address these elements starting with the address of the container div, **document.chart.document.objectID**.

Experienced JavaScript coders might think this is a roundabout way of assembling a browser-specific document object. I have used this method so that you can see exactly how the "address," or document object, is assembled depending on the browser.

Let's see how the script would work in action. Let's say the id of the **img** object being addressed is **sag** (the Sagittarius **img**). In Netscape 4.x, the document object "address" will look like this:

document.chart.document.sag

In Internet Explorer 4.x, the "address" will look like this:

document.all.sag

Finally, in Netscape 6 the "address" will look like this:

document.getElementById('sag')

All three "addresses" point to the same **img** object.

2 Create the rollover script for the center graphic (the **img** with the **id mid**).

This function is similar to the rollover script for the star signs, except that it refers to the **index** value of the **midImg** array.

```
// the rollover function for the middle image
function midroll(index) {
        if (loaded ==true) {
                // if all image objects have loaded
                if (document.layers) {
                        midsource = eval(doc + 'chart' +doc2+'mid');
                } else {
                        midsource = eval(doc + 'mid'+doc2);
                }

                        midsource.src = midImg[index].src;
        }
}
```

CREATING THE SCRIPT TO DISPLAY THE HOROSCOPE TEXT

In this step, we will create the script that shows or hides the appropriate **div** element that holds the corresponding horoscope text for each star sign.

1 First, define a global variable named active and set the initial value to **null**.

This variable will hold the value of any currently visible, **div** element.

2 Start to declare the function. The function is passed one argument, **signID**, or the **id** value of the star sign whose horoscope should be displayed.

3 Create the first part of the function. It will only execute if the value of the variable **active** is not **null** or in other words, if there is already an active (visible) horoscope text **div**. If so, the DOM of the active (visible) **div** element is evaluated and assigned to the variable, **activelayer**. Then the active (visible) **div** element is made invisible by changing its **visibility** style value to "**hidden**."

```
/* the global variable "active" checks to see which layer is
currently active.
*/

var active = null;

function showHoroscope(signID) {
        /*first check if a layer is active and make it invisible */
        if (active != null) {
                activeLayer = eval (doc+active +"horoscope" +sty);
                activeLayer.visibility = "hidden";
        }
        /*now make the selected DIV visible */
        newLayer = eval (doc + signID + "horoscope" + sty);
        newLayer.visibility = "visible";
        /*set the new layer's ID to "active" */
        active = signID;
}
```

4 Create the next part of the function. The DOM of the **div** element to be displayed is evaluated and assigned to the variable, **newlayer**. Then, the selected **div** element is shown by changing its **visibility** style value to **"visible"**. Finally, the variable, **active**, is assigned the value of **signID**.

Note: This function uses a global (persistent) variable to hold the value of the **active**, or currently visible, horoscope text **div** element. This is necessary to ensure that only one **div** element at a time is visible.

Let's see this in an example. The user clicks the Libra graphic button, displaying the Libra horoscope. The value of the variable, **active**, is set to **lib**.

Next, the user clicks the Gemini button. Because the current value of **active** is **lib**, the Libra horoscope text **div** (**id: libhoroscope**) is hidden. The Gemini horoscope text **div** (**id: gemhoroscope**) is made visible, and the value of the variable **active** is now set to **gem**.

You can track how the value of **active** changes at each stage of the function by inserting **alert()** calls at key places. Using **alert()** calls is a great way of debugging your scripts. (Remember to take out the **alert()** calls before uploading your final project!)

```
var active = null;

function showHoroscope(signID) {
    /*first check if a layer is active and make it invisible */
    if (active != null) {
        alert('the current value of  active is ' + active);
        activeLayer = eval (doc+active +"horoscope" +sty);
        activeLayer.visibility = "hidden";
    }

    /*now make the selected DIV visible */
    newLayer = eval (doc + signID + "horoscope" + sty);
    newLayer.visibility = "visible";

    /*set the new layer's ID to "active" */
    active = signID;
    alert('the new value of  active is ' + active);
}
```

When the user clicks the Gemini button with the Libra text visible, the current value of **active** is **lib** (top). After clicking, the Libra text **div** is hidden, the Gemini text **div** is made visible, and the value of **active** is set to **gem** (bottom).

WRITING TEXT DYNAMICALLY INTO THE DOCUMENT

We want to display the current date on the page because we are displaying a daily horoscope. The **writedate() function** writes in the day's date plus some text onto the page dynamically.

> **Note:** To load the external JavaScript file, put the following in the **\<head\>..\</head\>** section of your HTML page:
>
> **\<script src="today.js" type="text/javascript" language="JavaScript"\>\</script\>**

1 Define the **function writedate()**.

The string **doc + "header" + doc3** is evaluated. For Netscape 4 this is **document.header**; for IE it is **document.all.header**; and for Netscape 6 it's **document.getElementById('header')**. These all point to the **div** element with the **id header**.

2 Define the variable **headertext**. This will hold the HTML text string that will be will be written into the **div header**.

The **shortdateE** object, which is predefined in the file, today.js, has been used. This displays the current date in a Weekday, Month, Date, Year format.

Note that the delimiters (**"**) in the HTML text string have been escaped with a backslash (\). The string has been divided into manageable pieces and concatenated.

3 Create the code for Netscape 4.

For this browser, it's necessary to write the text into the **div** header with the **document.write()** method.

> **Note:** To assemble the date string itself, we'll use a function that we've defined in a separate JavaScript page, today.js. This file is included on the CD and on the companion web site. We haven't gone into the details of how to construct the date string, which uses the built-in **date()** object. You can use this script on any page where you'd like to include the current date and/or time. If you're interested in how the date strings were constructed, see the notes on the today.js page itself and the companion web site.

The current date and time displayed with this script will be the date/time set on the user's computer, not the date/time on the server. This is an important difference! If the user's date/time settings are inaccurate, the displayed date/time will be too. For situations where the date/time must be accurate—or at least match your records, such as for an auction page—don't use client-side (JavaScript) date/time setting because you never know if the user's computer settings are accurate. Use the server-side date/time setting instead and make sure that these settings are correct.

```
/* write in the header with today's date Note that the shortdateE object is pre-defined in
the external JavaScript file today.js. */
function writedate() {
        headerLayer = eval (doc + "header" + doc3);
        headertext = "<img src=\"images\/spacer.gif\" width=\"280\" height=\"1\"
 border=\"0\"><\/br>";
        headertext += "<h2>Your daily horoscope<br><small>for ";
        headertext += shortdateE;
        headertext += "<\/small><\/h2>";
        if (document.layers) {
                headerLayer.document.write(headertext);
                headerLayer.document.close();
        } else {
                headerLayer.innerHTML = headertext;
        }
```

4 Create the code for Internet Explorer 4.x and Netscape 6.x for Mozilla.

For these browsers the **innerHTML** property is used. The **innerHTML** of the **div** header is set to the value of the variable, **headertext**.

COMPENSATING FOR THE NETSCAPE NAVIGATOR 4.X WINDOW RESIZE BUG

When a browser window is resized in Netscape Navigator 4.x, any CSS–positioned **div** element will collapse. In this section, we'll define the function that compensates for this bug.

Include this function on any page that has positioned elements, whether the elements are positioned only with CSS style rules or with JavaScript that changes the style values dynamically.

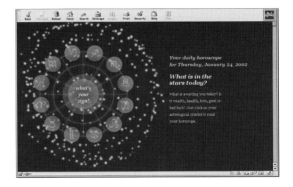

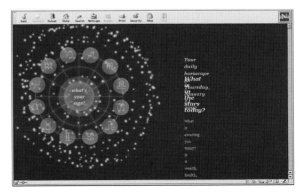

When the window is resized in Netscape Navigator 4.x, the text elements collapse.

1. First, check the current value of **window.innerWidth** (the inner width of the browser window) and **window.innerHeight** (the inner height of the browser window) when the document is loaded.

2. Define the function, **reloadpage()**.

   The function will only be triggered if the **document.layers** object is recognized (only in Netscape Navigator 4.x).

   When the window is resized, if the new **innerWidth** does not equal the old **innerWidth**, and/or the new **innerHeight** does not equal the old **innerHeight**, the page is reloaded. Reloading the page makes the elements "settle" back the way they should.

```
//Netscape resize problem

if (document.layers) {
        var win_width = window.innerWidth;
        var win_height = window.innerHeight;
}

function reloadpage() {
        if (document.layers) {
                if (window.innerWidth != win_width || window.innerHeight != win_height){
                        location.reload();
                }
        }
}
```

CALLING THE FUNCTIONS IN THE HTML

To complete the page, we will insert the necessary function calls in the HTML markup.

1. Invoke the **preload()**, **writedate()**, and **showdef()** scripts as an **onload** event in the **<body>** tag. Pass the value **'def'** (for **defhoroscope**, the default text) for **showdef**. Invoke the **reloadpage()** function as an **onresize** event.

```
<body onload="writedate();showHoroscope('def')" onresize="reloadpage()">
```

2. Invoke the rollover scripts and the **showdef()** script from the **<a>…</a>** tags surrounding each star sign image. The horoscope sign rollover script, **rollit()**, is invoked with **onmouseover**, **onmouseout** and **onclick** events; the middle circle image rollover script **midroll()** is invoked on **onmouseover** and **onmouseout** events; and the **showdef()** script is invoked on **onclick**.

```
<!-- sample tag. Change the values as appropriate. This one is for Pisces. -->
<a href="#" onmouseover="rollit('pis','over');midroll(10)"
onmouseout="rollit('pis','off');midroll(0)"
onclick="rollit('pis','click');showHoroscope('pis');"><img border="0" name="pis" id="pis"
alt="Pisces" src="images/pis.jpg" width="60" height="72"></a>
```

HOW IT WORKS: CHANGING THE src AND style PROPERTIES OF AN OBJECT

In this project, we've created two kinds of scripts. One is the rollover script, where the **src** of an **img** object was changed. This should be quite familiar to you by now.

The second type of script we've created here is one that changes the **style** property of an object. Here, we've changed the **visibility** style of the horoscope text **div** elements. Much of dynamic HTML involves changing various style properties with JavaScript. One of the programs facing web designers and programmers today is that older browsers don't support the scripting of style properties. In Netscape 4.x for example, only a very limited number of style-related properties are scriptable. This scenario will change as more people adopt the use of newer, more scriptable browsers.

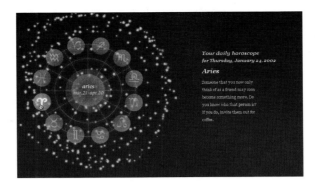

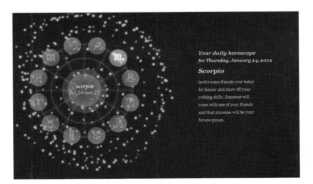

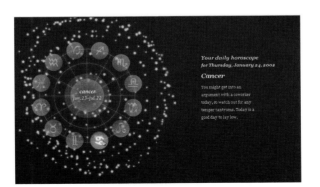

When the user mouses over a sign, the sign lights up, and the middle text changes. When the user clicks, the sign lights up, and the horoscope text changes.

POSITIONING ELEMENTS DYNAMICALLY

"Be very, very careful what you put

into that head because you will

never, ever get it out."

—THOMAS CARDINAL WOLSEY

THE PROFILE PAGE

In this project, you'll use JavaScript to position

elements on a page. With this method it's

possible to create a precise layout that fits the

browser window perfectly.

Project 9

Positioning Elements Dynamically

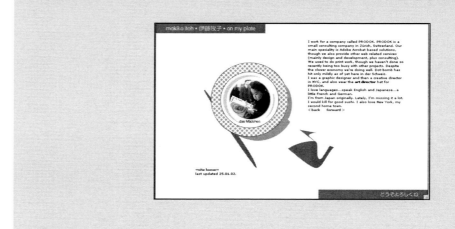

GETTING STARTED

The W3C recommends that web designers get away from using tables for layout and use CSS positioning instead. Ideally, that should be possible. However, current browsers do not support CSS positioning consistently enough to allow for the kind of precise control that many designers want.

One way to deal with this issue is to dynamically position elements within the browser window with JavaScript. This allows for far more control over the layout than any other method available.

This project is a one-page design that I created as a personal profile page. The JavaScript dynamic positioning method is well suited for a rather stylized page such as this. The main elements of the page are contained in absolutely positioned **div** elements, which are then positioned relative to the browser window size.

In this project, you will learn

- How to plan the layout of a page that will be positioned dynamically

- How to obtain the inner dimensions of the browser window

- How to move elements into place dynamically, relative to the browser window size

- How to use alert messages to check and debug your script during development

PLANNING THE PAGE LAYOUT

For the past few years, web designers have become accustomed to laying out pages with tables. In contrast, this project page is laid out with **div** elements, which are only moved into place when the JavaScript is implemented. Therefore, it is important to have a clear picture of the final page design that you intend to create.

1 Create your design in an image editor such as Photoshop, and enclose the main elements in blocks. Note how you want the elements to be positioned. Mark the layout page with rules if necessary.

> **Note:** It can be useful to attach notes or annotations to your design, especially if you are working in a team environment. The second screenshot here shows the elements with the annotations feature in Photoshop 6.0 being used.

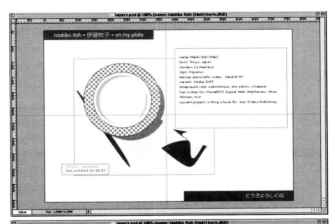

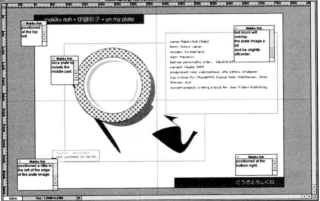

The layout in Photoshop 6.0 shown with and without the annotations visible. Lines indicate the vertical and horizontal center rules and the edges of the blocks of content that will be positioned dynamically. Annotations are used to include notes.

2 Slice the plate graphic to isolate the plate section, using the slicing feature of your graphics editor or by hand.

The graphic is sliced because the plate portion of the graphic will be scripted with an **img src** swapping function. Isolating just the part of the overall graphic that will be swapped instead of using the whole graphic makes the page function much more efficiently.

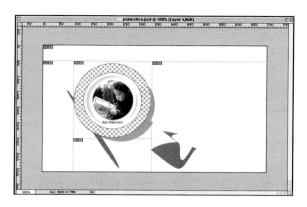

The graphic is sliced, taking care to isolate the plate image. Note that the top slice is empty.

3 Use the image-editing program to generate the image swap graphics. To ensure that the graphics are named logically for ease of scripting, name each rollover state that is generated by the image-editing program individually. Here, the "empty" plate graphic that loads initially is named plateplain.gif, the graphic with the little girl's picture is named platemaki.jpg, and so on.

The rollover state graphics are named logically. It's important to use file names that that will help to streamline your script writing process later. Note that the graphics with photos are saved as JPGs instead of GIFs.

4 Generate the sliced table code from the image-editing program. If necessary, clean it up so that all the attributes are quoted and get rid of any unnecessary cells, such as the one-pixel-wide spacer GIF cells, which are often generated.

For this page, we've eliminated the extraneous single-pixel GIFs on the edges of the table, as well as the empty white cell at the top.

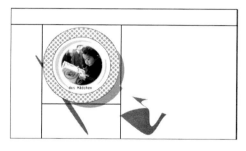

The sliced up graphic shown with table borders visible to show the table cells/slices. The top image shows the table as it's generated from the image-editing program. It has some single-pixel GIF cells, and the top cell is a large white blank. The bottom figure shows the same image with the unnecessary cells eliminated.

Note: The table code generated by image editing programs can be a little messy or invalid, which can potentially "break" a page that is laid out with CSS. Therefore, it's often necessary to clean it up. Things to look out for include unquoted attribute values such as **width=700** instead of **width="700"** and missing **alt** tags. In addition, if you are converting your pages to XHTML and wish to use these auto-generated sliced tables, you will have to convert the case of the tags from upper to lower case. Here's a tip: Using an HTML "lint" tool such as HTML Tidy can automate this process.

```html
<!-- ImageReady auto-generated table code -->
<TABLE WIDTH=700 BORDER=0 CELLPADDING=0 CELLSPACING=0>
        <TR>
                <TD COLSPAN=3>
                        <IMG SRC="plateslice_01.gif" WIDTH=700 HEIGHT=50></TD>
        </TR>
        <TR>
                <TD ROWSPAN=2>
                        <IMG SRC="plateslice_02.gif" WIDTH=96 HEIGHT=360></TD>
                <TD>
                        <IMG SRC="plateslice_03.gif" WIDTH=245 HEIGHT=250></TD>
                <TD ROWSPAN=2>
                        <IMG SRC="plateplain.gif" WIDTH=359 HEIGHT=360></TD>
        </TR>
        <TR>
                <TD>
                        <IMG SRC="plateslice_05.gif" WIDTH=245 HEIGHT=110></TD>
        </TR>
</TABLE>


<!-- The same table code after cleanup. The plate graphic has been renamed, and alt tags
(empty when the ALT text is irrelevant) have been added. The case has been changed to
lower case also; while this is not totally necessary, it is a good habit to get into,
especially if you intend to convert eventually to XHTML. -->
<table width="700" border="0" cellpadding="0" cellspacing="0">
<tr>
<td colspan="3"><img src="images/1.gif" width="700" alt="" height=
"50"></td>
</tr>

<tr>
<td rowspan="2"><img src="images/2.gif" alt="" width="96" height=
"360"></td>
<td><img src="images/plateplain.gif" alt="plate graphic" width="245" height="250"></td>
<td rowspan="2"><img src="images/4.gif" width="359" height=
"360" alt=""></td>
</tr>

<tr>
<td><img src="images/5.gif" width="245" alt="" height="110"></td>
</tr>
</table>
```

CREATING THE HTML BASE

The HTML code for this project is the shortest part of the whole code. Because all the major layout blocks will be positioned on the fly, they will be enclosed in **div** elements.

1 Create a new HTML page. For this page, use an HTML 4.01 Transitional **DOCTYPE** that does not point to a DTD URL.

```
<!DOCTYPE HTML PUBLIC "-//W3C//DTD HTML 4.01 Transitional//EN">
```

2 Create the HTML markup for the page layout. Create a **div** element with a unique **id** for each "block" that comprises the layout.

There are four elements on the page that will always be visible plus four text elements, which will be shown and hidden with script.

3 Arrange the **div** elements in a logical hierarchy from top to bottom so that the page can be read easily in a text-only or non-JavaScript (or non-CSS) capable browser. Paste the table slice HTML into the **div** with the **id mainbox**.

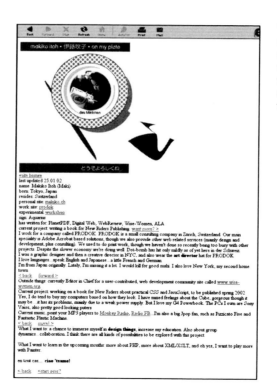

The plain HTML page before any CSS or JavaScript is added. It's always a good idea to check the page at this point to see if the contents are readable for users of alternative or older browsers.

Note: Using a **DOCTYPE** declaration that doesn't point to a URL goes against the way we've created our markup in previous projects. As we discussed in Project 1, "Designing a Page with CSS," this makes the browser render the page in "quirk" mode—in other words, it will render the page as best it can.

We need to do this because of the **onresize** event call we'll make in the **<body>** tag on the completed page. The HTML 4.01 DTD does not recognize the onresize attribute as being valid. Therefore, Internet Explorer 6.0 on Windows—which is the only version of Windows IE that recognizes the **DOCTYPE** declaration—will "fail" the page and not render it properly. The script will stop, and the elements will not be positioned.

The correct method of calling the **onresize** event handler is to call it within the **<script>...</script>** tags in the head section of the document. However, Netscape 4.x will not recognize this at all.

Instead of trying to create a separate page for each browser, we've used the quirk mode **DOCTYPE**. With this, Internet Explorer 6.0/Windows renders the page just as we intend. It's a compromise, but a practical solution.

```
<div id="topbanner"> <!-- this div contains the topbanner graphic -->
<img src="images/tophead.gif" alt="" width="342" height="30"
➥border="0">
</div> <!-- end of top banner div -->


<div id="mainbox"> <!-- this div contains the main graphic table -->

<table width="700" border="0" cellpadding="0" cellspacing="0">

<tr>
<td rowspan="2"><img src="images/2.gif" width="96" height="360"
➥alt=""></td>
<td><img src="images/plateplain.gif" width="245" height="250"
➥alt=""></td>
<td rowspan="2"><img src="images/4.gif" width="359" height="360"
➥alt=""></td>
</tr>
<tr>
<td><img src="images/5.gif" width="245" height="110" alt=""></td>
</tr>
</table>
</div> <!-- end of mainbox div -->

<div id="bottombanner">
<!-- this div contains the bottom banner graphic -->
<img src="images/bottom.gif" alt="" width="342" height="30"
➥border="0">
</div> <!--end of bottom banner div -->
```

```
<div id="tag"> <!-- this div contains the "back" link text -->

<a href="/">&laquo;home&raquo;</a>

</div> <!-- end of back link div -->

<div id="text1">

<!-- contents of text block 1. Omitted for clarity.-->
</div> <!--end of text1 div  -->

<div id="text2">

<!-- contents of text block 2. Omitted for clarity.-->

</div> <!--end of text2 div -->

<div id="text3">

<!-- contents of text block 3. Omitted for clarity.-->
</div> <!--end of text3 div -->

<div id="text4">

<!-- contents of text block 4. Omitted for clarity. -->

</div> <!--end of text4 div -->
```

CREATING THE CSS

The CSS specifies the style rules for each **div** element when the page first loads.
The style rules are, in turn, changed on the fly with JavaScript.

1 Create the CSS style rules that control font and link appearance.

On this page, all the **div** elements with text in them will have the same font appearance, so a rule for the **div** element is applied. Because the elements will be positioned precisely in relation to each other, the sizes are specified in absolute units (pixels).

```css
div {
        font-family: verdana, helvetica, sans-serif;
        font-size: 10px;
        line-height: 13px;
        color: #336699;
        }
body {
        background-color: #ffffff;
        margin: 0px;
        }
a:visited {
        color: #ffcc33;
        text-decoration: none;
        }
a:link {
        color: #cc9900;
        text-decoration: none;
        }
a:active {
        color: #996600;
        text-decoration: underline;
        }
a:hover {
        text-decoration: underline;
        }
```

2 Create the CSS style rules for the positionable **div** elements, giving each **div** its unique **id**. Note the following:

- All the elements have a **position: absolute** value, and they all start with an initial **top** and **left** **position** value of **0px**.

- The **text1**, **text2**, **text3**, and **text4 div** element ID selectors are grouped together because they all share the same CSS style rules. This keeps the code leaner and easier to edit.

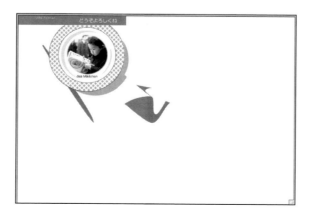

The page with the initial CSS rules, but before the scripting makes things happen. It doesn't look like much yet because the elements are bunched up in the top left corner, and the text is invisible.

170

- The **text1**, **text2**, **text3**, and **text4 div** elements have a higher **z-index** value than the main graphic **div** element (**mainbox**) because they will sit on top of it. In addition, the text **div**s have a **visibility** value of **hidden**. When the page loads initially, the text is invisible.

```
#topbanner {
        top: 0px;
        left: 0px;
        position: absolute;
        z-index: 2;
}

#tag {
        width: 300px;
        top: 0;
        left: 50px;
        position: absolute;
        z-index: 10;
}

#mainbox {
        text-align: left;
        width: 700px;
        height: 410px;
        top: 0px;
```

```
        left: 0px;
        position: absolute;
        z-index: 1;
}

#bottombanner {
        top: 0px;
        left: 0px;
        position: absolute;
        z-index: 3;
}
#text1, #text2, #text3, #text4 {
        width: 300px;
        top: 0px;
        left: 0px;
        position: absolute;
        z-index: 10;
        visibility: hidden;
}
```

DETECTING THE BROWSER AND CREATING YOUR OWN DOCUMENT OBJECT

In this step, we'll create our own document object that can be reused repeatedly for addressing elements on the page correctly.

1 Declare the global variables that will hold the browser detection values and pieces of the document object.

The variables **n4**, **ie**, and **n6** will be used to create browser-specific conditional "branches" in the script. The variables **doc**, **doc2**, **doc3**, and sty will hold text string values that form the pieces of our own document object.

```
var n4, ie, n6;

var doc,doc2,doc3,sty;
```

2 Detect for Netscape Navigator 4.x, Internet Explorer 4.x/5.x, and W3C DOM-compliant browsers and assign the appropriate values to the variables, with a series of **if**…**else if** statements.

```
if (document.layers) {
        doc = "document.";
        doc2 = ".document.";
        doc3 = "";
```

continues

You'll notice that this is the same as the browser detection and document object creation code we used in the previous project, but we've added three more variables. First of all, the appropriate text string values that make up the pieces of the document object depending on the browser in use area assigned to the variables **doc**, **doc2**, **doc3**, and **sty**.

In addition, if the object **document.layers** is recognized, the boolean value of **true** is assigned to the variable **n4**. If the **document.all** method is recognized, the value of the variable, **ie**, is declared to be **true**. Finally, if **document.getElementById** is recognized, the value of the variable, **n6**, is declared to be **true**.

continued

```
        sty = "";
        n4 = true;
        }
    else if (document.all) {
        doc = "document.all.";
        doc2 = "";
        doc3 = "";
        sty = ".style";
        ie = true;
    }
    else if (document.getElementById) {
        doc = "document.getElementById('";
        doc2 ="')";
        doc3 ="')";
        sty = "').style";
        n6 = true;
    }
```

Note: A boolean value is used as a "yes/no" checker in code. If certain criteria are met, then the boolean value is **true**; if not, the value is **false**. When a variable is initially declared with no value assigned, its boolean value is **false** by default, though in some cases you might want to explicitly define the value as **false** just for the sake of clarity.

FINDING THE DIMENSIONS OF THE PAGE

Previously in Project 7, we detected the size of the user's monitor to position browser windows. In this project, we will detect the inner dimensions of the browser window itself to position the page elements within it. To do this, it's necessary to create a function that detects the browser in use and then assigns the width and height values of the window using the browser-specific method of obtaining this value.

1 Declare the global variables, **win_width** and **win_height**. These variables will be assigned the window width and window height values.

2 Declare the global variables, **centerhor** and **centerver**. These variables will be assigned the values of the horizontal centerpoint and vertical centerpoint, respectively.

3 Create the function, **dimensions()**, which will detect the dimensions of the browser window.

The function consists of two **if...else** conditional statements. The first condition that must be met is **if(n4 || n6)**, which means if the boolean value of **n4** is **true or** the boolean value of **n6** is **true**. This conditional statement will be met if the browser in use is Netscape 4.x, Netscape 6.x, or Mozilla. If so, the variable, **win_width**, will be assigned the value of **window.innerWidth**, and the variable, **win_height**, will be assigned the value of **window.innerHeight**.

The second part of the **if...else** statement checks for the boolean value of **ie**. If **ie** is true, then **win_width** is assigned the value of **document.body.clientWidth**, and **win_height** is assigned the value of **document.body.clientHeight**.

```
// the variables for the window dimensions
var win_width,win_height;
var centerhor, centerver;


// Get dimensions of the window
function dimensions() {
     if(n4 || n6){
          win_width=window.innerWidth;
          win_height=window.innerHeight;
     } else if(ie) {
          win_width=document.body.clientWidth;
          win_height=document.body.clientHeight;
          }
          centerhor = win_width/2;
          centerver = win_height/2;
}
```

Note: The dimensions of the browser window (the inner dimensions without the chrome) are represented in two ways, depending on the browser. In Internet Explorer, the height is **document.body.clientHeight**, and the width is **document.body.clientWidth**; in Netscape 4 and 6 and also Mozilla, it is **window.innerHeight** and **window.innerWidth**.

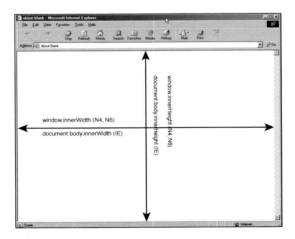

The inner dimensions of a browser window are the part without the surrounding "chrome" (the address bar, button bar, and so on.)

4 Create a function, **measurewindow()**, that will test the **dimensions()** function to see if the width and height of the window are being evaluated properly. The function displays the width and height values in an alert box.

```
//the temporary alert() function that displays the window
dimensions.

function measurewindow() {
alert('the window width is ' + win_width + '\n' +
```

continues

This is a temporary function that won't actually be part of the final page, but it helps us to check the numbers. Using the built-in **alert()** function to check key values of certain variables and objects is good way of debugging JavaScript code.

continued

```
'the window height is ' + win_height + '\n' +
'the horizontal center is ' + centerhor + '\n' +
'the vertical center is ' + centerver);
}
```

Note: The **\n** inserts a new line (line feed) into the text string so that the alert message doesn't end up as one long box.

5 Call the functions, **dimensions()** and **measurewindow()**, with an **onload** event by inserting the function call in the **<body>** tag.

```
<body onload="dimensions();measurewindow()">
```

6 After you have tested the **dimensions()** function and verified that the window dimensions are seen properly, delete the **onload** call in the **<body>** tag before proceeding to the next step. You might also want to delete the **measurewindow()** function too, though you might want to keep it for further debugging purposes until you're confident that the page is working properly.

When the page is loaded in a browser window, the alert box displays the dimensions.

CENTERING ELEMENTS ON A PAGE

Now that we have obtained the dimensions of the window, we can use this information to position elements dynamically. The first function simply centers an element both horizontally and vertically on the page.

1 Create the function, **centerIt()**. The function is passed three arguments: **elem**, which is the **id** of the element to be centered; **w**, which is the width of the element; and **h**, the height of the element.

2 Assemble the text string that represents the document object "address," evaluate this string with the built-in **eval()** function, and assign this value to the variable **docObj**.

For example, if the element **id** is **topbanner**, here is how the string will look in each browser:

Netscape 4:

```
document.topbanner
```

Internet Explorer:

```
document.all.topbanner.style
```

Netscape 6/Mozilla:

```
document.getElementById('topbanner').style
```

When this string is evaluated with the built-in **eval()** function, the correct document object for each browser is returned.

3 Create an **if…else** conditional statement. This is necessary because each of our target browsers uses a different way of referring to the **left** and **top** style rules for an element.

In Netscape 4 and 6, the left position property of an element is **left**, so the first part of the conditional statement, which will be executed if **n4** or **n6** are **true**, assigns the value of **centerhor** (the horizontal center of the window) minus **w**, divided by two (half the width of the window) to the **left** property of **docObj**. Similarly, the **top** property of **docObj** is assigned the value of **centerver** (the vertical center of the window) minus **h**, divided by two (half the height of the window).

In Internet Explorer, the left and top position properties of an element are **pixelLeft** and **pixelTop**, respectively. These properties are assigned the corresponding left and top values.

Note: You can check the document object that is returned by inserting an **alert()** call into the function that sees the value of **docObj**. If we insert the following line in the **centerIt()** function, right after the **eval()** line:

```
alert('the document object is ' + docObj)
```

Netscape 4.7 will display the following:

```
the document object is [object layer]
```

Internet Explorer will display:

```
the document object is [object style]
```

And Netscape 6 will display:

```
the document object is object[CSSStyleDeclaration]
```

This lets us know that we are addressing the correct object.

4 Close the function. Because there are so many brackets in this function, check carefully to see that the brackets pair up properly.

```
//center the elements on the page.

function centerIt(elem,width,height) {
        docObj = eval(doc + elem + sty);
        if (n4 || n6 ) {
                docObj.left = (centerhor - (width/2));
                docObj.top = (centerver - (height/2));
        }
        if (ie) {
                docObj.pixelLeft = (centerhor - (width/2));
                docObj.pixelTop = (centerver - (height/2));
        }
}
```

POSITIONING ELEMENTS ANYWHERE ON THE PAGE

In this step, we'll create a function that will position an element at a designated left and top coordinate in the window. Note that the document object creation method is the same as in the **centerIt()** function. Specify a left and top position.

1 Create the function, **placeIt()**. The function is passed three arguments: **elem**, which is the **id** of the element to be positioned; **leftPos**, which is the left position of the element; and **topPos**, the top position of the element.

2 Assemble the text string that represents the document object address and evaluate this string with the built-in **eval()** function. Then, assign this value to the variable, **docObj**.

3 Create an **if...else** conditional statement. This is necessary because each of our target browsers uses a different method of referring to the **left** and **top** style rules for an element.

```
//place the elements relative to the page.

function placeIt(elem,leftPos,topPos) {
        docObj = eval(doc + elem + sty);
        if (n4 || n6) {
                docObj.left = leftPos;
                docObj.top= topPos;
```

continues

If **n4** or **n6** are true, then the **left** property of **docObj** is assigned the value of **leftPos**, and the **top** property is assigned the value of **topPos**.

If ie is true, then the **pixelLeft** property of **docObj** is assigned the value of **leftPos**, and the **pixelTop** property is assigned the value of **topPos**.

continued

```
    } else if (ie) {
            docObj.pixelLeft = leftPos;
            docObj.pixelTop = topPos;
    }
}
```

SHOWING AND HIDING THE TEXT ELEMENTS

This function shows or hides the appropriate text element by changing the **visibility** style property. To see how this works in detail, see the previous project. This is especially useful on a page such as this where the position of the elements is precisely controlled: not only does the designer retain more control over the look of the page, but the user does not have to scroll up and down to read the page.

1 Create the function, **showhide()**. The function is passed two arguments: **elem**, which is the **id** of the element to be shown or hidden and **state**, which is the **visibility** state of the element.

2 Create the document object and assign this to the variable, **docObj**, by evaluating the string of **doc + elem + sty**, as we have done in the previous two sections. Assign the value of **state** to the **visibility** property of **docObj**. For example, if the value of **elem** is **text3** (the **div** element with the **id text3**), and the value of **state** is **'hidden'**, the **text3 div** element will be hidden.

```
//show or hide
function showhide(elem,state) {
    docObj = eval(doc + elem + sty);
    docObj.visibility = state;
}
```

IMAGE PRELOADING AND THE IMAGE SWAP FUNCTION

This section defines the code for pre-caching the images and creating the **img src** swap function for the plate image.

For more details on how image swapping works, see the previous project as well as Project 6, "Dynamic Frames."

1 Define the variable, **Loaded**, and set the value to **false**. This will be the "flag" that checks to see if the image objects are pre-cached into the browser cache.

2 Create the function, **preload()**. This function defines the **Image** objects that will be used for the **img src** swap function and defines the value of the **src** for each object as the path to the appropriate graphic. Once the Image objects are declared, set the value of **Loaded** to **true**. Note the naming of each variable: **plate1**, **plate2**, **plate3**, and **plate4**. This is important for our swapping function.

```
// the code that precaches the image swap graphics

var Loaded = false;

//preload images

function preload() {
        plate1 = new Image;
        plate1.src = "images/plateplain.gif";
        plate2 = new Image;
        plate2.src = "images/platemaki.jpg";
        plate3 = new Image;
        plate3.src = "images/platetib.jpg";
        plate4 = new Image;
        plate4.src = "images/platecube.jpg";
        Loaded = true;
}
```

3 Call the function, **preload()**, to load the **Image** objects.

4 Define the **img src** swapping function, **changeplate()**. The function is passed three arguments: **num**, which is the number of the image (the **"1"** part of **"plate1"**); **container**, which is the parent (container) element **id**; and **elem**, which is the **id** value of the **img** element whose **src** property will be changed.

For this function, the **if...else** conditional statement checks for the value of **n4** first. Nested elements are addressed in the **document.parentelementID. document.elementID** format in this browser, so the string **of doc + container + doc2 + elem** is evaluated to create the document object and assign that value to the variable **plateObj**.

```
// call the image precaching function.

preload();

//the image swapping function
function changeplate(num,container,elem) {
        if (Loaded) {
                if (n4) {
                        plateObj = eval (doc + container + doc2 +elem);
                }
                if (ie || n6) {
                        plateObj = eval (doc + elem + doc2);
                }
                plateObj.src = eval('plate' + num + '.src');
        }
}
```

Then the function checks that the **true**/**false** value of either **ie** and **n6** is true. It then evaluates the string of **doc + elem + doc2** to create the document object and assign that value to the variable **plateObj**. For Internet Explorer this string would be in the **document.all.elementID** format, and for Netscape 6 it would be in the **document.getElementById ('elementID')** format.

INITIALIZING THE PAGE AND POSITIONING THE ELEMENTS

The **initialize()** function essentially calls the other functions and positions the elements appropriately.

1 Call the **dimensions()** function we defined earlier to obtain the window width, height, horizontal center, and vertical center.

2 Establish some element-specific dimensions and assign them to variables, as follows:

- **bottomtop** is assigned the value of the top position of the bottom element.

- **bottomleft** is assigned the value of the left position of the bottom element, minus its width.

- **tagleft** is assigned the value of the left position of the tag element (300 pixels to the left of the horizontal center).

- **tagtop** is assigned the value of the top position of the tag element (100 pixels less than the window height or, in other words, 100 pixels from the bottom of the page.)

- **textleft** is assigned the value of the left position of the text1 through text4 elements (50 pixels to the left of the horizontal left).

```
function initialize() {
    dimensions();
    var bottomtop = win_height - 30;
    var bottomleft = win_width - 342;
    var tagleft = centerhor - 300;
    var tagtop = win_height - 100;
    var textleft = centerhor + 50;
    centerIt('mainbox',700,430);
    placeIt('bottom',bottomleft,bottomtop);
    placeIt('tag',tagleft,tagtop);
    placeIt('text1',textleft,50);
    placeIt('text2',textleft,50);
    placeIt('text3',textleft,50);
    placeIt('text4',textleft,50);
    showhide('text1','visible');
    showhide('text2','hidden');
    showhide('text3','hidden');
    showhide('text4','hidden');
}
```

3 Call the positioning functions for each element, as noted here:

- The **mainbox div** element is centered with its width and height values passed as arguments to the **centerIt()** function.

- The bottom **div** element is positioned with the **placeIt()** function with the bottomleft and bottomtop values passed to the function.

- The tag **div** element is positioned with the **placeIt()** function with the tagleft and tagtop values passed to the function.

- The **text1** through **text4 div** elements are positioned with the **placeIt()** function with the **textleft** value passed as the left position and an arbitrary number (50, or 50 pixels from the top) passed as the top position.

- Finally, the **text1 div** element is made visible with the **showhide()** function, and all the other text elements are hidden.

ADJUSTING THE HTML TO CALL THE FUNCTIONS

Finally, you'll adjust the HTML to call the functions.

1 Insert an onload event handler in the **<body>** tag that calls the **initialize()** function.

```
<body onload="initialize()" onresize="window.location.reload(false)">
```

2 Insert an **onresize** event handler in the **<body>** tag that calls the **window.location.reload(false)** argument.

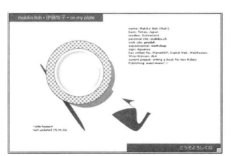

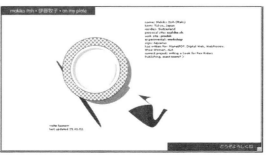

When the browser window is resized, the page elements realign themselves.

This **window.location.reload()** function is usually used to refresh the contents of a browser window. When you want to load a new URL from the web server, you would put the value within the brackets, for example **window.location.reload ('mypage.html')**.

For this project, however, we put a boolean value of **false** in the brackets as an argument to stop the window from reloading a new page. This will reload the current page again. Because this will call the **initialize()** function again, the elements will be repositioned in relation to the new window size.

3 Call the **showhide()** and **changeplate()** functions with an **onclick** event in the **<a>** navigational link elements at the bottom of each text box **div** element.

To give the page a further finish, call **window.status** message changes with **onmouseover** and **onmouseout** events.

The code here shows the markup for one of the text links. This "advances" the user to the **text2 div** element from the **text1 div** element. It hides the **text1 div** element, makes the **text2 div** element visible, and changes the **img src** of the plate graphic.

```
<a href="javascript://" onmouseover="window.status='next';return true" onclick=
➥"showhide('text1','hidden');showhide('text2','visible');changeplate('2','mainbox',
➥'plate')" onmouseout="window.status='';return true">link text</a>
```

HOW IT WORKS: DYNAMIC POSITIONING

In this project we've shown you how to address the positioning style properties of **div** elements. Note that we've used absolutely positioned elements (**position: absolute**). This gives us the most amount of control over the positioning of the elements given that absolutely positioned elements are placed independently of the flow of the page.

One word of caution: Don't try to position static position elements (where the position property value is not defined) with this method because this can cause Netscape 4.x to crash.

This might seem like a very cumbersome way of laying out a page. After all, it's possible to achieve similar results by using a table-based layout without any scripting necessary. One advantage of this method is that it allows the designer to break out of the table-cell mentality while still accommodating older browsers that don't handle CSS positioning rules very well. It also achieves the goal of separating the content and markup of a page from the visual layout. You should use this method sparingly, however, because all the script does is make the page rather heavy. It's best suited for rather stylized pages such as the one presented here.

DROP-DOWN
HIERARCHICAL MENUS

"Making the simple complicated is

commonplace; making the

complicated simple, awesomely

simple, that's creativity."

—CHARLES MINGUS

Dynamic Elements on a Table-Layout Page

In this project we'll create a page with a

drop-down navigation menu. The page uses

a familiar table-based layout together with

dynamically scripted elements.

Project 10

Drop-Down Hierarchical Menus

GETTING STARTED

A popular web site navigation interface is the drop-down menu. When properly implemented, drop-down menus can reduce the visual clutter on the page. On content-rich sites with many categories, they can be particularly useful.

In this project, we will implement a 2-level, text-based drop-down navigation menu for the prototype design for a music oriented web site.

The base layout is table-based. The navigation menu uses some dynamic scripting methods but is created as a self-contained unit. It's still more practical to use tables than CSS positioning to create page layouts, so it's important to know how to add dynamic elements that function properly on the base static page.

Note: Page design by Shirley Kaiser of SK Designs (**www.skdesigns.com**).

The entire project might seem complicated because it involves a number of steps, but if you have been following the projects in this book in sequence, you will see some familiar techniques used here, such as the following:

- Dynamic positioning of a **div** element
- Showing and hiding **div** elements
- Image source swapping

In addition, you will learn about

- Using dynamically positioned elements together with static page elements
- Changing the color style attributes of an element on the fly
- Using global variables to hold values that are passed from function to function
- Invoking and stopping functions using the **setTimeout()** and **clearTimeout()** methods
- Creating reusable code

CREATING THE HTML

For this project, the basic page layout is static and table-based. The drop-down menu elements, which will be dynamically positioned when the page is loaded, are created separately from the rest of the page.

1 Create the base page HTML.

The base page consists of a top logo/banner element and a two-column main text area. The logo/banner element has a background image.

The entire base page is contained within a **div** with the attribute, **align="center"**. No style attributes are assigned; in particular, a **position:** rule is not applied. By default, this creates a statically positioned **div** element, which appears where it is actually typed on the page.

The top banner is contained within one **table**, followed by a **p** element containing the text links. The main body of the page is contained in another **table**, which creates a two-column layout. Finally, the copyright notice is at the foot of the page in another **p** element.

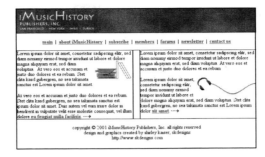

The base page layout with the table borders visible (top) and invisible (bottom).

```
<!-- plain (static position) DIV that holds the base banner and
contents. -->
<div align="center">
<table width="750" border="0" cellpadding="0" cellspacing="0">
<tr><td background="images/topmast1.gif" valign="middle"
align="left"><img src="images/logo.gif" width="248" height="80" alt=""
border="0"></td></tr></table>

<p class="textlinks"><br>
<b><a href="index.html" class="link">main</a>  | 
<a href="index.html" class="link">about iMusicHistory</a>
 |  <a href="subscribe.html" class="link">subscribe</a>
```

```
 | 
<a href="members.html" class="link">members</a>   | 
<a href="forums.html" class="link">forums</a>   | 
<a href="newsletter.html" class="link">newsletter</a>  | 
<a href="contact.html" class="link">contact us</a></b></p>

<table width="750" border="0" cellpadding="0" cellspacing="0">
<tr><td width="350" valign="top" align="left"><p>Lorem ipsum dolor sit
amet, consetetur sadipscing elitr,  sed diam nonumy eirmod tempor
invidunt ut labore et dolore magna aliquyam erat,<img
src="images/cdstack1.gif" width="112" height="59" alt="cd stack"
border="0" align="right" hspace="5"> sed diam voluptua.  At vero
```

continues

185

continued

```
eos et accusam et justo duo dolores et ea rebum. Stet clita kasd
gubergren, no sea takimata sanctus est Lorem ipsum dolor sit amet.</p>

<p>At vero eos et accusam et justo duo dolores et ea rebum. Stet clita
kasd gubergren, no sea takimata sanctus est ipsum dolor sit amet. Duis
autem vel eum iriure dolor in hendrerit in vulputate velit esse molestie
consequat, vel illum dolore <b><a href="subscribe.html" class="link">eu
feugiat nulla facilisis</a></b>.<a href="subscribe.html"><img
src="images/arrow_rt.gif" width="24" height="10" alt="&gt;" border="0"
hspace="3"></a></p></td><td
width="20">     </td>

<td width="350" valign="top" align="left"><p>Lorem ipsum dolor sit amet,
consetetur sadipscing elitr,  sed diam nonumy eirmod tempor invidunt ut
labore et dolore magna aliquyam erat, sed diam voluptua. At vero eos et
accusam et justo duo dolores et ea rebum.</p> <p><img
```

```
src="images/headphones1.gif" width="182" height="57" alt="headphones"
border="0" align="right" vspace="2">Lorem ipsum dolor sit amet,
consetetur sadipscing elitr,  sed diam nonumy eirmod tempor invidunt ut
labore et dolore magna aliquyam erat, sed diam voluptua.  Stet clita
kasd gubergren, no sea takimata sanctus est Lorem ipsum dolor <b><a
href="listen.html" class="link">sit amet</a></b>.<a
href="listen.html"><img src="images/arrow_rt.gif" width="24" height="10"
alt="&gt;" border="0" hspace="3"></a></p></td></tr></table>

<p class="copyright">copyright &copy; 2001 iMusicHistory Publishers,
Inc. all rights reserved.<br>
design and graphics created by shirley kaiser, skdesigns<br>
http://www.skdesigns.com</p>

</div>
```

2 Create the top menu element.

The top-level menu element consists of 5 graphical buttons. They are placed in a table, which in turn, is placed in a **div** element with the **id mainmenu**, which will be positioned when the page loads. Each graphic button is placed in an **<a>** link element.

Each **img** element has a unique **id** and **name**, **top_home**, **top_about**, and so on.

The graphics themselves are white text with transparent backgrounds because they will appear on top of the blue banner background on the page.

Note that each of the **img** elements has an "on" state graphic and an "off" state graphic.

Note: The **href** attribute for each **<a>** link in all the menu items is set to **#** in this example as a temporary placeholder.

```
<div id="mainmenu">
<table border="0" cellspacing="0" cellpadding="0">
<tr><td width="52"><a href="#"><img src="images/nav/home-off.gif" width="52" height="21"
alt="home" border="0" id="top_home" name="top_home"></a></td>
    <td width="84"><a href="#"><img src="images/nav/about-off.gif" width="84" height="21"
alt="about us" border="0" id="top_about" name="top_about"></a></td>
    <td width="84"><a href="#"><img src="images/nav/subscribe-off.gif" width="83" height="21"
alt="subscribe" border="0" id="top_subscribe" name="top_subscribe"></a></td>
    <td width="90"><a href="#"><img src="images/nav/members-off.gif" width="90" height="21"
alt="members" border="0" id="top_members" name="top_members"></a></td>
    <td><a href="#"><img src="images/nav/contact-off.gif" width="93" height="21" alt="contact
us" border="0" id="top_contact" name="top_contact"></a></td></tr></table>
</div>
```

The top-level menu table—shown with the table cell borders visible. The top illustration shows how the graphics look without a background image: They are white with a transparent background. The bottom two illustrations show how they look against a dark blue background similar to the color of the graphic to be used as a background image.

3 Create the first level of submenus.

Each top-level menu item except for **home** has a corresponding submenu. Each submenu consists of a single-column table with one menu selection per cell row.

Each submenu **div** element has a unique **id** attribute. The **div** elements will be dynamically positioned when the page loads.

Note that each **<td>** element has a **class** attribute of **"menu"** and a unique **id** attribute. This allows for CSS and JavaScript control of the **<td>** elements.

The text within each cell is contained within an **<a>** (link) element.

The first-level drop-down menu elements before CSS style rules are applied. Shown with the table cell borders visible for clarity.

```
<!-- first level of submenus -->
<div id="about">
<table border="0" cellspacing="0" cellpadding="0">
<tr><td class="menu" id="about1" width="100" height="15">
<a href="#">Our Company</a></td></tr>
<tr><td class="menu" id="about2" width="100" height="15">
<a href="#">Our Staff</a></td></tr>
</table>
</div>


<div id="subscribe">
<table border="0" cellspacing="0" cellpadding="0">
<tr><td class="menu" id="subscribe1" width="100" height="15">
<a href="#">Information</a></td></tr>
<tr><td class="menu" id="subscribe2" width="100" height="15">
<a href="#">Free Newsletter</a></td></tr>
<tr><td class="menu" id="subscribe3" width="100" height="15">
<a href="#">Premium Newsletter</a></td></tr>
</table>
</div>


<div id="members">
<table border="0" cellspacing="0" cellpadding="0">
<tr><td class="menu" id="members1" width="100" height="15">
<a href="#">Online Listening</a></td></tr>
<tr><td class="menu" id="members2" width="100" height="15">
<a href="#">Teachers' Area</a></td></tr>
<tr><td class="menu" id="members3" width="100" height="15">
<a href="#">Students' Area</a></td></tr>
</table>
</div>


<div id="contact">
<table border="0" cellspacing="0" cellpadding="0">
<tr><td class="menu" id="contact1" width="100" height="15">
<a href="#">Customer Service</a></td></tr>
<tr><td class="menu" id="contact2" width="100" height="15">
<a href="#">Sales Dept.</a></td></tr>
<tr><td class="menu" id="contact3" width="100" height="15">
<a href="#">General Inquiries</a></td></tr>
</table>
</div>
```

4 Create the second level of submenus.

The "**members**" category submenu has a second level of submenus. These are created exactly like the first level of submenus. Each submenu element is a **div** that contains a single-row **table**, with one menu item per table cell. Each **div** element has a unique **id** value, and the **td** elements have a **class** attribute value of "**menu**".

Note: Don't give the submenu **div** elements here **id** values that have underscores or hyphens in them, such as members_music or members-music. Using hyphens is illegal for CSS and JavaScript. Underscores are legal, but Netscape 4.x doesn't allow for them.

| - Medieval |
| - Renaissance |
| - Baroque |

| - Course Aids |
| - Quizzes |
| - Teacher Forum |
| - Class Forum |

| - Study Aids |
| - Ask a Teacher |
| - Student Forum |

The second-level drop-down menu elements before CSS style rules are applied. Shown with the table cell borders visible for clarity.

```html
<!-- second level of submenus, for 'members' category -->
<div id="membersmusic">
<table border="0" cellspacing="0" cellpadding="0">
<tr>
<td class="menu" id="membersmusic1" width="100" height="15">
<a href="#">- Medieval</a></td></tr>
<tr><td class="menu" id="membersmusic2" width="100" height="15">
<a href="#">- Renaissance</a></td></tr>
<tr><td class="menu" id="membersmusic3" width="100" height="15">
<a href="#">- Baroque</a></td></tr>
</table>
</div>


<div id="membersteacher">
<table border="0" cellspacing="0" cellpadding="0">
<tr><td class="menu" id="membersteacher1" width="100" height="15">
<a href="#">- Course Aids</a></td></tr>
<tr><td class="menu" id="membersteacher2" width="100" height="15">
<a href="#">- Quizzes</a></td></tr>
<tr><td class="menu" id="membersteacher3" width="100" height="15">
<a href="#">- Teacher Forum</a></td></tr>
<tr><td class="menu" id="membersteacher4" width="100" height="15">
<a href="#">- Class Forum</a></td></tr>
</table>
</div>


<div id="membersstudent">
<table border="0" cellspacing="0" cellpadding="0">
<tr><td class="menu" id="membersstudent1" width="100" height="15">
<a href="#">- Study Aids</a></td></tr>
<tr><td class="menu" id="membersstudent2" width="100" height="15">
<a href="#">- Ask a Teacher</a></td></tr>
<tr><td class="menu" id="membersstudent3" width="100" height="15">
<a href="#">- Student Forum</a></td></tr>
</table>
</div>
```

5 Combine all of the HTML segments created in the previous four steps to create the basic HTML markup for the page. Place the HTML for the drop-down menu elements below the HTML for the base layout. This is done so that non-CSS graphical browser users will see the main page first with the text links visible. The submenu elements are only viewable "below the fold," or on the second screen of the browser window. This makes the page more usable for people with older graphical browsers.

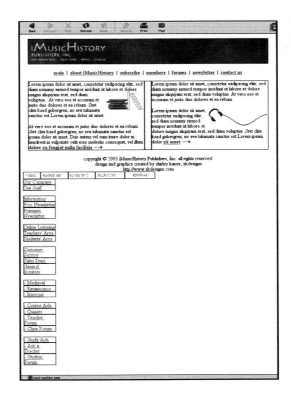

The completed page before any CSS rules or JavaScript are applied.

CREATING THE CSS

The CSS specifies the style rules for each **div** element when the page first loads. The style rules are, in turn, changed on the fly with JavaScript.

Because this site is planned to be many pages deep, it makes better sense to create an external stylesheet, which can be edited to change the look of the site all at once.

1 Open a blank text document and give it the filename dropdown_menus.css. Save this file in the same directory of the HMTL page.

This stylesheet will be linked to the main page.

2 Create the CSS style rules that control font, link, and color appearance for the base page elements.

One element to note is the **p** element class, **textlinks**. The **visibility** property has been set to **hidden**. This hides the text links for CSS-capable browsers, while on non-CSS browsers they will be visible.

```css
body {
     background-color: #ffffff;
     color: #000080;
     }

h3, p {
     font-family: verdana, sans-serif;
     }

h3 {
     font-size: 20px;
     }

p {
     font-size: 12px;
     line-height: 20px;
     }

p.textlinks {
     visibility: hidden;
     }

p.footnote {
     font-size: 10px;
     }

a.link:visited {
     text-decoration: underline;
     color: #990000;
     background-color: #ffffff;
     }

a.link {
     text-decoration: underline;
     color: #666666;
     background-color: #ffffff;
     }

a.link:hover {
     text-decoration: underline;
     color: #ffffff;
     background-color: #990000;
     font-weight: bold;
     }

/* this is to get rid of the default outline on links in
IE5.x/Mac and any other browsers that recognize the
outline:none style rule. */
a {
     outline: none;
     }
```

3 Create the **menu** class selector and specify the overall appearance of the submenus.

Each **<td>** element in the submenus has a **class="menu"** attribute. Create a **menu** CSS selector that specifies the appearance for the submenu items. In addition, create the style rules for any **a:link** items that are nested within an element with the **class** attribute, **menu**.

```css
.menu a:link {
        color: black;
        text-decoration: none;
        }
.menu a:visited {
        color: black;
        text-decoration: none;
        }

td.menu {
        background-color: #6699cc;
        color: black;
        height: 20px;
        font-family: verdana, sans-serif;
        font-size: 10px;
        padding-left: 3px;
        border: 1px solid #003366;
        }
```

4 Create the CSS style rules for the menu item **div** elements, giving each a unique **id** that corresponds to the **id** attribute in the HTML.

Note the following:

- All the menu **div** elements have a **position: absolute** value because they will be dynamically positioned with JavaScript.
- The **mainmenu div** element has the **left** and **top** values set, even though this will be changed with JavaScript when the page loads. This is to ensure that at least the top menu will be viewable in any browser that can handle CSS but may have problems with the JavaScript used on this page (such as Opera).
- The **visibility** of **mainmenu** is set to **visible**.

```css
#mainmenu {
        position: absolute;
        z-index: 1;
        left: 350px;
        top: 35px;
        height: 21px;
        visibility: visible;
        border: 2px solid #003366;
        }

#about, #subscribe, #members, #contact {
        position: absolute;
        z-index: 2;
        width: 100px;
        visibility: hidden;
        }

#membersmusic, #membersteacher, #membersstudent {
        position: absolute;
        z-index: 3;
        width: 100px;
        visibility: hidden;
        }
```

- The **id** selectors for the first level of drop-down menu elements are grouped together, as are the ID selectors for the second level of drop-down menu items. The **visibility** of the submenu **div** elements is set to **hidden**.

- The **z-index** of **mainmenu** is set to **1**. The **z-index** of the first-level submenus is set to **2**, and the second level submenus have a **z-index** of **3**.

5 Link the external stylesheet to the HTML page by including the **<link>** tag in the **head** section.

```
<link rel="Stylesheet" rev="Stylesheet" href="dropdown_menus.css" media="Screen">
```

The page after the CSS style rules are applied. Note that the textlinks are now invisible, as are the drop-down menu submenu elements.

CREATING THE DROP-DOWN MENU SCRIPT

The drop-down menu script is broken down into a number of small functions. All of these are put together to create the final script that makes the menu come to life.

You'll notice that we are reusing many functions that we've used in the previous projects in this section of the book. It's always a good idea to make your code reusable. Reusable code is one of the best timesavers.

Because this site is planned to be several pages deep, it makes better sense to create external JavaScript that can be edited to change the functionality of the site all at once.

The steps in this section don't go into detail when we are reusing code that we've already described in full detail in previous projects. To see how each reused function was created, refer to the Project number indicated.

1 Open a blank text document and name it drop-down_menus.js.

This external JavaScript document will be linked to the HTML page.

2 Detect the browser and create your own document object. The code used for this step is described in detail in Project 8, "Browser Detection and Displaying Elements Dynamically." This step is necessary for all cross-browser scripts.

```
/* define variables for "if n4 (Netscape 4), if IE (IE 4.x),
and if n6 (if Netscape 6/W3C-DOM compliant)" */

var n4, ie, n6;

/* detecting browser support for certain key objects/methods
and assembling a custom document object */


var doc,doc2,doc3,sty;

if (document.layers) {
    doc = "document.";
    doc2 = ".document.";
    doc3 = "";
    sty = "";
    n4 = true;
    }
else if (document.all) {
    doc = "document.all.";
    doc2 = "";
    doc3 = "";
    sty = ".style";
    ie = true;
}
else if (document.getElementById) {
    doc = "document.getElementById('";
    doc2 ="')";
    doc3 ="')";
    sty = "').style";
    n6 = "true";
  }
```

3 Reuse the code first introduced in Project 8 for getting the dimensions of the browser window and positioning elements on the page relative to those dimensions. The functions we'll use are **dimensions()** and **placeIt()**. Don't forget to declare the global variables as well as the functions.

To position the menu items appropriately, we want to detect the dimensions of the browser window when the page loads with the function, **dimensions()**. This function is described in full detail in Project 9, "Positioning Elements Dynamically."

```javascript
// the variables for the window dimensions
var win_width, win_height;
var centerhor, centerver;

//Get dimensions of the window
function dimensions() {
        if(n4 || n6){
                win_width = window.innerWidth;
                win_height = window.innerHeight;
        } else if(ie) {
                win_width = document.body.clientWidth;
                win_height = document.body.clientHeight;
        }
        centerhor = win_width/2;
        centerver = win_height/2;
}

//place the elements relative to the page.
function placeIt(elem,leftPos,topPos) {
        docObj = eval(doc + elem + sty);
        if (n4 || n6) {
                docObj.left = leftPos;
                docObj.top= topPos;
        } else if (ie) {
                docObj.pixelLeft = leftPos;
                docObj.pixelTop = topPos;
        }
}
```

4 Use the function that will precache the top menu graphical button images. The **preload()** function used here was created and described in detail in Projects 8 and 9. Only the variable names and the **src** image files have changed to the values specific to this page.

```
// preload navigation images
var loaded = false;
var navdir = "images/nav/";

function preload() {
        top_home_off = new Image;
        top_home_off.src = navdir + "home-off.gif";

        top_home_on = new Image;
        top_home_on.src = navdir + "home-on.gif";

        top_about_off = new Image;
        top_about_off.src = navdir + "about-off.gif";

        top_about_on = new Image;
        top_about_on.src = navdir + "about-on.gif";

        top_subscribe_off = new Image;
        top_subscribe_off.src = navdir + "subscribe-off.gif";

        top_subscribe_on = new Image;
        top_subscribe_on.src = navdir + "subscribe-on.gif";

        top_members_off = new Image;
        top_members_off.src = navdir + "members-off.gif";

        top_members_on = new Image;
        top_members_on.src = navdir + "members-on.gif";

        top_contact_off = new Image;
        top_contact_off.src = navdir + "contact-off.gif";

        top_contact_on = new Image;
        top_contact_on.src = navdir + "contact-on.gif";

        loaded = true;
}
```

5 Create the image source swapping function for the top-level menu buttons. The **onoff()** function swaps the **img** object source graphic. Three arguments are passed to the function: **container**, which is the **id** value of the **container** element of the **img** object; **elem**, which is the **id** value of the **img** object; and **state**, which indicates whether to use the "on" or "off" state graphic. You'll notice that this function is almost identical to the **changeplate()** **img** **src** swapping function we created in Project 9. We've just changed the function and variable names.

```
// img swapping function
function onoff (elemparent,elem,state) {
    if (loaded) {
        newstate = eval(elem +"_"+ state);
        if (n4) {
            menuObj = eval (doc + elemparent + doc2 + elem);
        } else if (ie || n6) {
            menuObj = eval (doc + elem + doc2);
        }
        menuObj.src = newstate.src;
    }
}
```

6 Create the function that changes the background color of an element.

For this page, we want to change the background color of the table cell that holds each drop-down menu text link when the user passes the mouse over that link. This is accomplished with the **changecolor()** function that changes the **backgroundColor** style attribute of an element.

Create two global variables, **offcolor** and **oncolor**, that will hold the appropriate color values.

The function first calls **stopall()**. This call is specific to this page and is explained later on in Step 10.

The rest of the function only executes if the browser is not Netscape 4,—that is, **if (!n4)**. This is because Netscape 4 does not allow for the changing of the background color of a **<td>** element with JavaScript.

The script evaluates the string of **doc + divname + sty** to create the **menuObj** object. If the browser used is Internet Explorer, this would be:

document.all.divname.style

```
// mouseover(on) and mouseoff(off) color values
var oncolor = "#99ccff";
var offcolor = "#6699cc";

function changecolor(divname,colorname) {
    stopall();
    if (!n4) {
        menuObj = eval(doc + divname + sty);
        menuObj.backgroundColor = colorname;
    }
}
```

And if the browser used is Netscape 6 or Mozilla, it would be:

```
document.getElementById('divname').style
```

Finally, the function changes the **backgroundColor** style attribute of the element.

7 Reuse the function, **showhide()**, that we created in Project 9, which changes the **visibility** style attribute of the **div** element with the **id** specified by **divname** to the attribute specified by **state**.

```
//show or hide
function showhide(elem,state) {
        docObj = eval(doc + elem + sty);
        docObj.visibility = state;
}
```

8 Create the function that closes the open menus.

To ensure that only one particular drop-down menu is visible at a time, it's necessary to create a function that closes open menus. To do this, we will create a function called **closeallmenus()**.

First, four global variables are defined: **active_submenu1**, **active_submenu2**, **active_menuelem**, and **active_topelem**. **active_submenu1** holds the **id** value of the currently open first-level submenu; **active_submenu2** holds the **id** value of the currently open second-level submenu; **active_menuelem** holds the **id** value of the currently selected menu item element; and **active_topelem** holds the **id** value of the currently selected top-level menu item element. All four variable values are initially set to **null**.

The function itself checks the value of each variable. If the value is not null **(!= null)**, the following line is executed.

If **active_submenu1** is not null, then the **showhide()** function is invoked and sets the **visibility** of the **div** element with the **active_submenu1** value **id** to **'hidden.'**

```
/* variables that hold the value of the currently active
(open) menu */
var active_submenu1 = null;
var active_submenu2 = null;
var active_menuelem = null;
var active_topelem = null;

/* function closes all active menus and turns back to 'off'
state */
function closeallmenus() {
        if(active_submenu1 != null) {
                showhide(active_submenu1,'hidden');
        }
        if(active_submenu2 != null) {
                showhide(active_submenu2,'hidden');
        }
        if(active_menuelem != null) {
                changecolor(active_menuelem,offcolor);
        }
        if(active_topelem != null) {
                onoff('mainmenu',active_topelem,'off');
        }
}
```

If **active_submenu2** is not null, then the **showhide()** function is invoked and sets the visibility of the **div** element with the **active_submenu2** value **id** to "**hidden**."

If **active_menuelem** is not null, then the **changecolor()** function is invoked and sets the background color of the menu item element with the **active_menuelem id** to the **offcolor** value.

If **active_topelem** is not null, then the **onoff()** function is invoked and sets the source of the img element with the **active_topelem id** to the 'off' graphic.

9 Create a function that calls the **closeallmenus()** function after a **timeout** delay.

A global variable **menu_close_timeout** that will hold the timeout function is specified with an initial value of **0**. This function will be invoked as an **onmouseout** event on all menu item **a** (link) elements.

The delay variable value here is set to **500 milliseconds**. This can be longer or shorter.

The **closeall()** function assigns the timeout function to the **menu_close_timeout** variable.

10 Create a function that will cancel the **timeout** function.

The function, **stopall()**, clears the **menu_close_timeout** function and therefore stops the menus from closing.

```
// the menu close timeout variable
var menu_close_timeout = 0;

// delay in milliseconds until the open menus are closed
var delay = 500;

// function calls the closeallmenus() function after a delay
function closeall() {
    menu_close_timeout = setTimeout('closeallmenus()',delay);
}
```

```
// stop all timeout functions (stops menus from closing)
function stopall() {
clearTimeout(menu_close_timeout);
}
```

11 Create the function that controls the opening and closing of submenus.

The **controlsubmenus()** function is the key function for the drop-down menus. It calls the functions **closeallmenus()**, **stopall()**, **showhide()**, **changecolor()**, and **onoff()** to control the opening and closing of submenus.

Four values are passed to this function: **submenu1**, **submenu2**, **menuelem**, and **topelem**.

First, the function cancels any currently active time-out functions by calling the **stopall()** function.

Then it closes any open (active) menus by calling the **closeallmenus()** function.

If the value of **submenu1** is not null, then the **showhide()** function is called, which sets the visibility of the **div** element with the **id** value of **submenu1** to **'visible'**. The value of **active_submenu1** is set to the value of **submenu1**.

If the value of **submenu2** is not null, then the **showhide()** function is called, which sets the visibility of the **div** element with the **id** value of **submenu2** to **'visible'**. The value of **active_submenu2** is set to the value of **submenu2**.

If the value of **menuelem** is not null, then the **changecolor()** function is called, which sets the background color of the menu element with the **id** value of **menuelem** to the **oncolor** value. The value of **active_menuelem** is set to the value of **menuelem**.

If the value of **topelem** is not null, then the **onoff()** function is called, which sets the **img src** graphic to the **'on'** state graphic. The value of **active_topelem** is set to the value of **topelem**.

```
// function controls submenus
function controlsubmenu(submenu1,submenu2,menuelem,topelem) {
        stopall();
        closeallmenus();
        if (submenu1 != null) {
                showhide(submenu1,'visible');
                active_submenu1 = submenu1;
        }
        if (submenu2 != null) {
                showhide(submenu2,'visible');
                active_submenu2 = submenu2;
        }
        if (menuelem != null) {
                changecolor(menuelem,oncolor);
                active_menuelem = menuelem;
        }
        if (topelem != null) {
                onoff('mainmenu',topelem,'on');
                active_topelem = topelem;
        }
}
```

CREATING THE FUNCTION THAT INITIALIZES THE MENU ELEMENTS

The function, **initialize()**, sets the positioning of the menu elements and preloads the images. This function will be called with an **onload** event.

1 Start to define the **initialize()** function. Call the **preload()** function to pre-load all images.

2 Call the **closeallmenus()** and **stopall()** functions to close all menus and to cancel any **timeout** functions.

3 Call the functions that determine the positioning of the menu items. The **dimensions()** function is called to determine the width and height of the browser window. If **win_width** (window width) is less than **800**, the value of the local variable **mainmenuleft** is set to **80** less than the value of **centerhor** (the horizontal center point of the browser window). If the browser window width is more than **800**, the value of the variable **mainmenuleft** is set to **50** less than the value of **centerhor**.

Note that the **mainmenuleft** variable holds the value of the left coordinate (in pixels) of the **mainmenu div** element.

The variables **offset1** through **offset4** hold the values of the **left** offset (in pixels) in relation to the **mainmenuleft** value, and determines the left coordinate (in pixels) of each set of submenus. The **offsetX** values roughly correspond to the width of the top menu graphical button widths.

The **mainmenu div** element is positioned with the **placeIt()** function and is given a left coordinate value of **mainmenuleft** and a top coordinate value of **35**.

Each submenu **div** element is positioned with the **placeIt()** function with the according offset value added to the value of **mainmenuleft** to determine the left coordinate. For example, if the value of **mainmenuleft** is **300**, then the **about** submenu **div** element is left-positioned at **300 + offset1** or **405px**.

The top coordinate value is set arbitrarily so that the appropriate submenu appears at the proper place.

Note: If you adapt this script to your own page, you will need to adjust the position coordinates of each submenu element to fit the specifics of the menu you are creating.

ADJUSTING THE HTML TO CALL THE FUNCTIONS

To activate the JavaScript, we will adjust the HTML markup to call the various functions we've defined.

1 Call the external JavaScript file and the external CSS file in the **<head>...</head>** section of your page.

```
<head>

<script src="dropdown_menus.js"
type="text/javascript"></script>
<link rel="Stylesheet" rev="Stylesheet"
href="dropdown_menus.css">

</head>
```

2 Insert an **onload** event handler in the **<body>** tag that calls the **initialize()** function. In addition, insert an **onresize** event handler that calls the **window. location.reload(false)** method to stop the page from loading a new page and thereby calling the **initialize()** function again. This method is described in more detail in Project 9.

```
<body onload="initialize()" onresize="window.location.reload(false)">
```

3 Call the appropriate functions in the **<a>** tags in the **mainmenu** elements.

For each menu element, the **controlsubmenu()** function is invoked **onmouseover**, and the **closeall()** function is invoked **onmouseout**.

Note that the values passed to the **controlsubmenu()** function differ. You also should note that the main difference depends on whether the menu button has a corresponding submenu or not.

For the **'home'** button, which does not have a submenu, the values **null**, **null**, **null**, and **'top_home'** are passed. This means that when the user mouses over the **'home'** button, only the **onoff()** function that turns the **'home'** button graphic to the **'on'** state is called, and the value of **active_topelem** is set to **'top_home'**.

```
<!-- top level menu -->
<div id="mainmenu">
<table border="0" cellspacing="0" cellpadding="0">
<tr><td width="52"><a href="index.html"
onmouseover="controlsubmenu(null,null,null,'top_home')" onmouseout="closeall()">
<img src="images/nav/home-off.gif" width="52" height="21" alt="home" border="0"
➡id="top_home" name="top_home"></a></td>
<td width="84"><a href="about.html"
onmouseover="controlsubmenu('about',null,null,'top_about')" onmouseout="closeall()">
<img src="images/nav/about-off.gif" width="84" height="21" alt="about us" border="0"
➡id="top_about" name="top_about"></a></td>
<td width="84"><a href="subscribe.html"
onmouseover="controlsubmenu('subscribe',null,null,'top_subscribe')"
onmouseout="closeall()"><img src="images/nav/subscribe-off.gif" width="83" height="21"
➡alt="subscribe" border="0" id="top_subscribe" name="top_subscribe"></a></td>
<td width="90"><a href="members.html"
onmouseover="controlsubmenu('members',null,null,'top_members')"
onmouseout="closeall()"><img src="images/nav/members-off.gif" width="90" height="21"
➡alt="members" border="0" id="top_members" name="top_members"></a></td>
```

continues

For the **'about'** button, which does have a submenu, the values **'about'**, **null**, **null**, and **'top_about'** are passed. When the user mouses over the **'about'** button, the **showhide()** function that makes the **'about' div** element visible is invoked, and the **onoff()** function that turns the **'about'** button graphic to the **'on'** state is called. The value of **active_submenu1** is set to **'about'**, and the value of **active_topelem** is set to **'top_about'**.

The three other buttons have submenus, so a value is passed for the first variable (**submenu1**) and the fourth variable (**topelem**), as with the **'about'** button.

When the user mouses out of the button, the **closeall()** function is called. This closes any open (active) submenu and returns the top menu button graphic to the **'off'** state. This is invoked with a short **timeout**, to allow for cancellation (with the **stopall()** function that is called within the **controlsubmenu()** function) if the user immediately mouses over another menu element.

4 Call the appropriate functions in the **<a>** tags in the submenu elements.

If the submenu element opens another submenu, the **controlsubmenu()** function is called with an **onmouseover** event call. If, on the other hand, the submenu element is a bottom-level element (it does not open any other submenus), the **changecolor()** function is called.

For example, the **about** submenu items do not open any more submenus. Therefore, the **changecolor()** function is called **onmouseover**, which first cancels the closing of any open menus (with the **stopall()** function) and then changes the background color of the appropriate table cell.

continued

```
<td><a href="contact.html" onmouseover="controlsubmenu('contact',null,null,'top_contact')"
onmouseout="closeall()"><img src="images/nav/contact-off.gif" width="93" height="21"
➥alt="contact us" border="0" id="top_contact" name="top_contact"></a></td></tr></table>
</div>
```

```
<!-- first level of submenus -->
<div id="about">
<table border="0" cellspacing="0" cellpadding="0">
<tr>
<td class="menu" id="about1" width="100" height="15"><a href="#"
onmouseover="changecolor('about1',oncolor)" onmouseout="changecolor('about1',offcolor);
closeall()">Our Company</a></td></tr>
<tr><td class="menu" id="about2" width="100" height="15"><a href="#"
onmouseover="changecolor('about2',oncolor)"
onmouseout="changecolor('about2',offcolor);closeall()">Our Staff</a></td></tr>
</table>
</div>

<div id="subscribe">
<table border="0" cellspacing="0" cellpadding="0">
<tr>
<td class="menu" id="subscribe1" width="100" height="15"><a href="#"
onmouseover="changecolor('subscribe1',oncolor)"
```

continues

```
onmouseout="changecolor('subscribe1',offcolor);
closeall()">Information</a></td></tr>
<tr><td class="menu" id="subscribe2" width="100" height="15">
<a href="#" onmouseover="changecolor('subscribe2',oncolor)"
onmouseout="changecolor('subscribe2',offcolor);closeall()">Free
➥Newsletter</a></td></tr>
<tr><td class="menu" id="subscribe3" width="100" height="15">
<a href="#" onmouseover="changecolor('subscribe3',oncolor)"
onmouseout="changecolor('subscribe3',offcolor);closeall()">Premium
➥Newsletter</a></td></tr>
</table>
</div>

<div id="members">
<table border="0" cellspacing="0" cellpadding="0">
<tr>
<td class="menu" id="members1" width="100" height="15"><a href="#"
onmouseover="controlsubmenu('members','membersmusic','members1',
➥'top_members')" onmouseout="closeall()">Online Listening</a></td></tr>
<tr><td class="menu" id="members2" width="100" height="15"><a href="#"
onmouseover="controlsubmenu('members','membersteacher','members2',
➥'top_members')" onmouseout="closeall()">Teachers' Area</a></td></tr>
<tr><td class="menu" id="members3" width="100" height="15"><a href="#"
onmouseover="controlsubmenu('members','membersstudent','members3',
➥'top_members')" onmouseout="closeall()">Students' Area</a></td></tr>
</table>
</div>

<div id="contact">
<table border="0" cellspacing="0" cellpadding="0">
<tr>
<td class="menu" id="contact1" width="100" height="15"><a href="#"
onmouseover="changecolor('contact1',oncolor)"
onmouseout="changecolor('contact1',offcolor);closeall()">Customer
➥Service</a></td></tr>
<tr><td class="menu" id="contact2" width="100" height="15"><a href="#"
onmouseover="changecolor('contact2',oncolor)"
onmouseout="changecolor('contact2',offcolor);closeall()">Sales
➥Dept.</a></td></tr>
<tr><td class="menu" id="contact3" width="100" height="15"><a href="#"
onmouseover="changecolor('contact3',oncolor)"
onmouseout="changecolor('contact3',offcolor);closeall()">General
➥Inquiries</a></td></tr>
</table>
</div>

<!-- second level of submenus, for 'members' category -->
<div id="membersmusic">
<table border="0" cellspacing="0" cellpadding="0">
<tr>
<td class="menu" id="membersmusic1" width="100" height="15">
<a href="#" onmouseover="changecolor('membersmusic1',oncolor)"
onmouseout="changecolor('membersmusic1',offcolor);closeall()">
➥- Medieval</a></td></tr>
<tr><td class="menu" id="membersmusic2" width="100" height="15">
<a href="#" onmouseover="changecolor('membersmusic2',oncolor)"
onmouseout="changecolor('membersmusic2',offcolor);closeall()">
➥- Renaissance</a></td></tr>
<tr><td class="menu" id="membersmusic3" width="100" height="15">
<a href="#" onmouseover="changecolor('membersmusic3',oncolor)"
onmouseout="changecolor('membersmusic3',offcolor);closeall()">
➥- Baroque</a></td></tr>
</table>
</div>

<div id="membersteacher">
<table border="0" cellspacing="0" cellpadding="0">
<tr>
<td class="menu" id="membersteacher1" width="100" height="15">
<a href="#" onmouseover="changecolor('membersteacher1',oncolor)"
onmouseout="changecolor('membersteacher1',offcolor);closeall()">
➥- Course Aids</a></td></tr>
<tr><td class="menu" id="membersteacher2" width="100" height="15">
<a href="#" onmouseover="changecolor('membersteacher2',oncolor)"
onmouseout="changecolor('membersteacher2',offcolor);closeall()">
➥- Quizzes</a></td></tr>
<tr><td class="menu" id="membersteacher3" width="100" height="15">
<a href="#" onmouseover="changecolor('membersteacher3',oncolor)"
onmouseout="changecolor('membersteacher3',offcolor);closeall()">-
➥Teacher Forum</a></td></tr>
<tr><td class="menu" id="membersteacher4" width="100" height="15">
<a href="#" onmouseover="changecolor('membersteacher4',oncolor)"
onmouseout="changecolor('membersteacher4',offcolor);closeall()">
➥- Class Forum</a></td></tr>
</table>
</div>

<div id="membersstudent">
<table border="0" cellspacing="0" cellpadding="0">
<tr>
```

continues

```
<td class="menu" id="membersstudent1" width="100" height="15">
<a href="#" onmouseover="changecolor('membersstudent1',oncolor)"
onmouseout="changecolor('membersstudent1',offcolor);closeall()">- Study
➧Aids</a></td></tr>
<tr><td class="menu" id="membersstudent2" width="100" height="15">
<a href="#" onmouseover="changecolor('membersstudent2',oncolor)"
onmouseout="changecolor('membersstudent2',offcolor);closeall()">- Ask a
➧Teacher</a></td></tr>
```

```
<tr><td class="menu" id="membersstudent3" width="100" height="15">
<a href="#" onmouseover="changecolor('membersstudent3',oncolor)"
onmouseout="changecolor('membersstudent3',offcolor);closeall()">- Student
➧Forum</a></td></tr>
</table>
</div>
```

The **members** submenu items open another submenu below it. Therefore, the **controlsubmenu()** function is called **onmouseover**, with four values passed to the function. For the first line ("Online Listening"), the values **members**, **membersmusic**, **members1**, and **top_members** are passed to the function.

This has the following result:

- The submenu, **members**, is kept open, and the value of **active_submenu1** is set to **members**.

- The second-level submenu **membersmusic** is opened, and the value of **activesubmenu2** is set to **membersmusic**.

- The background color of the menu item, **members1**, is set to the **oncolor** value.

- The graphic of the top menu graphic button, **top_members**, is set to the 'on' state, and the value of **activetopelem** is set to **topmembers**.

How the drop-down menu code works: When the user mouses over the Home button, the button graphic changes to the **'on'** state. When the user mouses over the other buttons, the button graphic changes to the **'on'** state, and the drop-down menu is revealed.

When the user mouses over the menu items in the Members drop-down menu, another menu is revealed to the side. When the user mouses out of the menu all together, the menu returns to the **'off'** state.

If the submenu element opens another submenu, the **changecolor()** function and the **closeall()** function are called with an **onmouseout** event call. If, on the other hand, the submenu element is a bottom-level element (it does not open any other submenus), only the **closeall()** function is called because the background color should not change back to its 'off' state when the next-level submenu is open.

> **Note:** Don't forget to insert the appropriate target URL value for **href** attribute of each **<a>** element.

OTHER DROP-DOWN MENU SCRIPTS

Drop-down menus are one of the most popular uses of Dynamic HTML, and there are many other ways of accomplishing this popular navigation interface. Dissecting these scripts can help you learn of the many different ways to accomplish things with CSS and JavaScript. See the companion web site for a list of other drop-down menu scripts.

HOW IT WORKS: THE TIMEOUT FUNCTIONS

In this project, we've introduced the powerful built-in timeout functions, **setTimeout()** and **clearTimeout()**.

The **setTimeout()** allows you to delay the execution of other functions by a specified amount of time, which is given in milliseconds. It also allows you to repeatedly execute (or loop) a function by calling it again and again.

The **clearTimeout()** function, on the other hand, stops the specified **setTimeout()** function. Here, we've used the **clearTimeout()** function in the **stopall()** function to effectively stop an open submenu from closing prematurely—before the user has had a chance to actually click a link.

A DIFFERENT VIEW IN NETSCAPE 4

Because Netscape Navigator/Communicator 4.x does not recognize border styles for **<td>** elements or allow for changing the background color of a **<td>** element with JavaScript, the menus look different in that browser. If this is not acceptable for your purposes, it is necessary to create **'on'** and **'off'** graphical text elements for each submenu menu item instead of using text. To simulate the mouseon/mouseoff color change, call the **onoff()** image source swapping function instead of the **changecolor()** function.

If the drop-down menus must look the same in all major browsers including Netscape 4.x, simply eliminate the **changecolor()** function and do not specify a **border** style for the **menu** class selector in your CSS.

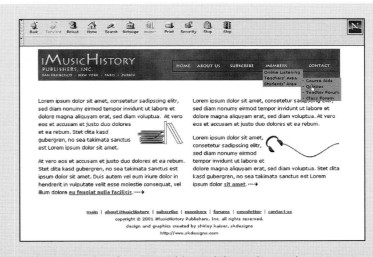

In Netscape 4.x, the submenus are plainer and do not change color on **mouseover**.

SCROLLING FRAMELESS WINDOWS

"When one door closes, another opens;

but we often look so long and so regretfully

upon the closed door that we do not see the

one which has opened for us."

—ALEXANDER GRAHAM BELL

CONSTRUCTING JAVASCRIPT OBJECTS

In this project we'll create another popular

page element—a scrolling inset "frame" using a

combination of CSS and JavaScript. Along the

way, we'll learn about constructing objects

with JavaScript.

Scrolling Frameless Windows

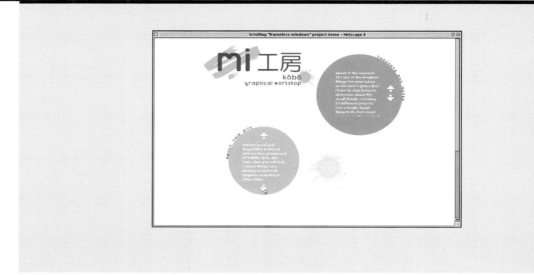

GETTING STARTED

One popular type of web page feature is a small stationary scrolling frame that is inset within the overall browser window. This allows elements on the browser window to always stay in view. While it's possible to create such a small scrolling window with nested frames, the **iframe** element in Internet Explorer or (in the case of the latest browsers) with **div** elements that have scrollbars, the default appearance of these frames or windows leave something to be desired.

By using JavaScript and CSS, it's possible to be far more creative with the design of the scrolling frame. The up and down scrolling "arrows" can be of any shape, as can the "frame" itself.

In this project, we will create a page with two scrolling "frames." Visually, the frames are circles instead of the ubiquitous rectangles, and the up and down arrows are positioned directly above and below the scrolling sections rather than to the right.

The following topics are covered in this project:

- JavaScript **object**s and the object constructor
- Using the CSS **clip** and **overflow** properties
- Looping functions with the **setTimeout()** method

JAVASCRIPT OBJECT CONSTRUCTORS

In programming terms, the **object** object in JavaScript is the most basic unit or building block. We've already created our own custom object with the document object creation script. In this project we'll go further into the JavaScript object constructor. Think of custom objects as being kind of like functions on steroids: once you know how to create your own, you will greatly enhance your scripting abilities.

The **scroller** object constructor, which is at the heart of this project, is a bit complicated because it contains multiple functions, which are themselves objects.

Object constructors are comprised of **property** and **method** definitions. Properties define the construction or framework of the object, while methods are functions that give the object its "brains," or functionality.

Why do we want to go to the trouble of creating custom objects? By creating an object that contains all of these plus all associated methods (functions), it becomes much easier to generate more than one instance of this object on the web page. In other words, when you construct a reusable object that contains all the reusable properties such as the document object model, values that are used over and over, there's a lot more scripting work required up front—but your workload later is greatly decreased.

Note that in this project we use the terms *custom* and *built-in* frequently. Built-in properties or methods are ones that are predefined in the version of JavaScript that's supported by the browser in use, and custom properties or methods are ones that we define ourselves.

CREATING THE **HTML** BASE

The HTML or XHTML markup of a dynamic web page is the shortest of all the documents that are assembled to create the final result. Because all of the layout element blocks will be positioned on the fly, they will be enclosed in **div** elements.

1 In the **head** section of the HTML document, insert the tags necessary to link the external CSS and JavaScript files.

Note that the HTML 4.01 Transitional **DOCTYPE** declaration is used—without a URL. This is to get around a quirk in Internet Explorer 6.0/Windows where a **DOCTYPE** declaration pointing to the URL of the Transitional DTD renders as if it were following a Strict DTD. Because the markup of this page is Transitional, this will cause the page to not display as intended. Therefore, the URL is omitted.

```
<!DOCTYPE HTML PUBLIC "-//W3C//DTD HTML 4.01 Transitional//EN">
<html>
<head>
<meta http-equiv="content-type" content="text/html; charset=iso-8859-1">
<title>Scrolling &quot;frameless windows&quot; project demo</title>
<link rel="Stylesheet" rev="Stylesheet" href="inc/scrolling_boxes.css">
<script src="inc/place.js" type="text/javascript"></script>
<script src="inc/scrolling_boxes.js" type="text/javascript"></script>
<script src="inc/place.js" type="text/javascript"></script>
<script type="text/javascript">
```

continues

There are three external files associated with this page: scrolling_boxes.css; the external stylesheet; and three external JavaScript files: docobj.js, place.js, and scrolling_boxes.js. All the linked files will be saved in the subdirectory, **inc**.

continued

```
<!--
/* page-specific JavaScript will be inserted here. */
//-->
</script>

</head>
<body>
```

2 Create a **div** element with a unique **id** for each element. There is a single **div** element enclosing each graphic on this page. Each of the **div** elements will be positioned with JavaScript.

```
<div id="logo">
<img src="images/logo.gif" alt="mi-kobo logo" width="348"
➥height="139" border="0">
</div>


<div id="aboutcircle">
<img src="images/bluecircle.gif" alt="about this site"
➥width="228" height="223" border="0">
</div>


<div id="newscircle">
<img src="images/pinkcircle.gif" alt="thoughts and notes"
➥width="276" height="262" border="0">
</div>

<div id="splash">
<img src="images/greensplash.gif" alt="click here to
➥proceed!" width="124" height="111" border="0">
</div>


<div id="backgroundimage">
<img src="images/bgsmear.gif" alt="" width="436"
➥height="252" border="0">
</div>
```

```
<!-- the following 4 DIVs are the up/down arrows for each
circle. -->

<div id="aboutup">
<a href="#"><img src="images/uparrow.gif" alt="up"
➥width="23" height="21" border="0"></a>
</div>


<div id="aboutdown">
<a href="#"><img src="images/downarrow.gif" alt="down"
➥width="23" height="21" border="0"></a>
</div>


<div id="newsup">
<a href="#"><img src="images/uparrow.gif" alt="up"
➥width="23" height="21" border="0"></a>
</div>


<div id="newsdown">
<a href="#"><img src="images/downarrow.gif" alt="down"
➥width="23" height="21" border="0"></a>
</div>
```

3 Create the tags for the scrolling text boxes. The scrolling text boxes consist of two **div** elements. The **div** element that contains the text itself is nested within a "container" **div**.

```html
<!-- the scrolling text boxes. -->

<div id="newsbox">
    <div id="newstext">
    <!-- the news text goes here. Omitted for clarity. -->
    </div>
</div>

<div id="aboutbox">
    <div id="abouttext">
    <!-- the about text goes here. Omitted for clarity. -->
    </div>
</div>


</body>
</html>
```

CREATING THE CSS

The CSS specifies the style rules for each **div** when the page first loads. The style rules are, in turn, changed on the fly with JavaScript.

1 In the document scrolling_boxes.css, create the basic CSS style rules for the **body** and **a** elements.

```css
a {
    outline: none;
    }
a:visited {
    color: #ffff00;
    background-color: transparent;
    }
a:link {
    color: #ffff00;
    background-color: transparent;
    text-decoration: none;
    }
a:hover {
    text-decoration: underline;
    }
```

```css
p {
    font-family: verdana, sans-serif;
    font-weight: bold;
    line-height: 14px;
    color: white;
    background: transparent;
    }
body {
    margin: 0px;
    background-color: #ffffff;
    color: #000000;
    }
```

2 Create the CSS rules for the graphical elements, giving each **div** element its own unique **id**. There are nine graphical elements on this page, each contained within a **div** element.

Note the following for these **div** elements as well as for the scrolling text box **div** elements explained in the upcoming step:

- The width and height of each **div** element is set to the size of the image graphic contained within each. If these values are not set, in some browsers the **div** element width defaults to the maximum width of the window.

- All of the elements have a **position: absolute** value because only absolutely positioned elements can be repositioned with CSS.

- The starting position for these **div** elements is at the top left corner of the page. They also are initially set to be invisible with the **visibility: hidden** rule until they are positioned on the page—otherwise, the viewer will see them bunched up in the corner of the page.

Tip: Another trick you can use is to position the elements off the page with negative top and/or left values, for example **top: -500px** and **left: -500px**.

- Be sure to set the **z-index** value of each element appropriately. For example, the up/down arrows should have a higher **z-index** than the circles—or you won't see them!

  The ID selectors **#aboutup**, **#aboutdown**, **#newsup**, and **#newsdown** are grouped together given that their style rules are identical.

```css
#logo {
        visibility: hidden;
        position: absolute;
        z-index: 100;
        top: 0px;
        left: 0px;
        width: 348px;
        height: 139px;
}
#aboutcircle {
        visibility: hidden;
        z-index: 2;
        top: 0px;
        left: 0px;
        position: absolute;
        width: 228px;
        height: 223px;
}
#newscircle {
        visibility: hidden;
        z-index: 2;
        top: 0px;
        left: 0px;
        position: absolute;
        width: 276px;
        height: 262px;
}
```

```css
#splash {
        visibility: hidden;
        z-index: 100;
        position: absolute;
        top: 0px;
        left: 0px;
        width: 124px;
        height: 111px;
}
#backgroundimage {
        visibility: hidden;
        z-index: 1;
        position: absolute;
        top: 0px;
        left: 0px;
        width: 436px;
        height: 252px;
}
#aboutup, #aboutdown, #newsup, #newsdown {
        visibility: hidden;
        z-index: 3;
        position: absolute;
        top: 0px;
        left: 0px;
        width: 23px;
        height: 21px;
}
```

3 Create the CSS rules for the scrolling text box **div** elements, giving each a unique **id**. In this case, the **id** values are **aboutbox**, **abouttext**, **newsbox**, and **newstext**.

> **Note:** It's important to maintain naming consistency for any **div** elements that you will be manipulating with JavaScript later. For this project, the important **div** element IDs are the ones associated with the scrolling text box—**aboutbox**, **abouttext**, **aboutup**, **aboutdown** (the up and down arrows) and **newsbox**, **newstext**, **newsup**, and **newsdown** (the up and down arrows).

The **...box** element is the "clipping box" for the nested **...text** element.

Two CSS style properties are important here: the **overflow** property and the **clip** property. The **overflow** property specifies that any content that overflows or exceeds the size of the **div** element box is hidden. The **clip** property specifies which region of the contents of this box is visible, with the offset from the containing box specified in this order: top, right, bottom, and left (think clockwise). In most cases, these two properties are used together as shown in the code. It's not necessary to include the **clip** values if they are the same as the dimensions of the element, as they are here, but you would need to define them if you want the **clip** area to be smaller.

```
#aboutbox {
        visibility: hidden;
        position: absolute;
        left: 0px;
        top: 0px;
        width: 140px;
        height: 130px;
        clip: rect(0px,140px,130px,0px);
        overflow: hidden;
        z-index: 3;
        background: transparent;
}

#abouttext {
        visibility: hidden;
        position: absolute;
        width: 138px;
        left: 0px;
        top: 0px;
        z-index: 3;
}
```

```
#newsbox {
        visibility: hidden;
        position: absolute;
        left: 0px;
        top: 0px;
        width: 140px;
        height: 150px;
        overflow: hidden;
        clip: rect(0px,140px,150px,0px);
        z-index: 3;
        background: transparent;
}

#newstext {
        visibility: hidden;
        position: absolute;
        width: 138px;
        left: 0px;
        top: 0px;
        z-index: 3;
}
```

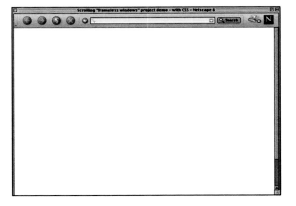

This screenshot is not a mistake. It's how the page looks after the CSS rules are applied. The elements are invisible until they are "activated" with JavaScript.

Creating the Basic Document Object Creation Script

In the following steps, we'll create the document object constructor script.

1 Create a new text file and save it with the name, **docobj.js**, in the **inc** directory. This document will hold the basic document object constructor script. The script looks for the **document.layers**, **document.all**, or **document.getElementById** objects within the browser and then defines the variables used to create the document object accordingly.

We've already used this script several times in other Projects. The only difference here is that we've now put it in its own file for the sake of modularity. We can use this for any web page where we need to create a cross-browser script.

```
/* define variables for "if n4 (Netscape 4),
if IE (IE 4.x),
and if n6 (if Netscape 6/W3C-DOM compliant)"
*/

var n4, ie, n6;

/* detecting browser support for certain key
objects/methods and
assembling a custom document object */


var doc,doc2,doc3,sty;

if (document.layers) {
        doc = "document.";
        doc2 = ".document.";
        doc3 = "";
        sty = "";
        n4 = true;
        }
else if (document.all) {
        doc = "document.all.";
        doc2 = "";
        doc3 = "";
        sty = ".style";
        ie = true;
        }
else if (document.getElementById) {
        doc = "document.getElementById('";
        doc2 ="')";
        doc3 ="')";
        sty = "').style";
        n6 = true;
        }
```

Defining the Global Variables for the Scroller Script

Defining global variables is the first step in creating the script that is the heart of this project—the construction of the scrolling text box objects.

1 Create a new text document and save it with the filename, scrolling_boxes.js, in the **inc** directory.

2 Define and initialize the key global variables.

First, define the variables to which the **setTimeout()** timer function will be assigned. By assigning a timer function to a variable, it becomes possible to clear the timer with **clearTimeout()**.

Next, define and initialize the variable that will control how fast the text box scrolls. The higher the number, the slower the scroll will be. It's set to 200 milliseconds in this project.

Finally, define and initialize the variable that will serve as a load checker. It's set to 0; once the objects are created and loaded, the value will be set to 1. This prevents a script from executing prematurely, which would result in a JavaScript error.

```
// the timer variables, for cleanup later.
var timer1, timer2;

// the scroll speed. The higher the number, the slower it scrolls.
var scrollspeed = 200;

// initialize the variable that will serve as a 'load checker'

var loaded = 0;
```

CREATING THE OBJECT CONSTRUCTOR FUNCTION

Next, you create the Object Constructor function.

1 Define the function **createObject**. This is the base object constructor.

Two arguments are passed to this function: **elem** (which will hold a section of the unique **id** value of the **div** element) and **container** (which holds the unique ID of the parent div element that the **div** you're addressing is nested in). Note that **container** is only required for nested objects and is only required for Netscape Navigator version 4.x.

```
//the object constructor's core function

function createObject(elem,container) {
```

2 The first part of the function holds three conditional **if-else** statements, which assign values to four key properties of the object. Define the first **if-else** "branch" by detecting if the **document.layers** object is supported. If so, then the browser is Netscape Navigator 4.x.

```
if (container) {
          container = doc +container+".";
```

215

Netscape Navigator version 4.x requires that any nested element be addressed in the **document. parentelementid.document.elementid** format. So if the element in question is nested (or is inside a "container" element), we'll need to construct the appropriate document object address.

If the argument, **container**, exists, then the value of **container** is set to the text string **document.container.**

3 Create the section of code that assigns values to some key properties of the object if the browser uses Netscape 4.x.

The **this.element** property is assigned the evaluated value of the string of **container + doc + elem**. For example, if the value of **container** is box1 and the value of **elem** is box2, then the string would be **document.box1.document.box2**. This gives us the basic document object for the element.

The **this.styleElem** property is assigned the same value. This gives us the style object for the element—in the case of Netscape 4.x this is the same as the document object.

The **this.elemheight** property is assigned the value of **this.styleElem.document.height**. This gives us the height style property for the object.

The **this.clipheight** property is assigned the value of **this.styleElem.clip.height**. This gives us the clip height property for the object.

Close off this section of the **if...else** statement with a closing bracket.

```
        this.element = eval(container+doc + elem);
        this.styleElem =  eval(container+doc + elem);
        this.elemheight = this.styleElem.document.height;
        this.clipheight = this.styleElem.clip.height;
}
```

Note: In JavaScript, the term, **this**, is used refer to the current object. You can then define properties and methods of the object in the **this.xxxxx** format. As you can see, it's possible to declare and define custom properties of an object, just as we can create our own variables or functions. Once we have defined a custom property, we can combine it with built-in properties to define another custom property. For example, the definition of the **this.clipheight** property for Netscape 4.x looks for the **clip.height** property, which is a built-in property of **div** elements of the **this.styleElem** property, which is a custom-defined property.

4 Create the section of code that defines the methods and properties for this object when the browser in use recognizes the **document.all** object (Internet Explorer version 4.x and up). Note that the built-in properties are different. This is why we need to define the custom properties for each type of browser in use.

```
else if (document.all) {
        this.element = document.all[elem];
        this.styleElem = this.element.style;
        this.elemheight = this.element.offsetHeight;
        this.clipheight = this.element.offsetHeight;
}
```

5 Create the section of code that defines the methods and properties for this object when the browser in use recognizes **document.getElementById** object (Internet Explorer 5.x and up, and Netscape 6.x / Mozilla).

```
else if (document.getElementById) {
        this.element = document.getElementById(elem);
        this.styleElem = this.element.style;
        this.elemheight = this.element.offsetHeight;
        this.clipheight = this.element.offsetHeight;
}
```

6 Create the final part of the **if...else** statement that will act as an "if all else fails" catchall. If the browser does not recognize **document.layers**, **document.all**, or **document.getElementById**, then the script returns a value of **false** and terminates. This avoids any JavaScript errors from occurring in browsers that don't support one of these methods.

```
else {
        return false;
}
```

7 Define custom functions as methods of the object.

Now that we have finished defining the properties, or construction, of the object, we will define its methods. *Object methods* are functions that are assigned to it and that make the object come alive. The functions that we will define in the following steps are assigned as methods of this object.

```
        this.scrollIt = scrollIt;
        this.scrollup = scrollup;
        this.scrolldown = scrolldown;
        this.scroller = scroller;
        this.hidearrow = hidearrow;
        return this;
}
```

CREATING THE `scrollIt()` FUNCTION

The **scrollIt()** function makes the inner textbox **div** element move up and down by a specified amount. This function is called by the **scrollup()** and **scrolldown()** functions.

1 Define the function, **scrollIt()**. The function is passed two arguments: **xpos** and **ypos** (the left and top coordinates of the text box).

```
function scrollIt(xpos,ypos) {
```

2 Define two properties: this.x is the value of the argument xpos, and this.y is the value of the argument ypos.

```
        this.x=xpos;
        this.y=ypos;
```

3 Assign the value of **xpos** to the **left** property of **this.styleElem** (the style property of the object) and the value of **ypos** to the **top** property of **this.styleElem**.

```
        this.styleElem.left = xpos;
        this.styleElem.top = ypos;
    }
```

CREATING THE `scrollup()` AND `scrolldown()` FUNCTIONS

Two functions call the **scrollIt()** function: **scrollup()** and **scrolldown()**. Both of these functions are, in turn, called by the **scroll()** function. Note that the **scroll()** function passes the values for **incr**, **containerbox**, and **textbox** to these two functions as arguments.

1 Define the global variables **var**, **minheight**, **containerbox**, and **textbox**.

```
var minheight, containerbox, textbox;
```

These variables will have values assigned to them within the functions.

2 Create the function, **scrolldown()**.

This is the function that will move the textbox **div** up, giving the appearance that the user is scrolling up the window. The argument **incr**, or scroll increment, is passed to this function from the **scroll()** function.

```
/* function to make the textbox div move up, giving the
viewer the illusion that she is
scrolling the frame down. */

function scrolldown (incr) {
```

3 Assign a value to the variable, **minheight**. This is the minimum height that should be showing—the height of the element minus the clip height of the container **div** element.

```
minheight = this.elemheight - containerbox.clipheight;
```

4 Check the value of the property, **this.y**, or the **top** coordinate of the element. If it's greater than the negative value of **minheight**, then the **this.scrollIt()** method is invoked with the value **0** and the value of **this.y** minus the value of **incr** passed as arguments.

```
if (this.y > - minheight) {
    this.scrollIt(0, this.y-incr);
```

5 Invoke the timer function. If the value of the variable loop is 1, then the **textbox.scrolldown** method is invoked for **this.elem** with the value of **incr** passed to it and a delay of the value, scrollspeed. Note that the values of loop and textbox will be passed to this function from the **scroller()** function.

```
    if (loop == 1) {
        timer1 =
setTimeout(("textbox.scrolldown("+incr+")"),scrollspeed);
        }
    }
}
```

Note: Note the way in which the **setTimeout()** is declared. The first argument is actually a string that contains the method or function to be executed with the appropriate argument value inserted. The assembled string in this case is **textbox.scrolldown(incr)**. The **setTimeout()** function evaluates the string and then executes it after the specified delay (in this case, the value of **scrollspeed**).

6 Create the function **scrollup()**. The **scrollup()** function is the same as the **scrolldown()** function, except the direction is reversed. If the value of **this.y** is less than **0**, then the **this.scrollIt()** method is invoked with **0** and the value of **this.y** minus the value of **incr** passed as arguments.

```
/* function to make the textbox div move up, giving the viewer the illustration that
she is scrolling the frame down. */


function scrollup (incr) {
    if (this.y < 0) {
        this.scrollIt(0,this.y-incr);
        if (loop == 1) {
            timer2 = setTimeout("textbox.scrollup("+incr+")",scrollspeed);
            }
        }
    }
}
```

CREATING THE scroller() FUNCTION

The **scroller()** function is what makes the text box move, and it's the one that we will call on our web page by calling it with a mouse event. The function also checks to see if the page is loaded before executing.

1 Create the function, **scroller()**.

Two arguments are passed to it: **elem**, which is a section of the **id** value of the element, and **incr**, the increment value (in pixels) by which the element should move—the higher this value, the more the text box will scroll.

```
/* Calls the scrolling functions. Also checks whether the
page is loaded or not. */
function scroll(elem,incr){
```

2 Assign the variable, **containerbox**, the evaluated value of the text string "box" + elem. Assign the variable, **textbox**, the evaluated value of the string, **"text"** + **elem**.

```
containerbox = eval("box" + elem);
textbox = eval("text" + elem);
```

When the page is initialized and the objects are created, this will assign the object value to each variable.

3 Check the value of the variable, **loaded**. If this is set to 1 (in other words, if the objects have been created), then the value of the variable **loop** is set to 1.

```
if (loaded==1){
    loop=1;
```

4 Call the function, **hidearrow()**, which hides the up or down arrow if the textbox has scrolled to the top or bottom limit. This function is defined later on in this project. It is passed the argument, **elem**.

```
hidearrow(elem);
```

5 Check the value of **incr**. If this is a positive value, then invoke the **scrolldown()** method for the **textbox** object with the value of **incr** passed to it as an argument; if it is negative, invoke the **scrollup()** method for the **textbox** object.

```
if(incr > 0){
        textbox.scrolldown(incr);
    } else {
        textbox.scrollup(incr)
    }
    }
}
```

CREATING THE `stopscroller()` FUNCTION

The **stopscroller()** function is called with a **mouseout** event. It stops the scrolling action by clearing the **setTimeout()** loops we invoked with the **scroller()** function, using the **clearTimeout()** method.

1 Define the function, **stopscroller()**. Two arguments are passed to it: **elem**, or the **id** value of the element, and **arrowdir**, the direction of the arrow graphic.

```
//Stops the scrolling (called on mouseout)
function stopscroll(elem,arrowdir){
```

2 Set the value of the variable loop to 0. If the **setTimeout()** timer, **timer1**, exists, clear it with **clearTimeout()**. If the **setTimeout()** timer, **timer2**, exists, clear it with **clearTimeout()**.

```
    loop=0;
    if (timer1){clearTimeout(timer1);}
    if (timer2){clearTimeout(timer2);}
```

3 Finally, call the **hidearrow()** function and close the function with a closing bracket.

This section completes the definitions for the scroller object and the functions that are defined as its methods.

```
    hidearrow(elem,arrowdir);
}
```

CREATING THE `hidearrow()` FUNCTION

Strictly speaking, the **hidearrow()** function is not necessary for the scrolling frame to work. It does, however, enhance the user interface. It hides the up or down arrow when the text box has scrolled to its limit—or, in other words, when there's no more content to show.

1 Create the function, **hidearrow()**. The argument **elem**, which will hold a portion of the **id** value of the element, is passed as an argument.

```
/* The function to make the arrow disappear when there is no
more to scroll. */
function hidearrow(elem) {
```

2 Create an **if...else** statement that sees if the **document.layers** property is recognized—or, in other words, if the browser is Netscape 4.x.

3 Obtain the value of height and then turn it into an integer with the built-in **parseInt()** method. This value is assigned to the property, **textelem_top**.

4 Create the next part of the **if...else** statement.

The other browsers that we're concerned with allow for direct addressing of a nested element. The value we want to see is the **top** style value; this also is turned into an integer with the **parseInt()** method.

> **Note:** The built-in **parseInt()** method is used to convert text string data into an integer. Because the Netscape browsers return a value such as **"60px"** for the position or size of an element rather than 60, you need to convert this to an integer to do any math on it.
>
> It's important to note that when you put text within quote marks, JavaScript will see this as data of type text—even when the text is a number. For example, let's say you declared a variable like this:
>
> **var** boxsize = "60";
>
> Even though to us humans, 60 looks like a number, to JavaScript it is a text string. You must convert this to an integer with **parseInt()** like this:
>
> **var** boxsizenum = **parseInt**(boxsize);
>
> Now you can perform math on the new **boxsizenum** variable.

```
if (document.layers) {
   textelem_top = parseInt(eval(doc+elem+"box"+doc2+elem+"text.height"));
}
```

```
else {
      textelem = eval(doc + elem + "text" + sty);
      textelem_top = parseInt(textelem.top);
}
```

5 Assign the document object to the variable, **uparrow**, by using the **eval()** method to evaluate the string, **doc + elem + "up" + sty.** When the value of elem is **"about"**, here is how the string will look in each browser:

In Netscape 4: **"document.aboutup"**

In Internet Explorer 4.x :
"document.all.aboutup.style"

In Netscape 6/Mozilla:
"document.getElementById('aboutup').style"

This address points to the **div** element, **aboutup**, in the case of Netscape 4.x and to the **style** property of the **div** element, **aboutup**, in Internet Explorer 4.x and Netscape 6.x/Mozilla.

Assign the document object to the variable, **downarrow** in the same manner.

```
uparrow = eval (doc + elem + "up" + sty);
downarrow = eval (doc + elem + "down" + sty);
```

6 Evaluate the value of the **textelem.top** property in a series of **if...else** statements.

If the value is less than **0** and greater than the negative value of the variable, **minheight**, then the **uparrow** is visible.

If it's less than or equal to the negative value of **minheight**, then both arrows are visible.

Otherwise, (in other words, if **textelem_top** is **0**) the **uparrow** is hidden and the **downarrow** is visible.

```
if(textelem_top < 0 && textelem_top > -minheight) {
  uparrow.visibility = "visible";
    downarrow.visibility = "visible";
}

else if (textelem_top <= -minheight) {
  uparrow.visibility = "visible";
  downarrow.visibility = "hidden";
    }
else {
  uparrow.visibility = "hidden";
    downarrow.visibility = "visible";
  }
}
```

The **hidearrow()** function hides the up arrow when the text box cannot be scrolled up (left). When the text box can be scrolled both ways, both arrows are visible (middle); when there's no more to scroll down, the down arrow is hidden (right).

CREATING THE toTop() FUNCTION

The **toTop()** function simply returns the text box to position 0,0. It's invoked when the user clicks the up arrow.

1 Define the **toTop()** function, passing the argument, **elem**.

```
// jumps to the top of the scrolling text. Called onclick.

function toTop(elem) {
```

2 Assign the variable, **textelem**, the evaluated value of the text string, **"text" + elem**. If the value of **elem** is **"about"**, the resulting string is "textabout"; when this is evaluated, it points to the **textabout** object.

Use the **textelem.scrollIt()** method with the arguments **0,0** to make the text box scroll to the top (left 0, top 0).

With the **toTop()** function complete, the **scrolling_boxes.js** script file is done.

```
        textelem = eval('text'+elem);
        textelem.scrollIt(0,0);
    }
```

CREATING THE place.js DOCUMENT

The functions in place.js are for placing the **div** element on the web page relative to the dimensions of the browser window, plus a function to control the visibility of an element. These functions have already been covered in detail in Project 8, "Browser Detection and Displaying Elements Dynamically," so it won't be described step by step here. The only difference is that we've put them all in an external document to make everything modular.

1 Create a new text document and save it with the place.js in the inc directory.

2 Place the following functions and their required variables in this file:

- **dimensions()**: the function that obtains the current dimensions of the browser window.

```
/* the functions that place elements on a page.
Always use together with docobj.js!
*/


// the variables for the window dimensions
var win_width,win_height;
```

continues

- **centerIt()**: the function that centers an element in the browser window

- **placeIt()**: the function that places an element at specified top/left coordinates on the page.

3 Make sure that this script is used in conjunction with docobj.js by associating both files to the base HTML document. The docobj.js file holds the document object constructor functions, which are the basis of the functions in place.js. Without them, these scripts will fail.

continued

```javascript
var centerhor, centerver;

// Get dimensions of the window
function dimensions() {
        if(n4 || n6){
                win_width=window.innerWidth;
                win_height=window.innerHeight;
        } else if(ie) {
                win_width=document.body.clientWidth;
                win_height=document.body.clientHeight;
        }
}


//center the elements on the page.
function centerIt(elem,width,height) {
        docObj = eval(doc + elem + sty);
        if (n4 || n6 ) {
                docObj.left = (centerhor - (width/2));
                docObj.top = (centerver - (height/2));
        }
        if (ie) {
                docObj.pixelLeft = (centerhor - (width/2));
                docObj.pixelTop = (centerver - (height/2));
        }
}


//place the elements relative to the page.
function placeIt(elem,leftPos,topPos) {
        docObj = eval(doc + elem + sty);
        if (n4 || n6) {
                docObj.left = leftPos;
                docObj.top= topPos;
        } else if (ie) {
                docObj.pixelLeft = leftPos;
                docObj.pixelTop = topPos;
        }
}


//show or hide an element
function showhide(elem,state) {
        docObj = eval(doc + elem + sty);
        docObj.visibility = state;
}
```

CREATING THE `initialize()` FUNCTION

The `initialize()` function brings everything together when the page loads. First, it creates the scroller objects. Then it places the **div** elements relative to the size of the browser window.

1 Create the function, `initialize()`, on the HTML page within the **<script>...</script>** tags in the **<head>** section. First declare the global variables that are used in the function and then start to define the function.

```
// The function that creates the objects and places everything.
var boxnews, textnews, boxabout, textabout;
function initialize() {
```

Note: The `initialize()` function is put on the HTML page instead of in an external script file because it contains the page-specific arguments passed to the functions. By keeping the external scripts generic and having the page-specific functions on the HTML page, the reusability of the external documents is increased.

2 Create the objects that define the scrolling news textbox (this appears in the larger circle): **boxnews**, which defines the container box for the news text, and **textnews**, which defines the text box.

Reset the position of the **textnews** object to left 0, top 0 with **scrollIt(0,0)**. This resets the scrolling text to the top.

```
boxnews = new createObject('newsbox');
textnews = new createObject('newstext','newsbox');
textnews.scrollIt(0,0);
```

Note: Here you can see your previous scripting efforts paying off. Creating a new object with the properties and methods needed for the scroller object is simply a matter of typing the following:

```
reference = new createObject(arguments);
```

3 Create the objects that define the scrolling about textbox (this appears in the smaller left-hand circle): **boxabout**, which defines the container box for the about text, and **textabout**, which defines the text box.

Reset the position of the aboutnews object to left 0, top 0 with **scrollIt(0,0)**.

```
boxabout = new createObject('aboutbox');
textabout = new createObject('abouttext','aboutbox');
textabout.scrollIt(0,0);
```

4 Call the **hidearrow()** function to hide the **aboutup** (the **about** section up arrow) and the **newsup** (the **news** section up arrow) **div** elements.

```
hidearrow('about');
hidearrow('news');
```

5 Set the value of the variable, **loaded**, to **1**. This tells the scripts that the objects are created and loaded.

```
loaded=1;
```

6 Start the positioning section of the **initialize()** function. First call the **dimensions()** function to get the dimensions of the browser window:

dimensions();

7 Call the functions, **centerIt()** and **placeIt()** that place all of the elements on the page.

You might have to adjust the numbers to suit your layout. Play around a bit with the numbers until the elements are positioned as you want them.
Remember the first number argument passed to the **placeIt()** and **centerIt()** functions is the left position, and the second number is the top position.

```
//place all the elements

centerIt('backgroundimage',436,252);
placeIt('logo',centerhor-320,20);
placeIt('newscircle',centerhor+30,50);
placeIt('newsbox',centerhor+90,100);

placeIt('newsup',centerhor+250,150);
placeIt('newsdown',centerhor+250,180);

placeIt('aboutcircle',centerhor-250,centerver-20);
placeIt('aboutbox',centerhor-250+50,centerver+30);

placeIt('aboutup',centerhor-250+105,centerver);
placeIt('aboutdown',centerhor-250+105,centerver + 170);

placeIt('splash',centerhor,centerver+70);
```

8 After the elements have been placed on the page, make them visible with the **showhide()** function.

```
// make all the elements visible

showhide('backgroundimage','visible');
showhide('logo','visible');
showhide('newscircle','visible');
showhide('aboutcircle','visible');
showhide('splash','visible');
showhide('newsdown','visible');
showhide('aboutdown','visible');
showhide('aboutbox','visible');
showhide('abouttext','visible');
showhide('newsbox','visible');
showhide('newstext','visible');

}
```

ADJUSTING THE HTML TO CALL THE FUNCTIONS

To activate the objects and functions we've defined, call the functions in the HTML markup.

1 Insert an **onload** event call in the **<body>** tag that calls the **initialize()** function, which will create the scrolling objects. In addition, insert an **onresize** event call that forces the page to reload if the browser window is resized.

```
<body onload="initialize()" onresize="window.location.reload(false)">
```

2 Insert the **onmouseover**, **onmouseout**, and **onclick** event calls in the **a** link elements surrounding the up and down arrow **img** elements.

For the up arrows:

- The **scroller()** function is called **onmouseover**, with the appropriate scrolling section name (either **'about'** or **'news'**) and a negative integer value passed as arguments.

- The **stopscroll()** function is called **onmouseout**, with the appropriate scroller name (either **'about'** or **'news'**) and the value, **'up'** (the direction of the arrow), passed as arguments.

```
<div id="aboutup">
<a href="javascript://" onmouseover="scroll('about',-7)"
onmouseout="stopscroll('about','up')" onclick="toTop('about')"><img
➥src="images/uparrow.gif" alt="up" width="23" height="21" border="0"></a>
</div>

<div id="aboutdown">
<a href="javascript://" onmouseover="scroll('about',7)"
onmouseout="stopscroll('about','down')"><img src="images/downarrow.gif" alt="down"
➥width="23" height="21" border="0"></a>
</div>

<div id="newsup">
<a href="javascript://" onmouseover="scroll('news',-7)"
```

continues

- The **toTop()** function is called **onclick**, with the appropriate scrolling section name (either 'about' or 'news') passed as the argument.

For the down arrows:

- The **scroller()** function is called **onmouseover**, with the appropriate scrolling section name (either **'about'** or **'news'**) and a positive integer value passed as arguments.

- The **stopscroll()** function is called **onmouseout**, with the appropriate scrolling section name (either **'about'** or **'news'**) and the value, **'down'** (the direction of the arrow), passed as arguments.

continued

```
onmouseout="stopscroll('news','down')" onmouseup="toTop('news')">
➥<img src="images/uparrow.gif" alt="up" width="23" height="21" border="0"></a>
</div>

<div id="newsdown">
<a href="javascript://" onmouseover="scroll('news',7)"
onmouseout="stopscroll('news','down')" onmousedown="scroll('news',100)"><img
➥src="images/downarrow.gif" alt="down" width="23" height="21" border="0"></a>
</div>
```

Note: The number passed to the **scroller()** function as the **incr** (increment) argument is the number of pixels the text box should be moved by—either in a positive (down) or negative (up) direction. The larger the number, the faster the text box will move.

HOW IT WORKS: THE SCROLLER IN ACTION

Let's load the page in a browser to see exactly what happens.

1 When the page loads, the **initiate()** function creates the four objects necessary for the two scrolling 'frames'. Each scrolling 'frame' consists of a container box and a text box.

2 The upper position of the text box is set to 0, 0—or to the top of the container box. At the same time, the up arrow is hidden. This tells the user that there's no text to scroll up to.

When the page loads, the elements are positioned dynamically, and the text boxes are set at the 0,0 position, or the top of the page. The up arrows are invisible.

3 Test the scrolling functions by mousing over a down arrow. The text starts scrolling up—in other words, the text box is moving up. This gives the illusion that the user is scrolling the "frame" down.

When the user mouses over the down arrow, the text starts scrolling.

4 Let's see how this works in conjunction with the **clip** values. Because the **clip** dimensions are fixed for the container box, we only see a portion of the text with any **overflow** hidden. This gives the illusion of a scrolling "window." It's actually a "hole" through which we see a portion of the text box exposed.

How clip works with the scrolling functions. The grayed out portions are the hidden areas, and the white portion shows the visible clip area. When the text box scrolls up (in the direction of the arrow) with the scrolling functions, a different area of the text becomes visible, giving the illusion that the "frame" is scrolling down.

5 Once the end of the text box is reached, the scroll stops.

6 When the user mouses out of the arrow, if the end of the text box is reached, the down arrow disappears. If there's more content to be seen, both arrows are visible.

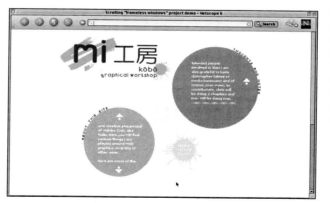

When the user mouses out of the arrow, if there's more text to be scrolled, both arrows are visible. If there's no more text at the bottom, the down arrow disappears; if there's no more text at the top, the up arrow disappears. The figure shows the left text "frame" with more to be scrolled up and down and the right text "frame" scrolled all the way to the bottom.

NETSCAPE NAVIGATOR VERSION 4.x JAVASCRIPT/CSS LIMITATIONS

Netscape Navigator/Communicator version 4.x is a rather out-dated browser. One way it shows its age is when there is a page such as this that incorporates several scripts and a lot of CSS. Although the individual scripts themselves work and no errors are generated, the page simply might not display properly.

Such is the case with this project. The functions, including the object constructor, do work in Netscape version 4.x; however, this page simply seems to exceed the limits of what can be incorporated onto one page.

The only workaround for this seems to be to simplify the page to the "tolerance level" of the browser. Some ways in which you can simplify the page include:

- Decreasing the number of dynamically positioned elements.

- Decreasing the number of functions that rely on timeout looping statements.

- Reducing the number of JavaScript functions on the page. Because there are several functions required for the text scroller, if you want to spawn more than one scroller window (meaning one container object and one text box object for each scroller), you might have to reduce the number of other scripts used on that page.

- Relying on table-based layouts with the amount of CSS minimized. Table-based layouts don't seem to tax this browser nearly as much as layouts that rely primarily on CSS. See the previous project for how to combine a dynamic element within a table-based layout.

TRANSITIONAL CSS AND JAVASCRIPT STRATEGIES

"In life, always do right. This

will gratify some people and

astonish the rest."

—MARK TWAIN

A TABBED INTERFACE

Creating web sites that take advantage of the

CSS and JavaScript capabilities of modern

browsers, while still accommodating older

browsers, is a headache faced by every site

creator. In this project we'll explore some ways

of dealing with this issue.

Project 12

Transitional CSS and JavaScript Strategies

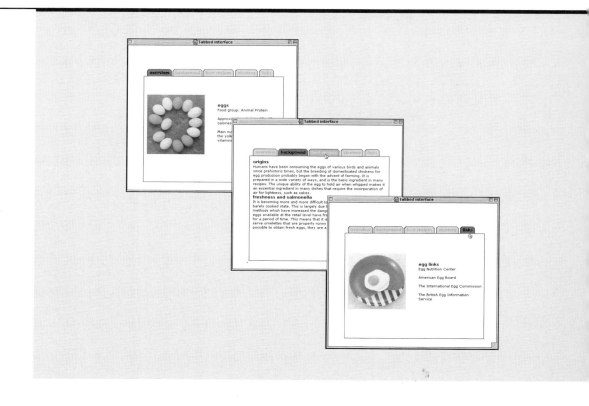

GETTING STARTED

Web site navigation interfaces that use a tab metaphor are very common. (Perhaps the best-known site that uses a tab-navigation interface is Amazon.com.) Yet in most cases, the navigation tabs are merely graphical links that load other pages from the server.

In this project, we show you how to create a tabbed "index-card" type of interface using a combination of CSS and JavaScript. All of the "pages" are actually contained in the one page; once the whole page is loaded into the browser, the user can very quickly "flip" through each "page" without having to reload content from the server.

Because we are using CSS and JavaScript, which are only recognized by the newer browsers, we've also taken steps to ensure that the page is still readable in older browsers.

Here are the main points we'll cover in this project:

- Creating "gracefully degrading" pages using a combination of CSS and JavaScript
- Modularizing the code
- Using arrays to streamline the script
- Manipulating the stacking order, or z-index, of elements

GRACEFULLY DEGRADING PAGES

The latest advanced graphical browsers offer a wealth of JavaScript and CSS features that were previously unavailable or too buggy to be practical. What's more, these modern browsers finally (in large part) follow a common set of standards as specified by the World Wide Web Consortium. This is a great development for those of us on the creative side of the World Wide Web.

There's still one thorny problem to face, however: How do you take advantage of these new methods and features but still accommodate users of version 4 and older browsers? Statistics for browser usage are in a constant state of flux, but as of this writing, a small yet still significant number of web surfers are using version 4 browsers.

Up until now, you have probably been accommodating users of older or alternate browsers using "browser sniffing" methods

to redirect them to other pages, writing alternate content onto the page, and so on. However, this can greatly increase the time and cost needed to create and maintain a site.

In extreme cases, you may even have closed off users of older and alternate browsers by telling them that your site can only be accessed with certain browsers. This only invites resentment from your site visitors, who may never return to your site.

The method introduced in this project is called *graceful degradation*. Essentially, this means that you while you may design your page so that it's optimized for modern browsers, at the same time you ensure that the content of your site is viewable in older or non-graphical browsers. The goal is to make the same pages viewable and useable by the widest audience. See the "How It Works" sidebars at the end of this project to see how this is accomplished.

CREATING THE BASE GRAPHICS FOR THE TABS AND ASSEMBLING THE TAB TABLE

Each navigational tab is made up of three tiny graphics and the label text, assembled into a small table.

1 Create the basic outline shape of the tab. Make the inside of the tab itself transparent and make the outside corners the same color as the background color of your page.

2 Slice the image. You only want to obtain the two side segments. Save each slice as a GIF with transparency.

Note that the corners outside of the tab have a white background. This background color should match the background color you intend to use on your page.

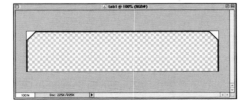

The tab showing the transparent area (the checkered area) in Photoshop.

3 Select a 1-pixel wide segment of the middle section. Save this as a GIF with transparency.

The three graphics: the tab sides, and the one-pixel-wide center graphic. The checkered area is the transparent area.

4 Pre-assemble the tab elements into an HTML/XHTML table.

The tab consists of a small table with three table cells. Each table cell has a different background image. The left and right side table cells have a fixed width, but the middle table "stretches" to accommodate the text that is placed inside it.

The graphic **dot.gif** is a 1×1 pixel transparent GIF that is used to hold the side **td**s open.

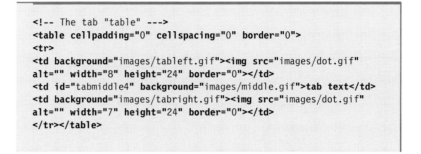

```
<!-- The tab "table" --->
<table cellpadding="0" cellspacing="0" border="0">
<tr>
<td background="images/tableft.gif"><img src="images/dot.gif"
alt="" width="8" height="24" border="0"></td>
<td id="tabmiddle4" background="images/middle.gif">tab text</td>
<td background="images/tabright.gif"><img src="images/dot.gif"
alt="" width="7" height="24" border="0"></td>
</tr></table>
```

Note: Why not simply use the tab graphics as **img src** files instead of as background images for the table cells? This is possible, of course, but we're going to use a bit of CSS trickery to make the graphics invisible in older browsers, as you'll see later in this project.

Note: Normally, when you create a GIF with transparent areas, you make the areas surrounding the actual image transparent. However, if you make GIFs with the main areas set as transparent and the "background" areas in the same color as the background of your page, the "background" areas essentially act as masks. Then you can use CSS to "color" the main area of the element. This is a great way to create graphical elements that you can reuse again and again.

The tab "table" shown with the table borders visible (left), borders off (center), and with a background color set. The background color "shows through" the transparent areas of the GIFs.

Planning the Project and Dividing It into Logical Modules

This project is divided into modules. Instead of putting everything into one document, each specific task is put into its own document, and the result is assembled at the end. The CSS is divided into two separate stylesheets: one containing rules that are compatible with CSS-aware (version 4 and higher) browsers and the other containing rules that are recognized only in browsers that recognize more advanced CSS rules (version 5.0 and higher of Netscape 6.x, Mozilla, and Internet Explorer). The JavaScript is also divided into two: one that contains two document object constructor functions that can be used over and over again for many projects and another that contains the functions specific to this project. The markup itself is XHTML, which follows current W3C recommendations.

1 Create a new text file to contain the XHTML markup. Save this in the root directory of your site as an HTML/XHTML file. Here we've named it tabpage.html.

2 Create a new directory under the root and name it **inc**.

3 In the **inc** directory, create a new text file that will contain the basic style rules that are recognized by most CSS-aware browsers. Save this file with the name common.css.

4 In the same directory, create a new text file that will contain more advanced CSS style rules that are only recognized by the latest graphical browsers. Save this file with the name advanced.css.

5 In the same directory, create a new text file that will contain the base document object constructor JavaScript. Save it with the filename docobj.js.

In the same directory, create a new text file that will contain the tab navigation Javascript. Save it with the filename tabs.js.

CREATING THE XHTML BASE

We've used XHTML instead of HTML for the markup for this project. (If you're unsure about XHTML markup conventions, refer back to Project 4, " Creating a Complex Layout with CSS-P.")

1 Create the **DOCTYPE** declaration for XHTML 1.0 Transitional in your markup document tabpage.html.

2 In the **head** section of the document, tabpage.html, insert the tags necessary to link the external CSS files.

Note that we created two external stylesheets in the previous step: common.css and advanced.css. Because advanced.css contains rules that will only apply to later browsers, including some rules that may cause problems in version 4 browsers, we'll use the **@import** method of linking an external stylesheet. For common.css we will use the **<link>** tag.

Note the order: **@import** comes before the **<link>**. This is because any **@import** rule must precede all other style rules specified for a document.

```
<!DOCTYPE html PUBLIC "-//W3C//DTD XHTML 1.0 Transitional//EN"
        "http://www.w3.org/TR/2000/REC-xhtml1-
20000126/DTD/xhtml1-transitional.dtd">
<html xmlns="http://www.w3.org/1999/xhtml" xml:lang="en"
lang="en">
<head>
     <meta http-equiv="content-type" content="text/html;
     ➥charset=iso-8859-1" />
     <title>Project 13: Tabbed interface demo</title>

    <style type="text/css" title="supplement">
     <!--
     @import "inc/advanced.css";
     -->
     </style>
     <link rel="Stylesheet" rev="Stylesheet" href="inc/common.css"
/>
```

Note: As you saw in Project 4, older browsers, such as Netscape 4.x, do not recognize the **@import** rule. We're using this seeming deficiency to our advantage here, to make sure that any CSS style rules that aren't interpreted properly are isolated from Netscape 4.x. All these rules are put in the advanced.css stylesheet.

For more information about the **@import** rule, see the W3C specifications at **http://www.w3.org/TR/REC-CSS2/cascade.html#at-import**.

3 In the **head** section of the markup document, tabpage.html, insert the **<script></script>** tags to link the external JavaScript files.

```
<script src="inc/docobj.js" type="text/javascript"></script>
    <script src="inc/tabs.js" type="text/javascript"></script>

</head>
```

4 In the **body** section of the document, create the markup for the contents.

Arrange the content logically so that it can be easily read even if the browser in use does not recognize CSS or JavaScript. The text inside the tabs becomes the header for each section.

Each of the three table cells that make up a tab have a **class** or **id** designation: the left side table cells have a **class** attribute value of **tableft**; the right side table cells have a **class** value of **tabright**; and the middle section table cells have the id values **tabmiddle1**, **tabmiddle2**, and so on.

Each **div** has a unique **id**.

```
<body>

<div id="tab1">
<table cellpadding="0" cellspacing="0" border="0">
<tr>
<td width="8" height="24" class="tableft"><img src="images/dot.gif"
➥alt="" width="8" height="24" border="0"></td>
<td id="tabmiddle1">overview</td>
<td class="tabright"><img src="images/dot.gif" alt="" width="7"
➥height="24" border="0"></td>
</tr></table>
</div>


<div id="box1">
<!-- content of the first text box. Omitted for clarity. -->
</div>


<div id="tab2">
<table cellpadding="0" cellspacing="0" border="0">
<tr>
<td width="8" height="24" class="tableft"><img src="images/dot.gif"
alt="" width="8" height="24" border="0"></td>
<td id="tabmiddle2">background</td>
<td class="tabright"><img src="images/dot.gif" alt="" width="7"
➥height="24" border="0"></td>
</tr></table>
</div>
```

```
<div id="box2">
<!-- content of the second text box. Omitted for clarity. -->
</div>

<div id="tab3">
<table cellpadding="0" cellspacing="0" border="0">
<tr>
<td width="8" height="24" class="tableft"><img src="images/dot.gif"
➥alt="" width="8" height="24" border="0"></td>
<td id="tabmiddle3">best recipes</td>
<td class="tabright"><img src="images/dot.gif" alt="" width="7"
➥height="24" border="0"></td>
</tr></table>
</div>


<div id="box3">
<!-- content of the third text box. Omitted for clarity. -->
</div>


<div id="tab4">
<tr>
<td width="8" height="24" class="tableft"><img src="images/dot.gif"
➥alt="" width="8" height="24" border="0"></td>
<td id="tabmiddle4">etcetera</td>
<td class="tabright"><img src="images/dot.gif" alt="" width="7"
➥height="24" border="0"></td>
</tr></table>
</div>
```

CREATING THE MAIN CSS STYLESHEET (`common.css`)

The stylesheet, common.css, holds all the CSS style rules that are recognized by older browsers—as well as the newer browsers.

1 Create the style rules that control the text appearance rules for the basic elements on the page, such as **a** (link) elements, **p** (paragraph) elements, and **h1** (header) elements.

Group the **h1** and **p** selectors together to specify the style rules that they share in common and then specify the unique style rules for each separately. Grouping together selectors to specify any common style rules together is a good way of streamlining your stylesheets—and also makes it easier to change the styles for these elements at once if necessary.

Group the ID selectors, **#tabmiddle1**, **#tabmiddle2**, **#tabmiddle3**, **#tabmiddle4**, and **#tabmiddle5**, together and specify the styles rules for them all at once.

Note: Because the **div** elements that act as text boxes on this page and the tabs are precisely sized in pixels, specify the **font** and **line-height** sizes in pixels also rather than in relative units such as em or percent.

```css
a {
        outline: none;
}

a:link {
        text-decoration: none;
        color: #000000;
}

a:visited {
        text-decoration: none;
        color: #000000;
}

a:hover {
        text-decoration: underline;
}

h1, p {
        background: transparent;
        color: #000000;
        font-family: verdana, helvetica, sans-serif;
        margin-left: 3em;
        margin-right: 3em;
}

h1 {
        font-size: 13px;
        margin-bottom: 0px;
}

p {
        font-size: 11px;
        line-height: 14px;
}

#tabmiddle1, #tabmiddle2, #tabmiddle3, #tabmiddle4, #tabmiddle5 {
        font-family: verdana, helvetica, sans-serif;
        font-size: 16px;
        font-weight: bold;
}
```

CREATING THE SUPPLEMENTAL CSS STYLE RULES (advanced.css)

The stylesheet, advanced.css, contains the style rules that are recognized only by browsers that recognize **@import**. It contains all of the positioning rules for the page, as well as some rules that override those in common.css.

1 Create new **margin: property** style rules for the **p** and **h1** elements.

In the common.css stylesheet, we specified **3em margin** values for these, but on our "real" layout we want **0px** margins. Therefore, we'll override the rules previously specified in common.css by creating new rules that are declared **!important**.

```
h1, p {
        margin: 0px !important;
        }
```

2 Create the style rules for the **.tableft** and **.tabright** class selectors that specify the **background-image** property rules for each.

```
.tableft {
        background-image: url(../images/tableft.gif);
        }

.tabright {
        background-image: url(../images/tabright.gif);
        }
```

3 Create the style rules for the **#tabmiddle1**, **#tabmiddle2**, **#tabmiddle3**, **#tabmiddle4**, and **#tabmiddle5** ID selectors.

These are the middle table cells of each tab table. Note that the **font-size: 12px** rule is specified as **!important**. This overrides the **font-size: 18px** rule set in common.css.

```
#tabmiddle1, #tabmiddle2, #tabmiddle3, #tabmiddle4,
➥#tabmiddle5 {
        background-image: url(../images/middle.gif);
        text-align: center;
        font-size: 12px !important;
        font-weight: bold;
        color: #999999;
        cursor: arrow;
        }
```

4 Create the style rules for the **#tab1**, **#tab2**, **#tab3**, **#tab4**, and **#tab5 div** elements.

These are the **div** elements that hold the tab tables. Note that all the **div** elements are specified as **position:absolute**. The initial **z-index** is set to 0.

```
#tab1, #tab2, #tab3, #tab4, #tab5 {
        position:absolute;
        height: 24px;
        top: 77px;
        z-index: 0;
        background-color: #cccccc;
        color: #999999;
        }

#tab1 {
        left: 60px;
        }

#tab2 {
        left: 140px;
        z-index: 0;
        }

#tab3 {
        left: 235px;
        }

#tab4 {
        left: 335px;
        }

#tab5 {
        left: 410px;
        }
```

5 Create the style rules for the ID selectors **#box1**, **#box2**, **#box3**, **#box4** and **#box5**.

These are the **div** elements that contain the main content. The content boxes all have a one-pixel wide black **border** and are absolutely positioned like the tab boxes. The **height** and **width** are specified in absolute (pixel) values.

```
#box1, #box2, #box3, #box4, #box5 {
        position: absolute;
        top: 100px;
        left: 50px;
        width: 415px;
        height: 320px;
        z-index: 0;
        padding: 10px;
        background-color: #ffffff;
        border: 1px solid #000000;
        }
```

242

CREATING THE BASIC DOCUMENT OBJECT CREATION SCRIPT (docobj.js)

In this section we'll create a document object construction script, which is a slight variation on the one we have used in the previous JavaScript projects. This script is more modular given that the document object constructor is defined as two functions. These functions can then be called by subsequent functions to create the necessary document object strings.

1 Open the file, docobj.**js**.

2 Create the function, **getDocObj()**. This function returns the text string that points out the correct document object of an element, depending on which browser is in use. Two arguments can be passed to the function: **elem**, or the **id** of the element in question, and parent, the **id** of the parent element if the element is nested.

If the browser in use is Netscape 4.x and it recognizes the **document.layers** property, the script then looks to see if the argument, **parent**, is specified. If it is, then the string of **"document."+parent+".document."+elem** is returned. If **parent** is not specified, then the string of **"document." + elem** is returned.

Otherwise, if the browser in use is Internet Explorer 4.x and up and it recognizes the **document.all** method, the string of **"document.all." + elem** is returned.

Otherwise, if the browser in use is W3C-DOM compliant (and is not Internet Explorer), the string of **"document.getElementById('"+elem+"')"** is returned.

```
function getDocObj(elem,parent) {
    if (document.layers) {
        if (parent) {
            return "document."+parent+".document."+elem;
        } else {
            return "document."+elem;
        }

    } else if (document.all) {
        return "document.all."+ elem;
    } else if (document.getElementById) {
        return "document.getElementById('"+elem+"')";
    }
}
```

3 Create the function, **getStyleObj()**. This function returns the string that points to the **style** property of an element, depending on which browser is in use. This function is the same as **getDocObj()** except that it adds the **".style"** string to the base document object string—in the case of Internet Explorer 4.x and up and W3C-DOM-compliant browsers. Note that the string for Netscape 4.x is identical in both functions.

```
function getStyleObj(elem,parent) {
    if (document.layers) {
        if (parent) {
            return "document."+parent+".document."+elem;
        } else {
            return "document."+elem + ".style";
```

continues

243

continued

```
            }
    } else if (document.all) {
            return "document.all."+elem + ".style";
    } else if (document.getElementById) {
            return "document.getElementById('"+elem+"').style";
    }
}
```

THE CROSS-BROWSER DOCUMENT OBJECT CONSTRUCTOR REVISITED

To use the **getDocObj()** and **getStyleObj()** functions in other functions, use the **eval()** method to evaluate the results. This will obtain the actual document object. For example:

eval(getDocObj(elementid));

will return the document object of the element with the **id** specified, while

getDocObj(elementid);

will only return the text string.

The advantage of putting the document object constructors into functions is that it modularizes your code and reduces the typing you have to do when defining other functions. Experienced programmers in any object-oriented language like to create a library of custom reusable objects and functions like this.

Let's take an example from the previous project—the **placeIt()** function.

This is the old code. We've used this method so far so that you can see exactly how a custom document object is assembled:

```
function placeIt(elem,leftPos,topPos) {
    docObj = eval(doc + elem + sty);
    if (n4 || n6) {
            docObj.left = leftPos;
            docObj.top= topPos;
    } else if (ie) {
            docObj.pixelLeft = leftPos;
```

```
            docObj.pixelTop = topPos;
    }
}
```

Now this is the new code that uses the **getStyleObj()** function (the changed code is highlighted):

```
function placeIt(elem,leftPos,topPos) {
    docObj = eval(getStyleObj(elem));
    if (n4 || n6) {
            docObj.left = leftPos;
            docObj.top= topPos;
    } else if (ie) {
            docObj.pixelLeft = leftPos;
            docObj.pixelTop = topPos;
    }
}
```

As your understanding of JavaScript increases, try to build up your own library of reusable objects and functions too.

The document object text string for Netscape 4.x is not really needed for this project because none of the JavaScript functions that follow are intended to work in that browser. The **getDocObj()** function also is not used in the subsequent functions. However, I have presented the complete **getDocObj()** and **getStyleObj()** functions here because they are very useful when you have to create cross-browser scripts.

Creating the Tab Navigation Script (tabs.js)

The file, tabs.js, contains the JavaScript that makes the tab navigation work.

The tab navigation script basically does two things: it changes the stacking order or **z-index** of the elements and changes the background color and textcolor of the tab. This is done by simply changing the style property values of elements.

1 Open the file tabs.js.

2 Define the arrays, **tabArray** and **boxArray**. These arrays hold the style object text strings that are obtained with the **getStyleObj()** function, which will be used in the tab navigation functions.

The **tabArray()** array holds the style property strings for the **tab1** through **tab5 div** elements. The **tabTextArray()** array holds the style property strings for the **tabmiddle1** through **tabmiddle5 td** elements. The **boxArray()** array holds the style property text strings for the **box1** through **box5 div** elements.

It's important to put the array values in the proper order because the functions we'll define later will point to the **index** in each array.

Note: The data in array position 0 for each array has been set to **null**. This is just a matter of convenience—all arrays start at index number 0, but I always tend to forget this because I like to start counting at 1. But remember that the total number of items in the array is 6.

Defining text strings as array values can make writing scripts that require repeating or looping statements much more efficient.

```javascript
/* The tab navigation script. Always use in conjunction with
docobj.js! */

// Set up array of tab element style property strings

var tabArray = new Array(6);
tabArray[0] = null;
tabArray[1] = getStyleObj('tab1');
tabArray[2] = getStyleObj('tab2');
tabArray[3] = getStyleObj('tab3');
tabArray[4] = getStyleObj('tab4');
tabArray[5] = getStyleObj('tab5');

var tabTextArray = new Array(6);
tabTextArray[0] = null;
tabTextArray[1] = getStyleObj('tabmiddle1');
tabTextArray[2] = getStyleObj('tabmiddle2');
tabTextArray[3] = getStyleObj('tabmiddle3');
tabTextArray[4] = getStyleObj('tabmiddle4');
tabTextArray[5] = getStyleObj('tabmiddle5');

// Set up array of text box element style property strings
var boxArray = new Array(6);
boxArray[0] = null;
boxArray[1] = getStyleObj('box1');
boxArray[2] = getStyleObj('box2');
boxArray[3] = getStyleObj('box3');
boxArray[4] = getStyleObj('box4');
boxArray[5] = getStyleObj('box5');
```

3 Define some global variables that are used in the functions.

The variable, **active**, is used as a holder to see which element is the one on top.

The other variables hold color values and are used to color the tabs and tab text.

4 Start to define the function, **tabcolor()**. This function sets the appearance of the tab.

Three arguments are passed to the function: **tabnum**, or the number of the tab; **color1**, which is the background color of the tab; and **color2**, which is the text color of the tab.

5 Continue to define function, **tabcolor()**. Declare the value of the local variable tab to be the evaluated result of the value in the **tabArray[tabnum]** array element. For example, if the value of **tabnum** is 3, the value of **tabArray[tabnum]** is the result returned by **getStyleObj('tab3')**.

Declare the value of the local variable, tabtext, to be the evaluated result of the value in the **tabTextArray[textnum]** array element. If the value of tabnum is 3, the value of **tabTextArray[tabnum]** is the result returned by **getStyleObj('tabmiddle3')**.

6 Continue to define the function, **tabcolor()**, by setting the **backgroundColor** property of **tab** to the value of **color1** and the **color** property of **tabtext** to the value of **color2**.

7 Finally, define the code that changes the appearance of the cursor. Because the **tabcolor()** function will be used with mouse events associated with a **td** element, the cursor will not change its appearance by default—unlike mouse events that occur when associated with an **a** link element. Therefore, we'll

```
var active = null;
var activebgcolor = "#993399";
var activetextcolor = "#000000";

var inactivebgcolor = "#cccccc";
var inactivetextcolor = "#999999";

var overbgcolor = "#cc99cc";
var overtextcolor = "#ffcc99";
```

```
function tabcolor(tabnum,color1,color2) {
    var tab = eval(tabArray[tabnum]);
    var tabtext = eval(tabTextArray[tabnum]);
    tab.backgroundColor = color1;
    tabtext.color = color2;
```

continues

change the cursor style to the "pointing hand." Because the syntax is different for Internet Explorer and Netscape 6/Mozilla, we have a branching statement: the **cursor** style is set to **"hand"** in IE and **"pointer"** in Netscape 6.

8 Define the function, **choosebox()**.

This is the core function that sets the z-index of the content **div**s and tabs. It also calls the **tabcolor()** function.

One argument passed to it is **tabnum**, which contains the appropriate array index number for the three arrays we defined previously.

First, check to see if the browser in use supports **document.all** or **document.getElementById**. If not, the function will not continue.

Next, check to see if the value of the variable **active** is **null**. If it is not, then that means that one of the layers is "active"—or was the last selected one. Therefore, the 'active' elements are reset to their 'inactive' states.

Assign the local variables **activetablayer**, **activetabtext**, and **activeboxlayer** the evaluated values of the **tabArray[active]**, **tabTextArray [active]**, and **boxArray[active]** array elements, respectively. Then set the **zIndex** property value of **activetablayer** and **activeboxlayer** to **0** and reset the **backgroundColor** and **color** values of the **tabTextArray[active]** element by calling the **tabcolor()** function, passing **active**, **inactivebgcolor**, and **inactivetextcolor** as the arguments.

continued

```
if (document.all) {
        tabtext.cursor = 'hand';
} else {
        tabtext.cursor = 'pointer';
}
}
```

CONVERTING HYPHENATED CSS STYLE PROPERTIES TO JAVASCRIPT

Most CSS style properties can be used as-is in JavaScript, with the exception of style properties with hyphens such as **background-color**, **z-index**, and **font-family**. We can't use hyphens for variable, function, custom defined property, or method names because the hyphen can be interpreted as a **minus** sign.

Fortunately, the rule for "converting" such CSS property names to JavaScript is simple: Take away the hyphen and capitalize the first letter of the word after the hyphen. So **background-color** becomes **backgroundColor**, **z-index** becomes **zIndex**, and so on. (Remember that while CSS is case-insensitive, JavaScript is case sensitive!)

9 Continue to define the function, **choosebox()**. This section of the function sets the newly selected elements to the 'active' state.

Assign the local variables, **tablayer**, **tabtext**, and **boxlayer**, the evaluated values of the **tabArray[num]**, **tabTextArray[num]**, and **boxArray[num]** array elements, respectively. Then set the **zIndex** property value of **tablayer** and **boxlayer** to 10 and reset the **backgroundColor** and **color** values of the **tabTextArray[tabnum]** element by calling the **tabcolor()** function, passing **tabnum**, **activebgcolor**, and **activetextcolor** as the arguments.

Finally, set the new value of **active** as **tabnum**. This makes the currently selected elements the **active** elements.

```
// the central tab navigation function

function choosebox(tabnum) {
    if (active) {
        var activetablayer = eval(tabArray[active]);
        var activetabtext = eval(tabTextArray[active]);
        var activeboxlayer = eval(boxArray[active]);
        activetablayer.zIndex = 0;
        activeboxlayer.zIndex = 0;
        tabcolor(active,inactivebgcolor, inactivetextcolor);
    }

    tablayer = eval(tabArray[num]);
    tabtext = eval(tabTextArray[num]);
    boxlayer = eval(boxArray[num]);
    tablayer.zIndex = 11;
    boxlayer.zIndex = 10;
    tabcolor(tabnum,activebgcolor, activetextcolor);
    active = tabnum;

}
```

10 Define the function, **tabover()**.

The **tabover()** function simply calls the **tabcolor()** function if the value of **tabnum** does not equal the value of active (in other words, if the chosen element is not the one currently on top or "active"). The values of the variables, **overbgcolor** and **overtextcolor**, are passed to **tabcolor()** as arguments. The **tabover()** function is invoked with the **mouseover** event.

```
function tabover(tabnum) {
    if (tabnum != active) {
        tabcolor(tabnum,overbgcolor,overtextcolor);
    }
}
```

11 Define the function **tabout()**.

The **tabout()** is identical to the **tabover()** function, except that it passes the values of the variables, **inactivebgcolor** and **inactivetextcolor**, as arguments. This function is called with the **mouseout** event.

```
function tabout(tabnum) {
    if (tabnum != active) {
        tabcolor(tabnum,inactivebgcolor,inactivetextcolor);
    }
}
```

Modifying the XHTML Markup to Call the Functions

To activate the JavaScript, we will adjust the XHTML markup to call the various functions we've defined.

1 Insert an **onload** event call in the **<body>** tag that calls the **choosebox()** function, with **1** passed as the argument.

```
<body onload="choosebox(1)">
```

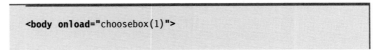

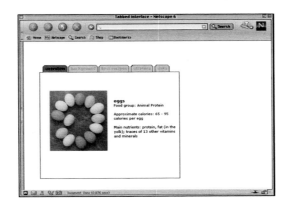

When the page first loads, the first tab (tab1) is set to "active," and the first content box (box1) is on top.

2 Insert the **onmouseover**, **onmouseout**, and **onclick** event calls from the **div** elements **tab1**, **tab2**, **tab3**, **tab4**, and **tab5**. The **tabover()** function is called **onmouseover**; the **tabout()** function is called **onmouseout**; and the **choosebox()** function is called **onclick**. The appropriate value for the tabnum argument is passed to the functions: for **tab1** it's **1**, for **tab2** it's **2**, and so on. The added event calls are highlighted in the code.

```
<div id="tab1" onmouseover="tabover(1)"
onmouseout="tabout(1)"
onclick="choosebox(1)">
<table summary="" cellpadding="0"
➥cellspacing="0" border="0">
<tr>
<td width="8" height="24" class="tableft">
➥<img src="images/dot.gif" alt=""
➥width="8" height="24" border="0" /></td>
<td id="tabmiddle1">overview</td>
<td class="tabright"><img
➥src="images/dot.gif" alt="" width="7"
➥height="24" border="0" /></td>
</tr>
</table>
```

```
</div>

<div id="tab2" onmouseover="tabover(2)"
onmouseout="tabout(2)"
onclick="choosebox(2)">
<table summary="" cellpadding="0"
➥cellspacing="0" border="0">
<tr>
<td width="8" height="24" class="tableft">
➥<img src="images/dot.gif" alt=""
➥width="8" height="24" border="0" /></td>
<td id="tabmiddle1">overview</td>
<td class="tabright"><img
➥src="images/dot.gif" alt="" width="7"
➥height="24" border="0" /></td>
</tr>
```

continues

continued

```
</table>

</div>

<div id="tab3" onmouseover="tabover(3)"
➥onmouseout="tabout(3)" onclick="choosebox(3)">
<table summary="" cellpadding="0" cellspacing="0"
➥border="0">
<tr>
<td width="8" height="24" class="tableft"><img
➥src="images/dot.gif" alt="" width="8" height="24"
➥border="0" /></td>
<td id="tabmiddle1">overview</td>
<td class="tabright"><img src="images/dot.gif" alt=""
➥width="7" height="24" border="0" /></td>
</tr>
</table>

</div>

<div id="tab1" onmouseover="tabover(1)"
➥onmouseout="tabout(1)" onclick="choosebox(1)">
<table summary="" cellpadding="0" cellspacing="0"
➥border="0">
<tr>
```

```
<td width="8" height="24" class="tableft">
<img src="images/dot.gif" alt="" width="8" height="24"
➥border="0" /></td>
<td id="tabmiddle1">overview</td>
<td class="tabright"><img src="images/dot.gif" alt=""
➥width="7" height="24" border="0" /></td>
</tr>
</table>

</div>

<div id="tab5" onmouseover="tabover(5)"
➥onmouseout="tabout(5)" onclick="choosebox(5)">
<table summary="" cellpadding="0" cellspacing="0"
➥border="0">
<tr>
<td width="8" height="24" class="tableft"><img
➥src="images/dot.gif" alt="" width="8" height="24"
➥border="0" /></td>
<td id="tabmiddle1">overview</td>
<td class="tabright"><img src="images/dot.gif" alt=""
➥width="7" height="24" border="0" /></td>
</tr>
</table>
</div>
```

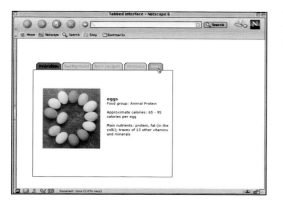

The user mouses over another tab, and the text and background colors change.

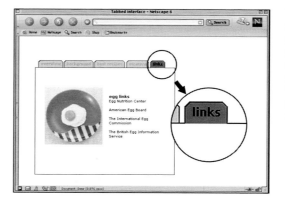

The user clicks the tab, and the new content box appears. Because the whole page is already loaded, the change occurs right away. The tab's appearance changes to the "active" state. Note how the tab is stacked on top of the content box.

How It Works: Gracefully Degrading Pages with CSS

In this project, we have dealt with the issue of creating a page that degrades gracefully in older browsers in two ways. The first is with a planned use of the varying support for CSS rules.

To review, our main goal for this project was to create a page that is readable to all and reasonably attractive to users of browsers with partial CSS support—while still avoiding the use of styling tags such as **<font>** within the markup itself.

The CSS for this page has been separated into two documents. The first one contains the rules that will be recognized by Netscape 4.x. This is so that the page looks reasonably attractive in that browser. Generally speaking, these are the style rules for font appearance as well as background and foreground colors. Some basic margin property values are also included.

The second stylesheet, advanced.css, contains the rules that are not well supported by Netscape 4.x or any other browser with only rudimentary support for CSS. Because advanced.css is associated with the base XHTML document using the **@import** property, the whole stylesheet will be ignored by those browsers that don't support **@import**. Some of the rules in advanced.css override the ones in common.css by declaring them to be **!important**. It's always important to remember to arrange the markup content in a way that is logical for people who are using non-CSS enabled browsers.

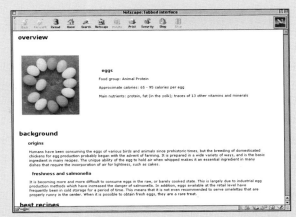

How the page looks in Netscape 4.x, which only recognizes the style rules included in common.css. Note how the "header" text for each section is actually the text contained in the tab tables. Here this text is set to a large size (font-size: 18px); this is overridden in the advanced.css stylesheet with !important (font-size: 12px !important).

How It Works: Gracefully Degrading Pages and JavaScript

In the previous projects, most of the functions we created had a number of **if...else** statements that specified different code for different browsers. In this project however, there are only two browser-specific **if...else** statements in the whole tabs.js script. The first one, in the **tabcolor()** function, deals with the fact that the syntax for cursor styles for Internet Explorer and Netscape 6 differ. The second one, at the beginning of the **choosebox()** function, specifies that the function will only execute if the browser in use recognizes **document.all** or **document.getElementById**.

The **tabover()** and **tabout()** functions, on the other hand, don't have any **if...else** statements that "sniff" the browser out. Instead, the functions are called from within **div** elements rather than from **a** (link) elements. Modern browsers allow for JavaScript events to be called from any element, while it's only possible to call JavaScript events from a limited set of elements in older browsers. Netscape 4.x, for example, will simply ignore the **onmouseover**, **onmouseout**, and **onclick** event calls in the **div** elements.

When creating a "gracefully degrading" site, the visitor should never get the impression that they are somehow getting a lesser version. Ideally, he should never know what he is missing—unless, of course, he revisits the site with another browser!

A COLLAPSING/EXPANDING MENU AND ENHANCED TABLE

"We are cups, constantly and quietly

being filled. The trick is, knowing

how to tip ourselves over and let the

beautiful stuff out."

—RAY BRADBURY

Changing Styles with the W3C DOM

This project shows you how to manipulate

styles to create a collapsing/expanding menu

and a user-friendly tabular display using W3C

standards-compliant XHTML markup, CSS, the

DOM, and JavaScript.

A Collapsing/Expanding Menu and Enhanced Table

GETTING STARTED

The example site in this project is for a fictional toy company. It's an e-commerce site with a large number of items for sale.

A collapsing/expanding menu helps to organize the items without overwhelming the user with a long list of choices. Previously, creating such a menu for browser use involved a lot of complicated scripting or even a Java applet. Using the latest W3C-standards-compliant methods, this can be accomplished with just a few lines of code. Tables that display a lot of information also can be manipulated with a few lines of script to make them more user-friendly.

The code presented in this project will only display as intended in browsers that support the latest W3C standards for markup, CSS, and the DOM, as well as JavaScript. However, the contents of the page are readable in older browsers.

The main points you will learn in this project:

- Creating a page using W3C standard methods.
- Extracting all elements on the page with a given tag name and class name.
- Changing the style values for a given property for elements with the same tag name and class name.

WHICH STANDARDS, WHICH BROWSERS?

Given that the World Wide Web Consortium sets a number of recommended specifications, it can be confusing to figure out what a "standards-compliant" browser is supposed to be capable of. For this project and the next, we'll concentrate on the browsers that at least support most specifications set by the W3C for the following:

- XHTML 1.0 Transitional for the markup, replacing HTML 4.01. The browser also should recognize the **DOCTYPE** declaration.

- CSS Level 1 and most of CSS Level 2.

- DOM Level 1.

In addition, the browser also should support a version of JavaScript (or JScript, in Microsoft terms) that conforms in large part to the latest standard version of ECMAScript, ECMA-262.

As of this writing, Internet Explorer 5.5 and above on Windows, Internet Explorer 5.x on the Mac, and Netscape 6.x meet these criteria, as does the latest "stable" release version (version 0.99 as of this writing) of Mozilla. Support for various features is not uniform—Internet Explorer on the Mac has better support for CSS than IE 5.5 or 6.0 on Windows, though IE 6.0 on Windows has a bit better DOM Level 2 support, for example. Other browsers tend to support some features well but not others—for example, Opera has excellent XHTML and CSS support, but its JavaScript/ECMAScript and DOM support lags a bit behind.

Because the browser landscape is constantly changing, visit the book web site for the latest information. Above all, always test your pages, especially in the browsers that your site visitors are likely to be using.

CREATING THE MARKUP AND CSS FOR THE COLLAPSING/EXPANDING MENU

The collapsing/expanding menu is modular—that is, it can be included on any page as a unit. Let's start by creating the menu on its own.

1 Set up the XHTML markup.

Each section of the menu has a **div** element with the class, **toplevel**, for the top line of the section and a **div** element with the class, **sublevel**. In addition, each submenu **div** element has an **id** value of **sub1**, **sub2**, and so on.

```
<!-- the menu -->

<!-- menu section 1 -->

<div class="toplevel">
<img src="images/plus.gif" class="square" alt="" width="15"
height="16" id="sq1" />
<span><a href="#">Vehicles</a></span>
</div>
```

The XHTML markup for the menu.

continues

The **toplevel div** elements contain an **img** element with a small plus sign GIF, and the **sublevel** menus start with an **img** element with a small "branch" GIF. Each **img** element has a **class** value of **square**, and each top-level **img** element also has an **id** value of **sq1**, **sq2**, and so on.

continued

```
<div class="sublevel" id="sub1">
<img src="images/branch2.gif" class="square" alt="" width="8" height="16" />
<a class="submenu" href="#">Pull cart</a>
<br />
<img src="images/branch2.gif" class="square" alt="" width="8" height="16" />
<a class="submenu" href="#">Tricycle</a>
<br />
<img src="images/branch2.gif" class="square" alt="" width="8" height="16" />
<a class="submenu" href="#">Bicycle</a>
<br />
<img src="images/branch1.gif" class="square" alt="" width="8" height="16" />
<a class="submenu" href="#">Scooter</a>
</div>


<!-- menu section 2 -->

<div class="toplevel">
<img src="images/plus.gif" class="square" alt="" width="15" height="16" id="sq2" />
<span><a href="#">Favorite Friends</a></span>
</div>


<div class="sublevel" id="sub2">
<img src="images/branch2.gif" class="square" alt="" width="8" height="16" />
<a class="submenu" href="#">Rag Doll</a>
<br />
<img src="images/branch2.gif" class="square" alt="" width="8" height="16" />
<a class="submenu" href="#">Teddy Bear</a>
<br />
<img src="images/branch1.gif" class="square" alt="" width="8" height="16" />
<a class="submenu" href="#">Raggety Ann and Andy</a>
</div>


<!-- menu section 3 -->

<div class="toplevel">
<img src="images/plus.gif" class="square" alt="" width="15" height="16" id="sq3" />
<span><a href="#">Fun and Games</a></span>
</div>


<div class="sublevel" id="sub3">
<img src="images/branch2.gif" class="square" alt="" width="8" height="16" />
<a class="submenu" href="#">Hula Hoop</a>
<br />
<img src="images/branch2.gif" class="square" alt="" width="8" height="16" />
<a class="submenu" href="#">Croquet Set</a>
```

continues

Contain each **toplevel** menu text within
<span></span> tags and **<a href=...></a>** tags.

Contain each **sublevel** menu text line within **<a href=..></a>** tags. Give the **a** elements a class value of **submenu**.

continued

```
<br />
<img src="images/branch2.gif" class="square" alt="" width="8" height="16" />
<a class="submenu" href="#">Balloons and Balloons</a>
<br />
<img src="images/branch1.gif" class="square" alt="" width="8" height="16" />
<a class="submenu" href="#">Sandcastle Building Set</a>
</div>


<!-- menu section 4 -->

<div class="toplevel">
<img src="images/plus.gif" class="square" alt="" width="15" height="16" id="sq4" />
<span><a href="#">Learning Toys</a></span>
</div>

<div class="sublevel" id="sub4">
<img src="images/branch2.gif" class="square" alt="" width="8" height="16" />
<a class="submenu" href="#">Classic Wood Blocks</a>
<br />
<img src="images/branch2.gif" class="square" alt="" width="8" height="16">
<a class="submenu" href="#">Learning Numbers</a>
<br />
<img src="images/branch2.gif" class="square" alt="" width="8" height="16" />
<a class="submenu" href="#">Logic Puzzle</a>
</div>
```

2   Set up the CSS for the menu.

Specify the appearance of each element with the appropriate styles. Note that the two class selectors have a **display** attribute value of **block**. We will be addressing the **display** style attribute later with JavaScript.

The menu displayed before (left) and after (right) CSS styles are applied.

257

Note: The **vertical-align** style attribute value of **middle** (applied to the **square** class of the element, **img**) makes the graphic align to the centerline of the text.

The color property values are stated in three characters instead of six. You may use six characters instead—both methods comply with CSS standards.

```css
body {
        font-family: verdana,
sans-serif;
        font-size: 11px;
        }

img.square {
        vertical-align: middle;
        }

.toplevel {
        display: block;
        font-weight: normal;
        margin-bottom: 0;
        }

.sublevel {
        display: block;
        font-weight: normal;
        margin-left: 20px;
        margin-top: 0;
        line-height: 14px;
        }


a:visited {
        text-decoration: none;
        color: #f03;
        font-weight: bold;
```

```css
        }

a:link {
        text-decoration: none;
        color: #f03;
        font-weight: bold;
        }

a:hover {
        color: #600;
        }

a.submenu:visited {
        color: #000;
        text-decoration: none;
        font-weight: normal;
        }

a.submenu:link {
        color: #000;
        text-decoration: none;
        font-weight: normal;
        }

a.submenu:hover {
        color: #f03;
        }
```

CREATING THE XHTML AND CSS FOR THE TABLE

The table displays a list of products that are for sale on this site.

1   Create the XHTML markup for the **form** buttons
    that will trigger the JavaScript actions. Give each
    input button a class value of **button**.

```html
<form action="">
<input class="button" type="button" value="show pictures" />
<input class="button" type="button" value="hide pictures" />

<input class="button" type="button" value="show only available
➥items" />
<br />
```

continues

continued

```
<input class="button" type="button" value="show all items" /><input class="button"
➥type="button" value="highlight items on sale" />
<input class="button" type="button" value="undo highlight" />
</form>
```

Note: Because this form is not submitted to a server-side script, give it an empty **action** value. You also may use **button** elements instead.

2 Create the XHTML for the table. Give the **table** an **id** value of **pricelist**.

The table has a **thead** (table header) that indicates the column headers: Item No., Item Name, Picture, Price, Sale Price, and Availability. Give the Picture **td** element a class value of **pic**.

The rest of the table is contained in a **tbody** (the table body). Give each Picture column **td** a **class** value of **pic**. Give all table rows (**tr** elements), where the item in the row is on sale, a **class** value of **onsale**. Give all table rows (**tr** elements), where the item is not in stock, a **class** value of **na** (for not available).

Note: While it's not necessary to use the **thead** and **tbody** elements for display purposes, it's structurally correct to use these in a true tabular display. It also allows the designer to apply style rules to just the header—we'll see an example in the next step.

The XHTML markup for the table.

```
<table id="pricelist" summary="Product List" cellspacing="2"
cellpadding="0">
<thead>
  <tr>
    <td>Item No.</td>
    <td>Item Name</td>
    <td class="pic">Picture</td>
    <td>Price</td>
    <td>Sale Price</td>
    <td>Availability</td>
  </tr>

</thead>

<tbody>
  <tr class="onsale">
    <td>V12532</td>
    <td>Pull Cart</td>
    <td class="pic"><img src="images/photos/cart-sm.jpg"
    ➥alt="pull cart" width="100" height="98" /></td>
    <td>$250.00</td>
    <td class="sale">$225.00</td>
    <td>Available</td>
  </tr>
  <tr>
    <td>V435325</td>
    <td>Tricycle</td>
    <td class="pic"><img src="images/photos/tricycle-sm.jpg"
    ➥alt="tricycle" width="100" height="94" /></td>
    <td>$350.00</td>
    <td>N/A</td>
    <td>Available</td>
  </tr>
  <tr class="na">
    <td>V450323</td>
    <td>Rocket Flyer Bicycle</td>
```

continues

259

```
<td class="pic"><img src="images/photos/bicycle-sm.jpg"
➥alt="Rocket Flyer Bicycle" width="100"
➥height="99" /></td>
<td>$525.00</td>
<td>N/A</td>
<td>On Order</td>
</tr>


<tr class="onsale">
<td>V102456</td>
<td>Scooter</td>
<td class="pic"><img src="images/photos/scooter-sm.jpg"
➥alt=" scooter" width="100" height="101" /></td>
<td>$400.00</td>
<td class="sale">$350.00</td>
<td>Available</td>
</tr>


<tr class="onsale">
<td>V12532</td>
<td>Croquet Set</td>
<td class="pic"><img src="images/photos/croquet-sm.jpg"
➥alt="croquet set" width="100" height="95" /></td>
<td>$150.00</td>
<td class="sale">$125.00</td>
<td>Available</td>
```

```
</tr>


<tr>
<td>V12532</td>
<td>Sandcastle Set</td>
<td class="pic"><img src="images/photos/sandset-sm.jpg"
➥alt="sandcastle set" width="100" height="91" /></td>
<td>$$25.00</td>
<td class="sale">N/A</td>
<td>Available</td>
</tr>


<tr class="na">
<td>V12532</td>
<td>Tool Set</td>
<td class="pic"><img src="images/photos/toolset-sm.jpg"
➥alt="toolset" width="100" height="97" /></td>
<td>$20.00</td>
<td class="sale">N/A</td>
<td>Out of Stock</td>
</tr>


</tbody>

</table>
```

3 Create the CSS rules for the table and the form input buttons.

The first rule specifies the styles that all **td** elements within the **pricelist** table should have.

The CSS for the table section of the page.

```
#pricelist td {
        border: 1px solid #000;
        padding: 2px;
        font-family: verdana, sans-serif;
        font-size: 11px;
        }

thead td {
        background-color: #ccc;
        font-weight: bold;
        }

input.button {
        font: bold 11px verdana, sans-serif;
        background-color: #39f;
```

continues

The second rule specifies the styles that all **td** elements within a **thead** element should have.

The final rule specifies the style for the **input** elements with the class **button**.

continued

```
color: #000;
margin-top: 2px;
margin-right: 5px;
margin-bottom: 5px;
}
```

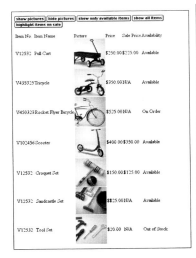 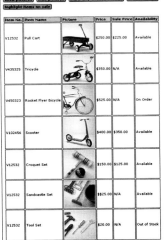

The table displayed before (left) and after (right) applying CSS styles.

CREATE THE COLLAPSING/EXPANDING JAVASCRIPT

In this step, we'll create the scripts that will be used for manipulating the menu and the table.

1 Open a new blank text document and name it display.js.

2 Define some global variables that will be used for browser detection. Some browser detection is necessary because of the way Internet Explorer 5.x/Mac, Internet Explorer 5.0 and 6.0/Windows, Netscape 6.x, and Mozilla interpret some style property values, as we'll see later.

```
/* just a bit of browser sniffing is necessary. */

var ie = (document.all) ? true:false;
var isWin = (navigator.platform.indexOf("Win") != -1) ?
true:false;
```

continues

continues

The first line detects for the **document.all** object and if true, sets the value of the variable **ie** to **true**. The second line detects for the string, **Win**, in the **navigator.platform** property. If it exists, it sets the value of the variable **isWin** to **true**.

The third line sets the value of the variable, **ieWin**, to **true** if both **ie** and **isWin** are true.

The fourth line checks for the string, **"MSIE 5.0"**, in the **navigator.appVersion** property. If it exists and the value of **isWin** is **true**, then it sets the value of the variable, **isWin50**, to **true**.

continued

```
var ieWin = (ie && isWin) ? true:false;

var ieWin50 = (isWin && (navigator.appVersion.indexOf('MSIE 5.0')
➡!= -1)) ? true:false;
```

Note: We have used the **?** conditional operator here instead of an **if...else** statement. The syntax for the conditional operator is as follows:

```
condition (true or false) ? expression1 : expression2;
```

If the condition evaluates to **true**, then the value of **expression1** is returned; if the condition evaluates to **false**, then the value of **expression2** is returned.

Because the two expressions here are **true** or **false**, strictly speaking, it's not necessary to state this as a conditional statement. If the condition is true, then the returned value should be **true**. I've shown it this way so that it's clear that we want a **true** or **false** value to be assigned to each variable.

OBTAINING THE CURRENT STYLE

As we've noted, when you specify a style property rule in a stylesheet, obtaining this value in browsers that follow the W3C DOM rules is a bit tricky. If you want to avoid the workaround we've used in the code, specifying any styles inline (in an element tag in the markup) will allow you to get the current style value.

Alternatively, you may use a method that is available in the W3C DOM Level 2 specifications, **getComputedStyle()**. For example, here we might use:

```
var submenuelem = document.getElementById(submenu);
var submenudisplay =
document.defaultView.getComputedStyle(submenuelem,"").get
➡PropertyValue("display");
```

Note that this method only works in browsers that support it—Netscape 6.x, Mozilla, and Internet Explorer 6.x on Windows. I've chosen not to use this method in the function because it just means that more browser-detection and branching would be necessary.

To obtain the current style in Internet Explorer 5.x and up, you can use **currentStyle** instead of **style**.

However, once the style is set programmatically with a script, the **style** attribute can be accessed in both Internet Explorer 5 and up and Netscape 6.x:

```
<div style="display:none;">..</div>
```

3 Define the **function** called **togglemenu()**.

The **togglemenu()** function opens or closes the submenus. This function is passed a single argument, **num**. This indicates the menu section number.

The first part sets two local variables. The variable, **sub**, is given a value of the string, **sub**, plus the value of the argument, **num**, and the variable, **square**, is given the value of the string, **sq**, plus the value of the argument, **num**. For example, if **num** is **1**, then **sub** is **sub1** (pointing to the element with the **id sub1**), and **square** is **sq1** (pointing the element with the **id sq1**).

The next part is a workaround for the fact that in browsers that strictly follow the W3C DOM specifications such as Netscape 6.x, when a style attribute value is specified in a stylesheet (as opposed to specifying it inline), the style value is not returned. To work around this, if the value of the style attribute, **display**, is **null** or **empty**, the value is set to **none**.

The final part of the function is the display toggle. If the submenu element's **display** style value is set to **none**, it's reset to **display**, and the **src** of the **square img** (the plus/minus GIF) is set to **"minus.gif"**. If the submenu element's display style value is set to **display**, it's reset to **none**, and the **square img src** is set to **"plus.gif"**.

4 Define the function, **getElementsByClassName()**.

As we've seen previously, in the latest W3C DOM-compliant browsers it's possible to access all the elements on the page by **id** (**getElementById**) or by the name of the element tag (**getElementsByTagName**). However, for some reason it's not possible to access elements by **class** name. Therefore, we'll create a function that does exactly that and call it **getElementsByClassName**.

The function, **togglemenu()**.

```
function togglemenu(num) {

        /* set local variables. */
        var submenu = "sub"+num;
        var square = "sq"+num;

        /* Set the display style to "none" if the value is
        ➥null */
        if (document.getElementById(submenu).style.display ==
        ➥null) {
                document.getElementById(submenu).style.display =
                ➥"none";
        }

        /* The toggle section.
        If the value of the submenu element's display is
        ➥"none", then it's set to "block"; if the value is
        ➥"block", it's set to "none".
        The plus/minus GIF is also reset accordingly.
        */
        if (document.getElementById(submenu).style.display ==
        ➥"none") {
                document.getElementById(submenu).style.display =
                ➥"block";
                document.getElementById(square).src =
                ➥"images/minus.gif";
        } else {
                document.getElementById(submenu).style.display =
                ➥"none";
                document.getElementById(square).src =
                ➥"images/plus.gif";
        }
}
```

The function, **getElementsByClassName()**, is useful for getting all elements with a given class name.

```
/* Get all the elements with a given class name */

function getElementsByClassName(tagname, classname) {

        /* only execute in 5+ browsers. If the browser doesn't
        ➥recognize document.getElementById, then false is
        ➥returned. */
        if (!document.getElementById){return false;}
```

continues

263

continued

Tip: Remember that in JavaScript, all functions, variables, and so on are case-sensitive! This applies particularly to this function.

The function is passed two arguments—**tagname** and **classname**.

The first line of the function stops the function from executing if the browser does not recognize the **document.getElementById** object by returning a value of **false**. This will stop the function from executing in all non-W3C DOM-compliant browsers, such as version 4 browsers.

Next, we'll get all the elements with the tag name, **tagname**, into the array object, **TagElements**. For example, if **tagname** is **td**, it will return an array of all the **td** elements on the page.

The next section defines a new array object called **elementsByClassName**. We use a **for** loop to step through all of the elements in the array, **TagElements**, looking for any with the class name of **classname**. For example, if the tag name is **td** and the class name is **pic**, then it will return an array of all the **td** elements on the page with the class name of **pic**.

5 Define the function, **changeclassstyle()**.

This function changes the value of a specified style property for all elements on a page with a given tag name and class name.

Four arguments are passed to this function: the **tag name**, **class name**, the **style property**, and the **new style** value.

The variable, **tochange**, is assigned the returned value of the function, **getElementsByClassName()**, passing it the values of **tagname** and **classname** as arguments— to get the array of all elements on the page with the

```
/* get all elements with the tag name tagname. */

var TagElements = document.getElementsByTagName(tagname);

/* define an array which will hold the elements with the class name classname. */
var elementsByClassName = new Array();

/* Look at all the elements in TagElements, and find the ones with the class name
classname. */

for (var i=0; i<TagElements.length; i++) {
    if (TagElements[i].className == classname) {
        elementsByClassName[elementsByClassName.length] = TagElements[i];
    }
}
    return elementsByClassName;
}
```

```
/* change the value of a style property for all elements on the
page with a given tag name and class name. */

function changestyle(tagname,classname,styleproperty,newstyle) {
    var tochange = getElementsByClassName
    ➥(tagname,classname);
    for (k=0; k < tochange.length; k++) {
        var currentelemstyle = eval("tochange[k].style." +
        ➥styleproperty);
        currentelemstyle = newstyle;
    }
}
```

The function,
changeclassstyle()

tag name, **tagname**, and the class name, **classname**.
For example, if **tagname** is **tr** and **classname** is
onsale, an array of all the **tr** elements with the
class name **onsale** will be returned.

The next section steps through the **tochange** array
with a **for** loop. For each element in the array, the
local variable, **currentelemstyle**, is assigned the evaluated result of the string, **tochange[k].style.**
styleproperty, which will return the style property
for that element's document object. This is assigned
the style property value of the argument, **newstyle**.

For example, if **tagname** is **td**, **classname** is **onsale**,
styleproperty is **backgroundColor**, and **newstyle** is
yellow, the script will change the background color
of all **td** elements with the **class onsale** to yellow.

6   Define the function, **changecursor()**. This function
is used to change the cursor style when the user
mouses over the plus/minus images used in the
menu.

One argument, **num**, which indicates the number of
the **img** element, is passed to the function. The local
variable square is assigned the string value of **"sq" +**
num. This is the **id** value of the **img** element that this
function will apply to.

The function has two **if...else** branching statements that assign a different value to the variable,
cursorstyle, for Internet Explorer 5.0/Windows
versus other target browsers. This is necessary
because the "pointed hand" cursor style is defined as
"pointer" in the W3C CSS specifications, but IE 5.0
Windows defines it as **"hand"**.

Finally, the cursor style of the element indicated is
changed to the value of **cursorstyle**.

Tip: Whenever there is a CSS property with a hyphen in it, such as
background-color, to address this property in JavaScript, eliminate
the hyphen and capitalize the first letter of the second word, as in
backgroundColor. This is because a hyphen is a minus operator in
JavaScript.

```
/* change the cursor style */
function changecursor(num) {
        var square = "sq" + num;
        if (ieWin50) {
                var cursorstyle = 'hand';
        } else {
                var cursorstyle = 'pointer';
        }
        document.getElementById(square).style.cursor =
        ➥cursorstyle;
}
```

The function,
changecursor().

7 Define the function, **init()**.

This function initializes the page and hides the sub-menus in the collapsing menu and the column with product photos in the table. The function will only execute if the browser in use recognizes the **document.getElementById** method.

The function, **changeclassstyle**, is called twice, first by passing the arguments **div** (**tagname**), **sublevel** (**classname**), **display** (**styleproperty**), and **none** (**newstyle**). This hides all the submenus. Then the same function is called passing the arguments **td** (**tagname**), **pic** (**classname**), **display** (**styleproperty**), and **none** (**newstyle**).

The function, **init()**.

```
function init() {
        if (document.getElementById) {
                changeclassstyle('div','sublevel',
                ➥'display','none');
                changeclassstyle('td','pic',
                ➥'display','none');
        }
}
```

ADJUSTING THE XHTML FOR THE MENU

To activate the collapsing/expanding menu script, we'll adjust the XHTML markup to call the appropriate functions.

1 Link to the **display.js** external JavaScript file by putting in the appropriate **<script>** tag in the **<head>** section.

```
<script src="inc/display.js" language="Javascript"
➥type="text/javascript"></script>
```

2 Insert an **onload** event call in the **body** tag that calls the function, **init()**.

```
<body onload="init()">
```

3 Insert an **onclick** event call in each plus/minus GIF **img** tag that calls the function, **togglemenu**, passing the appropriate menu section number as an argument.

Insert an **onmouseover** event call in each plus/minus GIF **img** tag that calls the function, **changecursor()**. The argument passed to the function corresponds to the **id** number of the applicable **img** element.

```
<img src="images/plus.gif" class="square" alt="" width="15"
height="16" id="sq1" onclick="togglemenu(1)"
onmouseover="changecursor(1)">
```

The img tag for the plus/minus GIF for menu section 1.

Note: When a scripting event calls in a tag other than **<a>**, remember that the default cursor does not change—so the user may be confused. Therefore, it's a good idea to change the cursor style to a pointer to indicate that the object can be clicked.

For more about cursor style properties, see **http://www.w3.org/TR/REC-CSS2/ ui.html#cursor-props**.

4 Insert an **onclick** event call in the **<span>** tag that surrounds the top menu level text that calls the function, **togglemenu()**, passing the appropriate menu section number as an argument.

```
<span onclick="togglemenu(1)"><a href="#">Vehicles</a></span>
```

The span tag for the top-level menu text for menu section 1.

Note: Why not call the **togglemenu()** function in the **<a>** tag? This is because this function should not be called in Netscape 4.x. Netscape 4.x and other older browsers that can't "see" any event calls from elements other than the **a** element. This is a way of "hiding" functions from these older browsers completely.

If you do choose to call the **togglemenu()** function from the **<a>** tag, make sure to create a branching statement in the **togglemenu()** function that will stop the function from executing in older browsers.

5 Test the results in a W3C DOM-compliant browser, such as Netscape 6.x or Internet Explorer 6.x.

When the page is loaded, the menus are all "collapsed" (left). The plus/minus sign or the top-level menu text is clicked, and the corresponding submenu is displayed (middle). Clicking the plus/minus sign or the top-level menu text again collapses the menu (right).

ADJUSTING THE **XHTML** FOR THE **TABLE**

Next, you'll adjust the XHTML for the table.

1 Insert the appropriate **onclick** event calls for each button.

The first **button** with the value, **show pictures**, calls the **changeclassstyle()** function and passes it the arguments, **td** (tagname), **pic** (classname), **display** (styleproperty), and **block** (newstyle) if the browser is Internet Explorer/Windows, and the arguments **td** (tagname), **pic** (classname), display (styleproperty), and **table-cell** (displaystate) for other W3C DOM-compliant browsers. This displays the picture column.

The second **button** with the value, **hide pictures** calls the **changeclassstyle()** function and passes it the arguments **td** (tagname), **pic** (classname), **display** (styleproperty), and **none** (displaystate). This hides the picture column.

The third **button** with the value, **show only available items**, calls the **changeclassstyle()** function and passes it the arguments **tr** (tagname), **na** (classname), **display** (styleproperty), and **none** (newstyle). This hides the rows where the item is out of stock.

The fourth **button** with the value, **show all items**, calls the **changeclassstyle()** function and passes it the arguments **tr** (tagname), **na** (classname), **display** (styleproperty), and **block** (newstyle) if the browser is Internet Explorer/Windows, and the arguments **tr** (tagname), **na** (classname), **display** (styleproperty), and **table-row** (displaystate) for any other W3C DOM-compliant browser. This displays all rows again, including items that are out of stock.

```
<form action="">
<input class="button" type="button" value="show pictures"
onclick="if (ieWin)
{changeclassstyle('td','pic','display','block') }
else {changeclassstyle('td','pic','display','table-cell')}" />
<input class="button" type="button" value="hide pictures"
onclick="changeclassstyle('td','pic','display','none')">
<input class="button" type="button" value="show only available
items" onclick="changeclassstyle('tr','na','display','none')" />
<br />
<input class="button" type="button" value="show all items"
onclick="if (ieWin)
{changeclassstyle('tr','na','display','block')}
else {changeclassstyle('tr','na','display','table-row')}">
<input class="button" type="button" value="highlight items on
sale" onclick="changeclassstyle('tr','onsale','backgroundColor',
'yellow')">
<input class="button" type="button" value="undo highlight"
onclick="changeclassstyle('tr','onsale','backgroundColor',
'transparent'">
</form>
```

The revised XHTML for the form buttons that accompany the product list table. The added code is highlighted.

The fifth button, "highlight items on sale," calls the **changeclassstyle()** function and passes it the arguments **tr** (tagname), **onsale** (classname), **backgroundColor** (styleproperty), and **yellow** (newstyle). This highlights the rows of items on sale by giving the rows a yellow background.

The sixth button, "undo," calls the **change-classstyle()** function and passes it the arguments **tr** (tagname), **onsale** (classname), **backgroundColor** (styleproperty), and transparent (newstyle). This undoes the highlighting of the rows of items on sale by changing the background color of the rows to transparent.

2 Test the results in a W3C DOM-compliant browser, such as Netscape 6.x or Internet Explorer 6.x.

Note: Netscape 6, Internet Explorer 5.0 on the Mac, and other browsers that interpret the display property rules strictly adhering to the W3C's CSS-2 specifications will not display the table cells or rows properly if you use the **display: block** value. Using **display: block** in these browsers makes the table cells or rows shift out of phase. Use **table-cell** for columns and **table-row** for rows in these browsers. However, Internet Explorer 5.x/6.0 on Windows does not recognize these other **display** property values, resulting in a JavaScript error. Therefore, it's necessary to use **display: block** for IE/Windows.

When the page is loaded, the column with the product photos is collapsed.

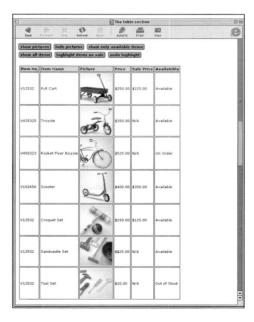

Clicking the show pictures button displays the product photo column.

Clicking the hide pictures button collapses the column again.

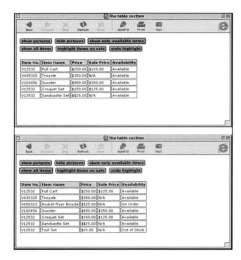

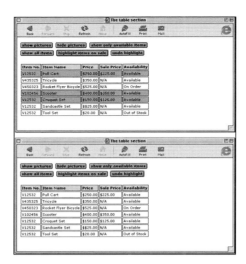

Clicking the "show only available" button hides the rows with out-of-stock items. Clicking the show all items button will display them again.

Clicking the "highlight items on sale" button changes the background color of rows with items on sale to yellow. Clicking the "undo highlight" button returns the background color to transparent.

Browser differences: if display: block is used in Netscape 6 to display table cells (left) or table rows (right), the table cells do not display correctly.

MODIFICATIONS: ADDING A SECTION INDICATOR

Let's incorporate the menu on a real web page. An addition is made to the **init()** function that opens the appropriate menu section if the corresponding section or web page is loaded.

1 Declare a global variable, **section**, right before the function, **init()**, is defined. (This isn't required, but it makes sense considering that this variable is referred to in the **init()** function.) Add the line to the **init()** function that looks at the value of **section**. If it's higher than **0**, then the **togglemenu()** function is called, passing the value of **section** as an argument.

```
var section;
function init() {
        if (document.getElementById) {
                changeclassstyle('div','sublevel','display','none');
                changeclassstyle('td','pic','display','none');
                /* the new line */
                if (section > 0) { togglemenu(section); }

        }
}
```

2 Modify the **onload** event call in the **<body>** tag and declare a value for the variable section. In this case, the value of **section** is **1** (for Vehicles).

```
<body onload="section=1; init()">
```

3 Test the page in a W3C DOM-compatible browser. When the page loads, the appropriate menu section is opened.

When the page is loaded, the corresponding menu section is opened.

DYNAMICALLY UPDATED PAGES

"Any fact facing us is not as

important as our attitude toward it, for

that determines our success or failure."

—DR. NORMAN VINCENT PEALE

CREATING PAGE ELEMENTS ON THE FLY

One of the most powerful features available in
browsers that support the W3C DOM is the
ability to create and delete elements dynamically. In this project, you'll use this capability to
generate and update page content on the fly
on multiple pages from a single source.

Dynamically Updated Pages

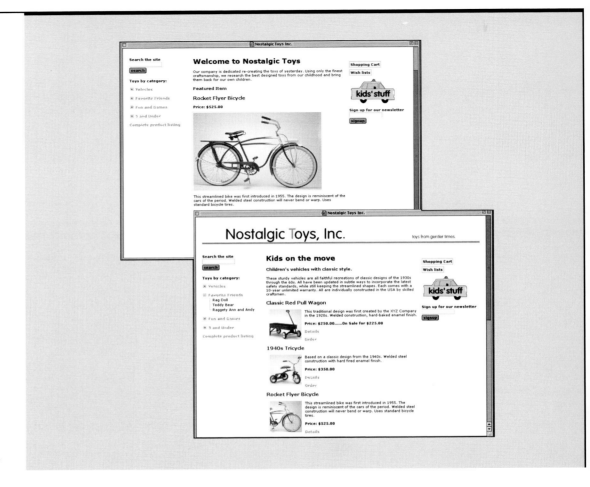

GETTING STARTED

The Nostalgic Toys site has a number of items in its product database, and it needs to display them in different ways on different pages. One of these pages is the home page, which shows a different featured item every time someone visits the site. Another page displays a complete listing of products and descriptions.

Up until now, the only way to display the same data in different ways was to do some HTML parsing on the server side. In W3C DOM compliant browsers, however, it's possible to handle the different display tasks on the client side. This has many advantages because the web interface

designer has a lot more flexibility in controlling and fine-tuning the page design, rather than having to rely on templates created by the server-side programmers.

This project covers the following topics:

■ How to put together a client-side "database" using JavaScript arrays

■ How to append and replace page content on the fly using the W3C DOM tree

Note: In this project, no attempt is made to accommodate older browsers because the methods only work in W3C DOM–capable browsers.

CREATING THE PRODUCT DATABASE

The first task is to create a small "database" of the data that will be written to the final, assembled page. All the data is contained in JavaScript arrays.

1 Open a new text file and save it with the name productdata.js in the **inc** subdirectory.

2 Declare the array variables.

There is one array for each category of data that you need to display: the product names, the product descriptions, the "more" or more detailed descriptions for each product, the original product price, the sale price for each product (if applicable), the small thumbnail photo of each product, and the large detail photo of each product. There is also an array that holds the height value of each large photo.

USING ARRAYS TO HOLD DATA

We've used arrays in several projects to hold a list of needed objects or data. Remember that it's possible to access each item in the array by referencing its index number. This means that arrays can be used as simple databases.

In this project, arrays are used as "mini-databases", to hold the data that will be displayed dynamically on a page.

```javascript
/* the product names */
var productname = new Array();

/* product descriptions */
var productdesc = new Array();

/* "more" descriptions for each product */
var moredesc = new Array();

/* the original product price. */
var origprice = new Array();

/* the sale price if applicable */
var saleprice = new Array();

/* the small photo of each product */
var smallimg = new Array();


/* the large photo of each product */
var largeimg = new Array();

/* the height of the large photo of each product. */
var largeimght = new Array();
```

3 Create each array value.

Each array has the same number of items; in this case **7**.

Note: Remember that array indexes always start with **0**.

The arrays **productname**, **productdesc**, **moredesc**, and **origprice** contain text strings. The array **saleprice** also contains text strings when an item has a sale price, otherwise the array item value is an empty text string.

The **smallimg** array contains an array of **Image** objects. Each **Image** object has a **height** and **width** specification that corresponds to the dimensions of the corresponding JPEG graphic. In addition, each **Image** object in the array is assigned an **src**. This effectively preloads the graphic into the browser cache.

The **largeimg** array is different from the **smallimg** array. Instead of containing **Image** objects, it just contains the URLs of the corresponding images as text strings. This does not precache the graphics. You don't want to precache the large graphics because they are used in a different way than the small graphics, as you'll see later.

The **largeimgHt** array contains an array of integers (numbers), which are the **height** values for each corresponding graphic. There is no array of **width** values for the graphics because all the graphics have the same width.

Note: In a production situation, an array data file might be generated on the server from a database. Alternatively, the data file could be generated in advance from a database program on any PC. If you don't have access to a database on your server, this is a way to get around that limitation.

The contents of productdata.js.

```
var productname = new Array();
productname[0] = "Classic Red Pull Wagon";
productname[1] = "1940s Tricycle";
productname[2] = "Rocket Flyer Bicycle";
productname[3] = "Scooter";
productname[4] = "Croquet Set";
productname[5] = "Sandcastle Building Set";
productname[6] = "Tool Set";

/* product descriptions */
var productdesc = new Array();
productdesc[0] = "This traditional design was first created by
the XYZ Company in the 1920s. Welded construction, hard-baked
enamel finish.";

productdesc[1] = "Based on a classic design from the 1940s.
Welded steel construction with hard fired enamel finish.";

productdesc[2] = "This streamlined bike was first introduced in
1955. The design is reminiscent of the cars of the period.
Welded steel construction will never bend or warp. Uses standard
bicycle tires.";

productdesc[3] =  "Scooters are back in style, and we've brought
back a classic design from the past.";

productdesc[4] = "Croquet, anyone? Associated with polite English
society, croquet has been around since the early 19th century.
Great fun for a party! This hand-turned hardwood set should last
a lifetime and more.";

productdesc[5] = "The perfect set of tools for building that
architectural masterpiece in the sand. Includes a pail, shovel,
rake, and hoe/smoother. Sturdy plastic is guaranteed for 10
years.";

productdesc[6] = "The perfect make-believe construction kit for
small children. Includes a wrench, spanner, screwdriver, hammer,
pincers and gauge.";

/* "more" descriptions for each product */

var moredesc = new Array();
moredesc[0] = "Carts or wagons of this type made of steel have
been made for more than 80 years, but the classic design looks
as contemporary as if it were made yesterday. The original
```

continues

designs were inspired by the sleek Art-Deco superliners and trains of the 1920s and 30s. Our interpretation of this classic adds some new features, such as a length-adjustable handle and cushioned wheels. The cart itself can support up to 200 lbs. A hard-fired powder enamel finish makes a virtually scratch-proof surface on both the cart and the handle. Wheels can be removed and replaced.";

moredesc[1] = "The sleek design of this tricycle was doubtlessly inspired by the jet fighters of World War II. First introduced in 1949 to cater to the baby boom generation, this model was in production until 1965. We've updated the construction of this tricycle with comfortably padded rubber coated handles, inflatable tires, and a padded seat. Recommended for children age 3 to 5. The tricycle can support up to 100 lbs.";

moredesc[2] = "Once your child graduates from the Tricycle, what better choice than this stylish bike? The Rocket Flyer was designed and manufactured by the Acme Bicycle Company from 1955 well into the 1970s, and was one of the most popular designs in their line. It's easy to see why - on this bike, your child will have the most stylish ride on the block. We have updated the construction in subtle ways, by exchanging the original hard seat to a spring-cushioned one, upgrading the single gear to three gears, and making it possible to attach training wheels to the back wheel. Recommended for children age 5 through 8. Supports up to 150 lbs.";

moredesc[3] = "Scooters were first introduced in the 1940s. This design dates back to 1962. The one-piece construction is extremely strong, and can support up to 200 lbs. We have modified the handle to be height-adjustable, so it can be ridden by the whole family. The graceful curving line of the handle to the base is sure to turn heads as your child - or even you - scoot down the street. Classic powder-blue finish is high-fired enamel and will never chip."

moredesc[4] = "This classic Croquet set is based on one manufactured by the Burton and Sons Company of London, England around the turn of the century. We've even replicated the presentation box it came in, printed with Edwardian-era pictures. Each piece is hand turned in beech, a hard wearing wood. Painted with non-toxic paint. The stakes are rustproof.";

moredesc[5] = "We were dissatisfied with the cheap quality of the plastic beach toys being manufactured today, and again went back to the past for inspiration. We found this in a 1950s catalog and fell in love with the sturdiness of the design. The handle of the pail will withstand even the toughest tug-of-wars, and the handles of the tools will not break even if you try. (We tried hard in our test labs and could only bend them a little!) This set is guaranteed for 10 years, and hours of creative fun in the sun.";

moredesc[6] = "What boy or girl doesn't want to emulate Dad in the workshop? With this fully functional, yet safe, tool set, he or she can. The tools are sized for small hands, and are constructed of a special hard-wearing plastic. Recommended for children aged 2 1/2 and up.";

```
/* the original product price. */

var origprice = new Array();
origprice[0] = "$250.00";
origprice[1] = "$350.00";
origprice[2] = "$525.00";
origprice[3] = "$400.00";
origprice[4] = "$150.00";
origprice[5] = "$25.00";
origprice[6] = "$20.00";

/* the sale price if applicable */
var saleprice = new Array();
saleprice[0] = "$225.00";
saleprice[1] = null;
saleprice[2] = null;
saleprice[3] = "$350.00";
saleprice[4] = "$125.00";
saleprice[5] = null;
saleprice[6] = null;

/* the small photo of each product */
```

continues

continued

```javascript
var smallimg = new Array();
smallimg[0] = new Image(100,94);
smallimg[0].src = "images/photos/cart-sm.jpg";
smallimg[1] = new Image(100,98);
smallimg[1].src = "images/photos/tricycle-sm.jpg";
smallimg[2] = new Image(100,99);
smallimg[2].src = "images/photos/bicycle-sm.jpg";
smallimg[3] = new Image(100,101);
smallimg[3].src = "images/photos/scooter-sm.jpg";
smallimg[4] = new Image(100,95);
smallimg[4].src = "images/photos/croquet-sm.jpg";
smallimg[5] = new Image(100,91);
smallimg[5].src = "images/photos/sandset-sm.jpg";
smallimg[6] = new Image(100,97);
smallimg[6].src = "images/photos/toolset-sm.jpg";


/* the large image of each product */
```

```javascript
var largeimg = new Array();
largeimg[0] =  "images/photos/cart-lg.jpg";
largeimg[1] =  "images/photos/tricycle-lg.jpg";
largeimg[2] =  "images/photos/bicycle-lg.jpg";
largeimg[3] =  "images/photos/scooter-lg.jpg";
largeimg[4] =  "images/photos/croquet-lg.jpg";
largeimg[5] =  "images/photos/sandset-lg.jpg";
largeimg[6] =  "images/photos/toolset-lg.jpg";

/* the height of the large image of each product. */
var largeimgHt = new Array();
largeimgHt[0] = 317;
largeimgHt[1] = 333;
largeimgHt[2] = 252;
largeimgHt[3] = 436;
largeimgHt[4] = 301;
largeimgHt[5] = 273;
largeimgHt[6] = 254;
```

CREATING THE XHTML MARKUP BASE FOR THE FRONT PAGE

The front page of the site displays a featured item, consisting of the product name, price, sales price (if applicable), a photo of the product, and a description. The page markup contains mostly empty markup elements, into which the contents will be inserted dynamically.

1 Insert the **DOCTYPE** declaration and appropriate **<html>** opening tag to indicate that this is an **XHTML** document.

```html
<!DOCTYPE html PUBLIC "-//W3C//DTD XHTML 1.0 Transitional//EN"
    "http://www.w3.org/TR/xhtml1/DTD/xhtml1-transitional.dtd">
<html xmlns="http://www.w3.org/1999/xhtml" lang="en">
```

2 In the **<head>** section, create the markup necessary to link the external CSS stylesheet styles.css to the external JavaScript files productdisplay.js and productdata.js.

```html
<head>
<meta http-equiv="content-type" content="text/html; charset=iso-8859-1" />
<title>Nostalgic Toys Inc.</title>
<style type="text/css" media="screen">
```

continues

Note: The file styles.css controls the appearance of the page. It was created in the previous project.

continued

```html
<!--
@import "inc/styles.css";
//-->
</style>
<script src="inc/productdisplay.js" language="Javascript"
type="text/javascript"></script>
<script src="inc/productdata.js" language="Java script"type="text/javascript"></script>

</head>
```

3 Create the markup for the section of the page that will contain the dynamically generated content. On the example site page, it's all contained in the **div** with the **id main**.

The first part of this section (the page header and the welcome text) is static.

After that are the empty elements, each with a unique **id** value.

The **h2** element with the **id featurehead** will contain the product name.

The **p** element with the **id featureprice** will contain the original price of the item, plus the sale price if applicable.

The **div** element with the **id productpic** will contain the product photo.

The **p** element with the **id featuredesc** will contain a short description of the product.

The **p** element with the **id featuremore** will contain the additional description of the product.

At the end of the section is a static link to the Order section. In a real life situation, this would lead to an order page; the markup here uses **#** as a placeholder.

```html
<!-- this part is static -->
<div id="main">
<h1>Welcome to Nostalgic Toys</h1>

<p>Our company is dedicated re-creating the toys of yesterday. Using only the finest
craftsmanship, we research the best designed toys from our childhood and bring them
back for our own children.</p>

<h3>Featured Item</h3>

<!-- end of static content. -->

<!-- start dynamic section with "holders" for the dynamic content. -->

<h2 id="featurehead"></h2>

<p id="featureprice" class="price"></p>

<div id="productpic"></div>

<p id="featuredesc"></p>

<p id="featuremore"></p>

<!-- end "dynamic" section -->

<!-- static link -->
<p>
<a href="#">Order this item</a></p>

</div>
```

CREATING THE MARKUP FOR THE PRODUCT LISTING PAGE

The second page you will create dynamically contains a list of items in a given category—in this example, vehicles.

1 Insert the **DOCTYPE** declaration and appropriate **<html>** opening tag to indicate that this is an **XHTML** document.

```
<!DOCTYPE html PUBLIC "-//W3C//DTD XHTML 1.0 Transitional//EN"
    "http://www.w3.org/TR/xhtml1/DTD/xhtml1-transitional.dtd">
<html xmlns="http://www.w3.org/1999/xhtml" lang="en">
```

2 In the **<head>** section, create the markup necessary to link the external CSS stylesheet styles.css to the external JavaScript files productdisplay.js and productdata.js.

This markup uses the **@import** method to load the external stylesheet styles.css, but you may choose to use the **<link rel>** method instead.

```
<head>
<meta http-equiv="content-type" content="text/html; charset=iso-8859-1" />
<title>Nostalgic Toys Inc. - Vehicles</title>
<style type="text/css" media="screen">
<!--
@import "inc/styles.css";
//-->
</style>
<script src="inc/productdisplay.js" language="Javascript" type="text/javascript"></script>
<script src="inc/productdata.js" language="Javascript" type="text/javascript"></script>

</head>
```

3 Create the markup for the section of the page that will contain the dynamically generated content. On the example site page, it's all contained in the **div** element with the **id main**.

The first part of this section (the page header and the category description) is static.

```
<!-- static section -->

<div id="main">
<h1>Kids on the move</h1>

<h3>Children's vehicles with classic style.</h3>

<p>These sturdy vehicles are all faithful recreations of classic designs of the 1930s
through the 60s. All have been updated in subtle ways to incorporate the latest safety
standards, while still keeping the streamlined shapes. Each comes with a 10-year unlimited
warranty. All are individually constructed in the USA by skilled craftsmen.</p>

<!-- end static section -->
```

continues

The next part contains 4 sections of elements—one for each product you want to display. Each section consists of the following:

- An empty **h2** element with the **id** value **head(number)**, where the **number** corresponds to the array index of the product you want to display. This will hold the product name text.

- A **div** element that holds an empty **img** element with the **id** value **img(number)**, where the **number** corresponds to the array index of the product you want to display. This will hold the small product photo.

- An empty **p** element with the **id** value **p(number)**, where the **number** corresponds to the array index of the product you want to display. This will hold the short description text for the product.

- An empty **p** element with the **id** value **pr(number)**, where the **number** corresponds to the array index of the product you want to display. This will hold the price of the product, plus the sale price if applicable.

- A **p** element with the **id** value **detail(number)**, where the **number** corresponds to the array index of the product you want to display. This contains a static link element. This is used to display the additional description text for the product.

- A **p** element that contains a static link to the **Order** section.

Take care to create enough static element sections for all the products you want to list. If you don't include enough sections, a JavaScript error will occur.

continued

```html
<!-- begin dynamic section, with empty
"holders" -->

<!-- first section -->
<h2 id="head0">
</h2>

<div class="floatleft">
<img id="img0"/></div>

<p id="p0">
</p>

<p id="pr0" class="price">
<span class="sale"></span></p>

<p id="detail0">
<a href="javascript:showdetail(0)">
Details</a></p>
<p><a href="#">Order</a></p>


<!-- second section -->

<h2 id="head1">
</h2>

<div class="floatleft">
<img id="img1"/></div>

<p id="p1">
</p>

<p id="pr1" class="price">
<span class="sale"></span></p>

<p id="detail1">
<a href="javascript:showdetail(1)">
Details</a></p>

<p><a href="#">Order</a></p>
```

```html
<!-- third section -->
<h2 id="head2"></h2>

<div class="floatleft">
<img id="img2"/></div>

<p id="p2">
</p>

<p id="pr2" class="price">
<span class="sale"></span></p>

<p id="detail2">
<a href="javascript:showdetail(2)">
Details</a></p>

<p><a href="#">Order</a></p>

<!-- fourth section -->

<h2 id="head3">
</h2>

<div class="floatleft">
<img id="img3"/></div>

<p id="p3">
</p>

<p id="pr3" class="price">
<span class="sale"></span></p>

<p id="detail3">
<a href="javascript:showdetail(3)">
Details</a></p>

<p><a href="#">Order</a></p>

</div>
```

CREATING THE DYNAMIC CONTENT GENERATION SCRIPT `productdisplay.js`

This script may seem long and complicated, but you will see that the same methods are used over and over to create different results.

1 Open a new blank text document and save it with the name productdisplay.js.

2 Create the function **newTextElement()**. This is the core function for creating and then inserting a new text element on the page.

Four arguments are passed to the function: **elemID** is the **id** value of the element to which the new text should be added; **arrayname** is the name of the array from which the text string data should be taken; **num** is the array index number; and **prefix** is any text string that should be inserted before the text in the text data array.

The next line evaluates the text string **arrayname**. This returns the object that is indicated by the string.

The next line finds the object on the page with the **id** value of **elemID** to the variable element.

The next line creates a new **TextNode** object by concatenating (adding) the text string of **prefix** plus the text string data in the array item with the index value of **num**.

Finally, the new **textNode** object is added to the object on the page with the **id** value of **elemID**.

```
/* Create, then append, a new TextNode object. */

        function newTextElement(elemID,arrayname,num,prefix) {
        arrayname = eval(arrayname);
        var newtext = document.createTextNode(prefix + arrayname[num]);
        document.getElementById(elemID).appendChild(newtext);
}
```

USING THE DOM TREE: createTextNode, createElement AND appendChild

The script productdisplay.js uses the W3C DOM tree to access parts of the page. It uses three built-in methods that are unique to the latest W3C DOM compatible browsers: **createElement**, **createTextNode**, and **appendChild**.

- **createElement** creates a new element or object of any type from scratch. The new element or object can then be inserted into the page at a specified location dynamically.

- **createTextNode** turns a text string into a new **TextNode** object, which can then be inserted into the page at a specified location dynamically.

- **appendChild** is one of the ways in which a new **TextNode** object—or any other valid object—can be inserted into the page. As the name implies, it appends a child element to a parent element.

For a more detailed explanation of the W3C DOM Tree, nodes, parents, siblings, and children, see the "How It Works" section later in this project.

3 Create the function **showcase()**. This function creates the dynamic content for the front page.

The argument **num**, which indicates the array index number of the product to be displayed, is passed to the function.

The first line creates, then appends, a new **TextNode** object to the element on the page with the **id featurehead** containing the text string value of the **productname[num]** index array item.

The second line creates, then appends, a new **TextNode** object to the element on the page with the **id featuredesc** containing the text string value of the **productdesc[num]** index array item.

The third line creates, then appends, a new **TextNode** object to the element on the page with the **id featuremore** containing the text string value of the **moredesc[num]** index array item.

The fourth line creates, then appends, a new **TextNode** object to the element on the page with the **id featureprice** containing the text **"Price: "** plus the text value of the **origprice[num]** index array item.

The next section sees if a value for **saleprice[num]** exists. If so, the script creates, then appends, a new **TextNode** object with the text **".....On Sale for"** plus the text value of the **saleprice[num]** index array item to the **featureprice** element.

4 Create the second half of the **showcase()** function. This section defines a new **img** element and then appends that to the **productpic** element on the page.

On the first line, a new element of the type **img** is created and assigned to the variable **PicObj** with the **createElement** method.

```
/* Create the dynamic content for the front page. */
function showcase(num) {
        newTextElement("featurehead","productname",num,"");
        newTextElement("featuredesc","productdesc",num,"");
        newTextElement("featuremore","moredesc",num,"");
        newTextElement("featureprice","origprice",num,
        ➡"Price: ");
        if (saleprice[num]) {
                newTextElement("featureprice","saleprice",
                ➡num,".....On Sale for ");
        }
```

The first part of the function **showcase()**.

```
        var PicObj = document.createElement("IMG");
        PicObj.id = "picture";
        PicObj.width = 400;
        PicObj.height =largeimght[num];
        PicObj.src = largeimg[num];
        document.getElementById('productpic')
        ➡.appendChild(PicObj);

}
```

The second half of the **showcase()** function.

On the next line, the **id** attribute for the new element is given a value of **picture**. We can give a fixed **id** attribute value to the new element because the function is called only once on the page.

Next, the **width** attribute is given a value of **400**. Then, the **height** attribute is given the value that is contained in the **largeimgHt[num]** array index.

Then, the **src** of the new element is defined as the URL text string of **largeimg[num]**.

Finally, the new element is appended to the element on the page with the **id productpic**.

5   Define the function **randomize()**.

This is simply a function that generates a random integer between two numbers. In this case, you need a random number in order to display a product at random when the page is loaded. This function uses the built in JavaScript **Math** methods. The function is not defined in detail here; if you want to know how it works, see the companion web site (**www.createwebmagic.com**). You can use the **randomize()** function in any situation where you need to generate a positive random number between two numbers.

6   Define the function **randomshowcase()**.

This function calls the **showcase()** function, passing it a random number between **0** and the length of the **productdesc** array minus **1** via the **randomize()** function.

```
/* obtain a random number between n and m */

function randomize(lownum, highnum) {
return Math.floor(Math.abs(Math.random() * (highnum - lownum + 1)
- 0.0000000001)) + lownum;
}
```

```
/* Display a random product on the first page. */
function randomshowcase() {
    showcase(randomize (0, productdesc.length-1));
    }
```

7 Define the function **createProductDesc()**.

This function creates the dynamic content for the product listing page.

The argument **num**, with the corresponding product array index number, is passed to the function.

The first section defines the variables that indicate the appropriate **id** value. For example, when the value of the argument num is **0**, **headnum** becomes **head0** (the **id** of the first header element), **picsrcnum** becomes **img0** (the **id** of the first image element), and so on.

The next section calls the function **newTextElement**, passing the appropriate values to create, and then append, the header, description, and price **TextNode** objects of each product listing.

The next section sees if the value of **saleprice[num]** is null (there is no sale price). If it isn't, it creates, then appends, a new **TextNode** object with the text "**.....On Sale for**" plus the text value of the **saleprice[num]** index array item to the price element.

8 Define the last part of the function **createProductDesc()**.

To display the appropriate product picture, instead of creating a new element, simply swap the **src** graphic of the element with the **id** value of **img[num]**.

9 Define the function **ProductList()**.

This function displays all of the product listings on the page.

Two arguments are passed to it; **arraystart** is the array index number of the first product to be listed and **arrayend** is the array index number of the last product to be listed.

The function then executes a **for** loop that is incremented by **1** and calls the function **createProductDesc**, passing the value of the counter variable **i** + **arraystart** to the function.

```
/* Create the dynamic content for the product listingpage.
*/

        function createProductDesc(num) {
                var headnum = "head" + num;
                var picsrcnum = "img" + num;
                var descnum = "p" + num;
                var pricenum = "pr" + num;
                newTextElement(headnum,productname,num,"");
                newTextElement(descnum,productdesc,num,"");
                newTextElement(pricenum,origprice,num,
                ➥"Price: ");
                if (saleprice[num] != null) {
                        newTextElement(pricenum,saleprice,num,
                        ➥".....On Sale for ");
                }
```

The first part of the function **createProductDesc()**

```
                document.getElementById(picsrcnum).src =
                ➥smallimg[num].src;

        }
```

The last part of the function **createProductDesc()**.

```
/* display the product listings */

function ProductList(arraystart, arrayend) {
        for (i=arraystart; i <= arrayend; i++) {
                createProductDesc(i);
        }
}
```

285

10 Define the function `showdetail()`

This function displays the **moredesc** (more detailed product description) text when the user clicks the **Details** link on the product listing page.

Once again, the array index number is passed to the function as an argument.

The variable **detailelem** is assigned the value of **detail** plus **num**. For example, if the value of **num** is **0**, **detailnum** is **detail0**.

The next line checks to see what the **nodeValue** of the **lastChild** (the last node of the element with the **id detailnum**) is. If the **nodeValue** is an empty text string, then the **newTextElement()** function is called to display the text string of the **moredesc[num]** array index value preceded by the text string **":::"**.

```
function showdetail(num) {
        var detailelem = "detail" + num;
        var lastNodeValue = document.getElementById
        ➡(detailnum).lastChild.nodeValue;
        if (lastNodeValue == null || lastNodeValue.charAt(0)
        ➡== "" || lastNodeValue.charAt(0) == "\n" ||
        ➡lastNodeValue.length < 3) {
                newTextElement(detailnum,moredesc,num,
                ➡"::: ");
        }
}
```

EMPTY TEXT NODES

Internet Explorer on both Windows and Mac, and Netscape 6 and Mozilla handle empty text nodes differently. Take this markup for example:

`<p>A paragraph.</p>`

`<p>Another paragraph.</p>`

The two line spaces between the two paragraphs is an empty text node. Internet Explorer 5+ on Windows interprets the nodeValue of this as a **null** string. Internet Explorer 5+ on Mac interprets this as a string of one character. Netscape 6.x and Mozilla interpret this as a string of two characters, including a **"\n"** (return) character.

Consider this next example:

`<p>A paragraph <b>with a bolded segment</b></p>`

In between the **</b>** and **</p>** is also an empty text node. In this case, Internet Explorer 5+ on both Mac and Windows will see the nodeValue of this as **null**, but Netscape 6 and Mozilla will see this as an empty text string. Remember that an empty text string is not **null**!

To deal with all of these different interpretations, the **if()** conditions in this script first check to see if the nodeValue is null, then check to see if it's an empty text string, if it contains a return character, and finally if its length is less than 3 characters. Note that the check for **null** must be the first condition checked, otherwise a JavaScript error will occur in Internet Explorer.

MODIFYING THE **XHTML** MARKUP TO CALL THE FUNCTIONS

To activate the JavaScript, you will adjust the XHTML markup to call the various functions you've defined.

1 On the front page, call the **randomshowcase()** function with an **onload** call within the **body** tag.

```
<body onload="randomshowcase()">
```

2 Display the results in a W3C DOM–ready browser, such as Netscape 6.x, Internet Explorer 5.x/Mac, or Internet Explorer 6.x/Windows. The product data is displayed on the fly.

Each time the page is loaded, a new product description is displayed on the fly.

3 On the product listing page, call the **ProductList()** function with an **onload** call within the **body** tag, passing the first and last array index numbers of the items to be listed as arguments. In this case, you want to display items **0** through **3**.

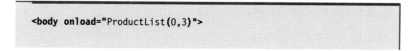

```
<body onload="ProductList(0,3)">
```

4 Display the results in a W3C DOM–ready browser. The product listings are displayed on the fly. Note that we're using the same set of data for both pages.

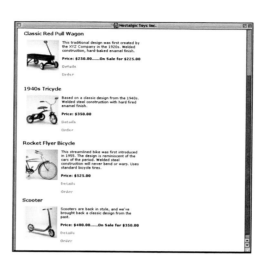

When the page is loaded, the products are displayed on the fly.

5 Test the Details links in a W3C-DOM ready browser. When the link is clicked, the appropriate "more" description text is displayed.

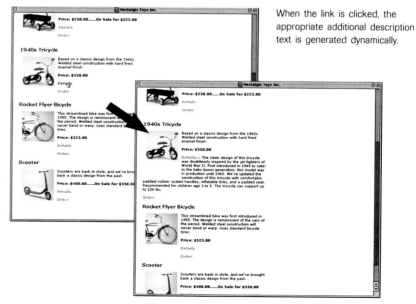

When the link is clicked, the appropriate additional description text is generated dynamically.

6 To finish the page, place the main **div** markup between the menu section and the right sidebar section in the layout you created in the previous project. Link to the display.js script that you also created in the previous project.

The featured item page and the product listing page, complete with the top banner and sidebars.

HOW IT WORKS: THE W3C DOM TREE

In previous projects, we've explored the **parent** and **child** model for web pages. The parent-child relationship governs how CSS style properties are inherited and also how certain elements are addressed in relation to each other, such as frames and browser windows.

The newer W3C DOM specification extends the family tree concept even further. Now not only are there **parents** and **children**, but there are also **siblings**. And, keeping with the tree concept, **nodes** have also been introduced.

As we've seen before, any element that's nested within another element is the **child** of that element. Conversely, the container element is the **parent**. **Sibling** elements are those that are on the same level. Finally, **nodes** are the individual parts that make up an element.

The code sample here shows the simplified markup of a small web page. The figure shows the page when it's viewed with the DOMInspector, a handy tool that's included in the most recent versions of the Mozilla browser (version 0.99 as of this writing—get the latest version from **http://www.mozilla.org**). You can find the DOMInspector in the Tasks – Tools menu. In the screenshot, the DOM Tree has been completely expanded.

Each branch of the tree is a **node**. Each tag, and each piece of text, is a **node**. Elements that are on the same level with each other (**siblings**) are on the same node level, and nested elements show up to the right, or under, their **parent** elements.

> **Tip:** To view a page in the Mozilla DOMTree Viewer, open the page first in a browser window, then copy-paste the URL into the DOMTree Viewer window.

```html
<html>
<head>
     <title>Node page view</title>
</head>
<body>
<div id="main">
<h1>Kids on the move</h1>

<h3>Children's vehicles with classic style.</h3>

<p>These sturdy vehicles are all faithful recreations of classic
designs of the 1930s through the 60s. All have been updated in
subtle ways to incorporate the latest safety standards, while
still keeping the streamlined shapes. Each comes with a 10-year
unlimited warranty.
</p>

<p>For more information, <a href="#">click here</a>. You'll be
<b>really</b> glad you did.</p>

</div>
</body>
</html>
```

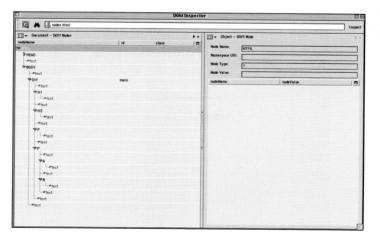

The Mozilla DOMTree Viewer is a handy way of examining the DOM tree of any web page.

Focus on the second **p** element on this page. This **p** element has five nodes that are its direct children: the first piece of text, the **a** element, the second piece of text, the **b** element, and the third piece of text. Two of these children have children of their own—the **a** element has a text child node, as does the **b** element. The first child node of the **p** element is called `firstChild`; the last child node is called `lastChild`.

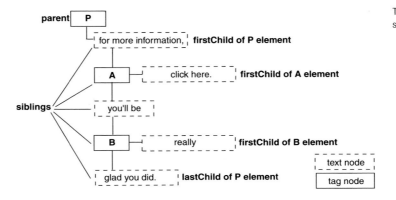

> **Note:** For this project, we've used the **appendChild** method to append (add) a text node to a specific element. In the newest W3C DOM–compatible browsers, it's possible to append, delete, and replace every node.
>
> With a good understanding of the DOM Tree, you can create any number of cool scripts that change a web page dynamically—all without having to access any server-side data.

MODIFICATION: GENERATING MARKUP TAGS ON THE FLY

In this project, you've established static markup elements on the XHTML page and created new text nodes that are appended to the static elements.

> **Note:** The process of creating a new HTML/XHTML element from scratch is rather like assembling small building blocks. Each tag element, and each text segment, is a separate node: each node must be created individually and then assembled to make the final element. This is quite a tedious process, so it makes sense to use this approach in cases where you are generating multiple elements dynamically. For example, on the front page there is only one listing, so the tag elements can be static, with only the text and picture changing. On the listings page, however, it makes more sense to generate each whole listings section including the tag elements since you may not know in advance how many items will be listed on the page.

1 Create a new XHTML document. Link the stylesheet styles.css, and the JavaScript files productdata.js and productdisplay2.js to it. Within the body of the document, create an empty **div** element with the id main.

```
<!DOCTYPE html PUBLIC "-//W3C//DTD XHTML 1.0 Transitional//EN"
    "http://www.w3.org/TR/xhtml1/DTD/xhtml1-transitional.dtd">
<html xmlns="http://www.w3.org/1999/xhtml">
<head>
<meta http-equiv="content-type" content="text/html; charset=iso-8859-1" />
<title>Product Listing with dynamically generated elements.</title>
```

continues

2 Open a new blank text document and save it with the name productdisplay2.js. This will be an edited version of the original productdisplay.js.

continued

```
<style type="text/css" media="Screen">      <body>
@import "inc/styles.css";
</style>                                      <div id="main">
<script src="inc/productdisplay2.js"
type="text/javascript"></script>             </div>
<script src="inc/productdata.js"             </body>
type="text/javascript"></script>             </html>
</head>
```

3 Create a function **newTagElement()**. This function creates a new markup tag element.

Four arguments are passed to this function: **tagname** is the name of the XHTML/HTML tag to be created, **elemname** is the full or partial **id** value of the element, **num** is the array index number, and **classVal** is the value to be assigned to the **class** attribute of the element.

The variable newelement is assigned a new element that's created with the **createElement()** method. The new element has the tag name of **tagname**.

Next, the newly created element is given an **id** value and a **class** value.

Finally, the function returns the newly created **newelement** object.

```
function newTagElement(tagname, elemname, num, classVal) {
        var newelement = document.createElement(tagname);
        newelement.id = elemname + num;
        newelement.className = classVal;
        return newelement;
}
```

4 Create the function **newTextElement2()**. This is a function for creating a new **TextNode** element. You may notice that it's a small modification of the function **newTextElement()** that you created in the original productdisplay.js script.

Three arguments are passed to the function: **arrayname** is the name of the array from which the text string data should be taken, **num** is the array index number, and **prefix** is any text string that should be inserted before the text in the text data array.

```
function newTextElement2(arrayname,num,prefix) {
        arrayname = eval(arrayname);
        var newtext = document.createTextNode(prefix +
        ➥arrayname[num]);
        return newtext;
}
```

292

The next line evaluates the text string **arrayname**. This returns the object that is indicated by the string.

The next line finds the object on the page with the **id** value of **elemID** to the variable element.

The next line creates a new **TextNode** object by concatenating (adding) the text string of **prefix** plus the text string data in the array item with the index value of **num**.

Finally, the function returns the newly created **newtext** object.

5 Create the function **createProductDesc2()**. This is the function that creates the dynamic content for the product listing page. (Again, we've called this function **createProductDesc2()** to differentiate it from the original **createProductDesc()** function.)

The argument **num**, with the corresponding product array index number, is passed to the function.

First of all, the local variable **maindiv** is assigned the **document.getElementById('main')** object—this points to the **div** element with the id main on the page.

6 Continue to define the function **createProductDesc2()**. For each element you want to create, a new tag element and a **TextNode** element is created.

Start with the header for each listing. Assign the local variable **headelem** a new tag element with the arguments **"div"**, **"head"** , **num** and **""** (the last is an empty text string because there is no class attribute for this element.) If the value of **num** is **2**, for example, it creates a **div** element with the id **head2**. Then, assign the local variable **headtext** a new **TextNode** element, with the arguments **productname** (pointing to the productname array in productdata.js), **num** and **""** (an empty text string, since there is no text prefix to this element.) Then, append **headtext** to **headelem** with the **appendChild** method.

Note: We've named this function **newTextElement2()** to differentiate it from the original **newTextElement()** function, to avoid confusion in this project. However, you may simply name it **newTextElement()** because this function doesn't appear in the same script as the original **newTextElement()** function. The same goes for the other functions in this script that we've named **createProductDesc2()**, and so on.

```
function createProductDesc2(num) {
    var maindiv = document.getElementById('main');
    var headelem = newTagElement("h2","head",num,"");
    var headtext = newTextElement2(productname,num,"");
    headelem.appendChild(headtext);
    var picdiv = newTagElement("div","pic",num,"floatleft");
    var imgelem = newTagElement("img","img",num,"");
    imgelem.src = smallimg[num].src;
    picdiv.appendChild(imgelem);
    var descelem = newTagElement("p","p",num,"");
    var desctext = newTextElement2(productdesc,num,"");
    descelem.appendChild(desctext);
    var priceelem = newTagElement("p","pr",num,"price");
    var pricetext = newTextElement2(origprice,num,"Price: ");
    priceelem.appendChild(pricetext);
    if (saleprice[num]) {
```

continues

For the product photo, it's necessary to create two tag elements: the **div** element and the **img** element. Assign the local variable **picdiv** to the new **div** element and the local variable **imgelem** to the new **img** element. Assign the value of **smallimg[num].src** to the **img** element's **src** property. This points to the graphic file indicated in the **smallimg** array in the productdata.js file. Then, the new **img** element is appended to the **div** element with the **appendChild** method.

To assemble the price listing, first create the **p** element and assign it to the local variable **priceelem**. Then, create the first **TextNode** element, which is the appropriate value in the **origprice** array in productdata.js, and append this to the price listing element. Next, check to see if a value for **saleprice[num]** exists; if it does exist, add a new **TextNode** element with the value of **saleprice[num]** from the **saleprice** array. This is appended to the price listing element.

To assemble the details element, first create the **p** element and assign it to the local variable **detailelem**. Then create the **a** element and assign this to the local variable **alinkelem**. Assign an **href** property value to this element, which is the string of **"javascript:showdetail2()"** with the value of **num** inserted within the parentheses. This is a call to the **showdetail()** function. Then, create a **TextNode** element with the text string **"Details"**. Append t he **TextNode** to the **a** element, then append the **a** element to the **p** element.

To assemble the order link element, first create the **p** element and assign it to the local variable **orderelem**. Then create the **a** element and assign this to the local variable **orderlinkelem**. Assign an **href** property

continued

```
        var saletext = newTextElement2(saleprice,
        ➥num,"......On Sale for ");
        priceelem.appendChild(saletext);
    }
    var detailelem = newTagElement("p","detail",num,"");
    var alinkelem = newTagElement("a","",num,"");
    alinkelem.href = "javascript:showdetail2(" + num + ")";
    var alinktext = document.createTextNode("Details");
    alinkelem.appendChild(alinktext);
    detailelem.appendChild(alinkelem);
    var orderelem = newTagElement("p","order",num,"");
    var orderlinkelem = newTagElement("a","",num,"");
    orderlinkelem.href="";
    var orderlinktext = document.createTextNode("Order");
    orderlinkelem.appendChild(orderlinktext);
    orderelem.appendChild(orderlinkelem);
    maindiv.appendChild(headelem);
    maindiv.appendChild(picdiv);
    maindiv.appendChild(descelem);
    maindiv.appendChild(priceelem);
    maindiv.appendChild(detailelem);
    maindiv.appendChild(orderelem);

}
```

value to this element, which is the URL string pointing to the order page (the markup here just uses **#**). Then, create a **TextNode** element with the text string **"Order"**. Append the **TextNode** to the **a** element, then append the **a** element to the **p** element.

Finally, append the entire product listing to the static **div** element **main** with the **appendChild** method, in the order in which the elements should appear.

7 Create the function **ProductList2()**. This is identical to the **createProductDesc()** function we created in productdisplay.js, except that it calls the function **ProductDesc2()** instead of **ProductDesc()**.

```
/* display the product listings */

function ProductList2(arraystart, arrayend) {
        for (i=arraystart; i <= arrayend; i++) {
                createProductDesc2(i);
        }
}
```

8 Create the function **showdetail2()**. This is very similar to the **showdetail()** function we created in productdisplay.js; however, since the function **createTextElement2()** only creates the **TextNode**, it's necessary to append it to the **detailelem div** element with the **appendChild** method.

```
/* show detailed product description */

function showdetail2(num) {
      var detailelem = "detail" + num;
      var lastNodeValue = document.getElementById(detailelem).lastChild.nodeValue;
      if (lastNodeValue.length < 2) {
              var detailtext = newTextElement2(moredesc,num,"::: ");
              document.getElementById(detailelem).appendChild(detailtext);
      }
}
```

9 Modify the XHTML document to call the function **ProductList2()** with an **onload** event call within the **body** tag.

```
<body onload="ProductList2(0,productname.length - 1)">
```

If you want to list all the products, call the **ProductList2()** function, passing **0** and **productname.length − 1** as arguments. The length of the array **productname** is **7**; this will list all products from array index **0** through **6**.

APPENDIX

WHAT'S ON THE CD-ROM

The accompanying CD-ROM is packed with all sorts of exercise files and products to help you work with this book and with CSS and JavaScript. The following sections contain detailed descriptions of the CD's contents.

For more information about the use of this CD, please review the ReadMe.txt file in the root directory. This file includes important disclaimer information, as well as information about installation, system requirements, troubleshooting, and technical support.

Technical Support Issues: If you have any difficulties with this CD, you can access our Web site at http://www.newriders.com.

SYSTEM REQUIREMENTS

This CD-ROM was configured for use on systems Windows NT Workstation, Windows 95, Windows 98, Windows 2000, Windows XP, Macintosh OS9 and Macintosh OSX. Your machine will need to meet the following system requirements in order for this CD to operate properly:

- **Memory (RAM).** 128MB. Some of the included software demos may require more RAM.

- **Monitor.** VGA, 800 x 600 or higher with 256 colors or higher (High Color (16 bit) or higher recommended for Windows; Thousands of Colors or higher recommended for Macintosh)

- **Storage Space.** 10 MB Minimum (will vary depending on the installation. You will need a lot more if you need to install the browsers.)

- **Other.** Mouse or compatible pointing device

Supported Browsers: All the projects in this book were tested to work in the latest versions of Microsoft Internet Explorer and Netscape on Windows 98SE, Windows 2000, Mac OS 9, and Mac OS X. As of this writing, these are: Internet Explorer 6.0 for Windows; Netscape 6.2 for Windows; Internet Explorer 5.1 for Mac; and Netscape 6.2 for Mac. It's highly recommended that you open the project files in one of these browsers, or the latest versions of the open-source browser Mozilla browser (www.mozilla.org), which is available for a wide variety of platforms. Netscape 6 is based on Mozilla. (Note that Mozilla is not included on the CD, since version 1.0 has not been released yet as of this writing.)

Many of the projects were also tested and are verified to work in Netscape Communicator 4.75. When a certain project is purposefully designed not to work in Netscape 4.x, that is clearly noted. It's important to know that Netscape versions 4.x and under and Netscape 6 are two entirely different browsers, based on completely different engines.

Although many of the projects will also work in alternate browsers, such as Opera and Konqueror, they have not been tested due to time constraints. While these are all fine browsers, we wanted to concentrate on what works in the browsers in widespread use. Visit **www.createwebmagic.com** for up to date news about the current state of browsers.

LOADING THE CD FILES

To load the files from the CD, insert the disc into your CD-ROM drive. If auto-play is enabled on your machine, the CD-ROM setup program starts automatically the first time you insert the disc. You may copy the files to your hard drive, or use them right off the disc.

> **Note:** This CD-ROM uses long and mixed-case filenames, requiring the use of a protected mode CD-ROM driver.

EXERCISE FILES

This CD contains all the files you'll need to complete the exercises in *JavaScript + CSS + DOM Magic*. These files can be found in the root directory's folder.

THIRD-PARTY PROGRAMS

This CD also contains several third-party programs and demos from leading industry companies. These programs have been carefully selected to help you strengthen your professional skills in web site creation in general, and CSS and JavaScript in particular.

Please note that some of the programs included on this CD-ROM are shareware—"try-before-you-buy"—software. Please support these independent vendors by purchasing or registering any shareware software that you use for more than 30 days. Check with the documentation provided with the software on where and how to register the product.

For Windows/PC:

- Internet Explorer 6.0. **www.microsoft.com**
- Netscape 6.2. **www.netscape.com**
- Macromedia Homesite, trial version. Homesite is the HTML editor of choice of many web designers and developers. **www.macromedia.com**
- Notetab Lite. A powerful text editor with a number of useful features for developers and programmers. This Lite version will operate as the fully featured Pro version for 30 days, after which you may continue to use it for free with limited features, or purchase an upgrade license. **www.notetab.com**
- Bradbury Topstyle Pro trial version. Topstyle is a powerful CSS creation helper application. I recommend that you use this program after absorbing the project lessons. **www.bradsoft.com**.
- Adobe Photoshop with ImageReady, trial version. The graphics program of choice for most professional designers. Photoshop and ImageReady were used to create most of the graphics in this book. **www.adobe.com**.
- Macromedia Fireworks trial version. A powerful graphics program dedicated to generating web graphics. Fireworks was also used for several projects in this book. **www.macromedia.com**

For Mac:

- Internet Explorer 5.1. **www.microsoft.com**
- Netscape 6.2. **www.netscape.com**
- BBEdit Lite. The Lite version of BBEdit Pro, the no. 1 text editor for Mac. **www.barebones.com**
- Pagespinner. Pagespinner is a text editor with some specific features that are useful for web site creators. **www.optima-system.com**
- Adobe Photoshop with ImageReady, trial version. The graphics program of choice for most professional designers. Photoshop and ImageReady were used to create most of the graphics in this book. **www.adobe.com**
- Macromedia Fireworks trial version. A powerful graphics program dedicated to generating web graphics. Fireworks was also used for several projects in this book. **www.macromedia.com**

READ THIS BEFORE OPENING THE SOFTWARE

By opening the CD package, you agree to be bound by the following agreement:

You may not copy or redistribute the entire CD-ROM as a whole. Copying and redistribution of individual software programs on the CD-ROM is governed by terms set by individual copyright holders.

The installer, code and images from the author are copyrighted by the publisher and the authors.

> **Note:** For more download files, errata, bonus chapters, and updated book information, visit *Javascript+CSS+DOM Magic's* companion website at **www.createwebmagic.com**.

INDEX

transitional DTDs, 18
transitional strategies (CSS and JavaScript tabbed interfaces), 233-235
  advanced.css stylesheet, 241-242
  assembling Tab table, 235-236
  common.css stylesheet, 240
  creating base graphics for tabs, 235-236
  dividing project into modules, 237
  document object construction scripts, 243-244
  modifying XHTML markup to call functions, 249-251
  tab navigation scripts, 245-248
  XHTML base, 238-239
troubleshooting CSS stylesheets, 16
two-column layouts, applying CSS style rules, 56-58

U-V

ul tag, 65
user-friendly tables, 253-255
  activating scripts, XHTML markup adjustment to call functions, 268-269
  creating manipulative scripts, 261-266
  modifications, adding section indicators, 271
  setting the CSS, 260
  XHTML markup, 258-259

Verdana, 8
version 4 browsers, applying CSS to HTML table-based layouts, 40
vertical-align style attribute, 258
visibility element, 148

W

W3C (World Wide Web Consortium), 255
  DOM-compliant browsers, 150, 155
  DOM tree (model for web pages), 289-291
  standards-compliant browsers, 255
web browsers. *See* browsers
web pages
  CSS applications, 8-16
  extending the script for functionality, 111-114
  framesets, 99-103
  preventing sites from being framed, 103-104
  reading and writing data from one frame to another, 107-110
  well-formed HTML. *See* well-formed HTML pages
  writing a frame dynamically, 104-107

well-formed HTML pages, 4-6
  CSS applications
    backgrounds, 10-14
    color styles, 10-14
    font styles, 8
    stylesheets, 15-16
  DOCTYPE declaration, 18-19
  HTML Tidy, 6
  layout, 7
    borders, 14-15
    margins, 14-15
    modifications, 19
    padding, 14-15
  text readers, 15-16
window objects (window browsers), 118
  anatomy of a browser window, 139
  changing the contents of the parent window, 126-127
  changing the window status message, 123-124
  closing a window, 120
  closing multiple windows, 132
  history arrays, 133
  loading a page into a new window, 121-123
  opening
    basic windows, 119
    centered windows, 124-126
    more than one window, 129
  Photo Album site, 137
  pushing a window back and moving it, 127-128
  scrolling windows automatically, 133-135
  writing content to a new window, 130-132
  writing information back to the opener, 136-137
window.blur( ) function, 128
window.location.reload( ) function, 181
window.moveTo function, 128
windows
  browser windows. *See* browser windows
  scrolling frameless windows. *See* scrolling frameless windows
World Wide Web Consortium. *See* W3C
writedate function, writing text dynamically into documents, 158
writeframe function, 105
writing
  content to a new window (browser windows), 130-132
  frames dynamically (DOM), 104-107
  information back to the opener (browser windows), 136-137
  text dynamically into the document, browser detection, 158-159

X-Z

XHTML
  base
    calling functions, 287-289
    creating page elements, front page, 278-279
    transitional CSS and JavaScript tabbed interface strategies, 238-239
  calling functions, transitional CSS and JavaScript tabbed interface strategies, 249-251
  creating base for complex layouts, 64-66
  markup
    adjusting to call functions, 266-269
    applying CSS style rules to page layouts, 45-47
    creating for collapsing/expanding menus, 255-257
    creating for user-friendly tables, 258-259
  versus HTML, 46
xmlns attribute (html tag), 46

"you are here" indicator, IMG SRC swapping, 94

z-index
  effect of tab navigation script, 245
  style property, applying style rules to page elements, 68

Solutions from experts you know and trust.

www.informit.com

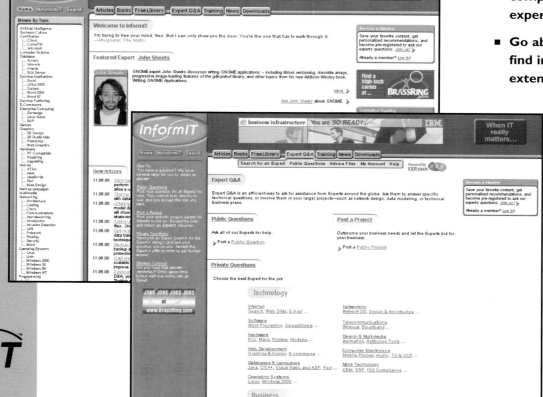

VIEW CART search ⊙

▸ Registration already a member? Log in. ▸ Book Registration

Publishing
the Voices
that Matter

OUR AUTHORS

PRESS ROOM

| web development | design | photoshop | new media | 3-D | server technologies |

EDUCATORS

ABOUT US

CONTACT US

You already know that New Riders brings you the **Voices that Matter**. But what does that mean? It means that New Riders brings you the Voices that challenge your assumptions, take your talents to the next level, or simply help you better understand the complex technical world we're all navigating.

Visit **www.newriders.com** to find:

▸ *Discounts* on specific book purchases

▸ Never before published chapters

▸ Sample chapters and excerpts

▸ Author bios and interviews

▸ Contests and enter-to-wins

▸ Up-to-date industry event information

▸ Book reviews

▸ Special offers from our friends and partners

Info on how to join our User Group program

▸ Ways to have your Voice heard

New
Riders

WWW.NEWRIDERS.COM

VOICES THAT MATTER

VISIT OUR WEB SITE

WWW.NEWRIDERS.COM

On our web site, you'll find information about our other books, authors, tables of contents, and book errata. You will also find information about book registration and how to purchase our books, both domestically and internationally.

EMAIL US

Contact us at: **nrfeedback@newriders.com**

- If you have comments or questions about this book
- To report errors that you have found in this book
- If you have a book proposal to submit or are interested in writing for New Riders
- If you are an expert in a computer topic or technology and are interested in being a technical editor who reviews manuscripts for technical accuracy

Contact us at: **nreducation@newriders.com**

- If you are an instructor from an educational institution who wants to preview New Riders books for classroom use. Email should include your name, title, school, department, address, phone number, office days/hours, text in use, and enrollment, along with your request for desk/examination copies and/or additional information.

Contact us at: **nrmedia@newriders.com**

- If you are a member of the media who is interested in reviewing copies of New Riders books. Send your name, mailing address, and email address, along with the name of the publication or web site you work for.

BULK PURCHASES/CORPORATE SALES

The publisher offers discounts on this book when ordered in quantity for bulk purchases and special sales. For sales within the U.S., please contact: Corporate and Government Sales (800) 382-3419 or **corpsales@pearsontechgroup.com**. Outside of the U.S., please contact: International Sales (317) 581-3793 or **international@pearsontechgroup.com**.

WRITE TO US

New Riders Publishing
201 W. 103rd St.
Indianapolis, IN 46290-1097

CALL/FAX US

Toll-free (800) 571-5840
If outside U.S. (317) 581-3500
Ask for New Riders
FAX: (317) 581-4663

New Riders